S0-AGX-532

The Shaping of Containment

The Shaping of Containment

HARRY S. TRUMAN, THE NATIONAL SECURITY COUNCIL, AND THE COLD WAR

Sara L. Sale
Missouri Southern State

Brandywine Press
Saint James, New York

Cover Photograph: 1951 NSC with President Truman
(Courtesy of Harry S. Truman Library)

Cover Design: Charles Peach

ISBN: 1-881089-15-0

Copyright © 1998 by Brandywine Press

All rights reserved. No part of this publication may be reproduced or transmitted in any form or by any means, electronic or mechanical, including
photocopying, recording, or any information storage and retrieval system,
without permission in writing from the publisher.

1st Printing 1998

Telephone Orders: 1-800-345-1776

Printed in the United States of America

For my mother,

Margaret Hyde Sale

and in memory of my father,

Onal Carter Sale

Contents

List of Maps

Nomenclatures

Abbreviations

AEC	Atomic Energy Commission
AIOC	Anglo-Iranian Oil Company
ARAMCO	Arabian American Oil Company
BOB	Bureau of the Budget
CIA	Central Intelligence Agency
DCI	Director of Central Intelligence
ERP	European Recovery Program
JCS	Joint Chiefs of Staff
MDAP	Mutual Defense Assistance Program
NATO	North Atlantic Treaty Organization
NCFE	National Committee for a Free Europe
NSC	National Security Council
OPC	Office of Policy Coordination
ORE	Office of Research and Evaluation
OSS	Office of Strategic Services
PPS	Policy Planning Staff
ROK	Republic of South Korea
SAC	Strategic Air Command
SANACC	State-Army-Navy-Air Force Coordination Committee
SPG	Special Procedures Group
UN	United Nations
USSR	Union of Soviet Socialist Republics

Note on Translation of Chinese Names

In the chapters where Chinese proper and place names are used readers will encounter the "pinyin" spelling, except in cases such as Hong Kong and Tsingtao where non-pinyin spellings are better recognized in the West. In 1958 the Chinese government adopted the pinyin transliterations and began to use them after Mao Zedong's death in 1976. Both the Mandarian translation and pinyin romanization are used in contemporary China.

Abbreviations of Notes Citations

The following references of abbreviated citations are used in the notes. Complete citations for sources in short form can be found in the Bibliography.

AWD-SGML	Papers of Allen W. Dulles, Seeley G. Mudd Library
Church Committee	U.S. Congress, *Supplementary Detailed Staff Reports on Foreign and Military Intelligence* Book IV
DLHP	Duke University Living History Program
FRUS	U.S. Department of State, *Foreign Relations of the United States*
GFK-SGML	Papers of George F. Kennan, Seeley G. Mudd Library
HSTL	Harry S. Truman Library
NA	National Archives
PCC-NME	Papers of Clark M. Clifford-National Military Establishment
PFE-SGML	Papers of Ferdinand Eberstadt, Seeley G. Mudd Library
PHT-NSC	Papers of Harry S. Truman-National Security Council
PHT-RPSB	Papers of Harry S. Truman-Records of the Psychological Strategy Board
PHT-WHCF	Papers of Harry S. Truman-White House Confidential Files

"Policies of the Government"	NSC, "Policies of the Government of the United States of America Relating to the National Security"
PPP:HST	*Public Papers of the Presidents of the United States, Harry S. Truman*
PPS Papers	Anna Kasten Nelson, ed., *The State Department Policy Planning Staff Papers*
PRN-SF	Papers of Richard E. Neustadt-Subject File
PSF-CF	President's Secretary's File-Chronological File
PSF-IF	President's Secretary's File-Intelligence File
PSF-KWF	President's Secretary's File-Korean War File
PSS-NSC	Papers of Sidney W. Souers-National Security Council
PSS-WHC	Papers of Sidney W. Souers-White House Counsel
PU	Princeton University
"Review of the World"	CIA, "Review of the World Situation As It Relates to the Security of the United States"
RG 59-PPS	Record Group 59-Records of the Policy Planning Staff
RG 59-RSS	Record Group 59-Records of the Secretary of State, Office of the Executive Secretariat
United States–Vietnam Relations	U.S. Department of Defense, *United States–Vietnam Relations 1945–1967*, Book 8

Introduction

In April 1949, *The Saturday Evening Post* published an article by journalists Joseph and Stewart Alsop entitled "How Our Foreign Policy Is Made." The subject of the Alsop brothers' examination was the National Security Council (NSC), which had been advising President Harry S. Truman since September 1947 on some of the most important foreign and military policy decisions of his administration. The Alsops noted in their investigation of Truman's working relationship with the NSC that in less than two years the council had become the president's primary "policy-making mechanism." Of the virtue of the NSC they concluded: "The United States does not have, as it has so often had in the past, two or three or half of a dozen foreign policies all insanely in operation at the same time—or no policy at all."[1]

During the turbulent years of World War II, the Alsops observed, foreign policy had been formulated in a rather haphazard manner. Truman's predecessor, Franklin D. Roosevelt, constructed a loosely organized process of foreign and military policymaking but it lacked effective coordination. When Truman became president he understood that if Roosevelt's policymaking apparatus remained unchanged, it would perpetuate the ongoing confusion and constant interbureaucratic rivalries that had existed since Pearl Harbor. Truman's experience in dealing with the complex matters and issues of foreign policy

1. Joseph and Stewart Alsop, "How Our Foreign Policy Is Made," *The Saturday Evening Post* (April 30, 1949): 31, 113–116.

had been limited, moreover, his critics together with some of his subordinates judged him to be an accidental president and a man of lesser talents in foreign affairs than Roosevelt. Truman knew that he could not afford serious policy differences within his administration, particularly between the Department of State and the military services, to circumvent his presidential decision-making during the crucial and uncertain years of the Cold War.

The idea for a NSC had originally taken shape in the political and economic corporatist visions of the United States held by Truman's Secretary of Defense James V. Forrestal, and his former business partner and long-time adviser, Ferdinand Eberstadt. From 1940 through 1947 Forrestal had served as undersecretary and secretary of the navy, while during World War II Eberstadt chaired the Army-Navy Munitions Board and became vice-chairman of the War Production Board. Both envisioned a postwar NSC composed of an organizational elite of national leaders, managers, and technocrats who would coordinate the country's political economy and national security. The problems of economic reconversion and military demobilization at the end of World War II convinced Eberstadt especially that the time was right for the creation of an NSC.[2]

Before World War II ended Truman had also developed his own ideas about military reorganization. In fact, when he was Roosevelt's vice-presidential running mate in 1944, Truman published an article in *Collier's* magazine, "Our Armed Forces Must Be Unified." It criticized the interservice rivalries that had plagued the army and the navy during World War II, and blamed the disaster at Pearl Harbor on the division of the armed services, with their separate commands and competing interests. He called for the integration of the military branches into a unified Defense Department, and he concluded: "Call it the War Department or the Department of National Security or

---

2. Jeffery M. Dorwart develops a superlative study of corporatism and the relationship of Ferdinand Eberstadt and James Forrestal in *Eberstadt and Forrestal: A National Security Partnership, 1909–1949* (College Station: Texas A & M University Press, 1991). For a firsthand account of the creation of the national security system see Clark Clifford with Richard Holbrooke, *Counsel to the President: A Memoir* (New York: Random House, 1991), 146–174. The best study of Forrestal is Townsend Hoopes and Douglas Brinkley, *Driven Patriot: The Life and Times of James Forrestal* (New York: Alfred A. Knopf, 1992).

what you will, just so it is one department." Later as president, Truman delivered a special message to Congress in December 1945 requesting a single department of national defense.[3]

Truman's proposals for unification of the armed services into a single Defense Department gave Forrestal reason to worry. He realized that if unification became reality, the Department of the Navy's aviation capabilities and Marine Corps could be absorbed by the other military branches, or the Navy itself could be decimated. Forrestal turned to his friend and adviser Eberstadt for help. Eberstadt began work on a corporatist plan that linked unification of the military services to a broader scheme for economic reconversion and for mobilizing national security. The Eberstadt Report (the Navy Plan), submitted to Forrestal in September 1945 recommended the formation of separate departments for Army, Navy, and Air Force, the three reporting to a secretary of defense. Eberstadt's plan suggested that he was not concerned with saving the navy, so much as he was determined to create a coordinated and tightly managed military establishment, responsible for constant national military preparedness.[4]

The Eberstadt Report's most important recommendation was for a "small group of people" to manage postwar national security organization through their coordination of foreign, military, and economic policy. Eberstadt argued that this organized elite, with its inherent corporate capabilities, could serve the president much like Great Britain's Committee on Imperial Defense which acted "as the secretariat of both the Defense Committee and the Cabinet." The small group of managers and advisers would emerge by 1947 as the NSC.

Forrestal and Eberstadt were corporatists who believed that the international catastrophe of the Great Depression had unleashed forces of ultranationalism, totalitarianism, and fascism that led the world into war and ultimately threatened the liberal, democratic values and economic security of the United States. For Forrestal, Eberstadt, and other corporatists at that

---

3. Harry S. Truman, "Our Armed Forces Must Be Unified," *Collier's*, (26 August 1944): 63–64.

4. Dorwart, *Eberstadt and Forrestal*, 91–107; U.S. Congress, Senate, Committee on Naval Affairs, *Unification of the War and Navy Departments and Postwar Organization for National Security*, 79th Congress, 1st sess. (Washington, D.C.: G.P.O., 1945), 20, 36–37, 42, 50.

time, lasting international order could be reestablished at the end of World War II, only by reconstructing the world system under the economic, political, and military hegemony of the United States. As Thomas J. McCormick correctly maintains: "Hegemony does not simply happen, individuals and groups of people make it happen." Forrestal and Eberstadt intuitively understood that a power base for American hegemonic interests had emerged in the United States, and that the economic, political, and military coordination of foreign policies necessary for a postwar international order could be conducted by the NSC.[5] Chapter 1 traces the establishment, organization, and operational reforms of the NSC during the years from 1947 to 1952, each historically important to engage the government in a series of international initiatives in the interest of United States hegemony.

Truman gave little thought to the NSC before 1947 besides accepting it as part of a compromise that produced a partial unification of the armed services. But from July through September 1947, when the NSC began to operate officially, he was suspicious of the corporatist organization that Eberstadt had envisioned for the council, fearing that it could subvert the powers of the presidency and redesign the national government. Yet all the while, he intuitively knew that he needed the NSC for its advice and the development of Cold War political and military policy. Within a few months after the council began to hold meetings, Truman overcame his skepticism and suspicion, took the initiative from Forrestal and Eberstadt, and began to control and use the NSC as his own presidential instrument for forming and coordinating Cold War policy.[6]

Truman rarely rejected the NSC's policy advice or objected to it. Of the 124 formal policy paper recommendations submitted to him for consideration, he approved or concurred with all but five. He made only two policy decisions without consulting the NSC. Domestic political implications in 1948 led him to recognize the new state of Israel despite the lack of NSC contribution or debate. Again in the absence of advice from the coun-

---

5. Thomas J. McCormick, *America's Half-Century: United States Foreign Policy in the Cold War* (Baltimore: The Johns Hopkins University Press, 1989), 5.
6. Alonzo L. Hamby, *Man of the People: A Life of Harry S. Truman* (New York: Oxford University Press, 1995), 311.

cil, in 1951, he ordered the transfer of nine atomic bombs to air force bases in the Pacific. This decision was made in great haste. Intelligence reports alerted Truman that the Soviet Union planned an offensive to assist the Chinese in pushing American troops out of Korea and Japan. At the same time he was preparing to relieve the Supreme Commander of United Nations Forces in Korea, General Douglas MacArthur. In an effort at once to thwart a major Soviet offense and to prevent MacArthur from receiving information about the nuclear shipment, Truman acted without meeting with the NSC. It was arranged, however, that the council would be consulted before any decision was made to use the bombs. On all other Cold War policies, the NSC advised Truman.

Two central problems confronted Truman and the NSC, and dominated United States foreign policy during the years from 1947 to 1952. Truman and the NSC had to determine how to respond to the apparent political and military expansion of the Soviet Union. They were also on alert to the possible collapse of Western capitalism after World War II, and the security crisis that could follow its collapse. The NSC's contribution in developing American foreign and national security policy in response to these two problems is the subject of this book.

Although the administration had decided as early as 1946 that the Soviet Union's duplicity and expansion threatened the ideological and hegemonic interests of the United States, the response toward the USSR and other Communist nations remained fluid throughout 1946 and much of early 1947. But in September 1946, a group of advisers chaired by Truman's White House aide, Clark M. Clifford, presented a report to the president that suggested the administration needed to "confine" the Soviet Union's geopolitical and military influence.[7] Instead, the doctrine of containment, articulated by the Department of State's leading Soviet specialist, George F. Kennan, became the primary response of policy coordinated by the NSC during Truman's presidency. Kennan's containment tenets

---

7. The Clifford-Elsey report, "American Relations with the Soviet Union," of September 1946 is printed in full in Arthur Krock, *Memoirs: Sixty Years on the Firing Line* (New York: Funk & Wagnalls, 1968), 419–482. For details of the writing of the Clifford-Elsey report see Clifford, *Counsel to the President*, 123–129.

were written in January 1947 and presented to Forrestal, who encouraged Kennan to submit the paper to *Foreign Affairs*. Published seven months later in the journal under the pseudo-nym Mr. "X," the article entitled "The Sources of Soviet Conduct" provided initial justification for the Truman Doctrine and the Marshall Plan. Kennan wrote of the ideological fanaticism that motivated Soviet expansion and of the Communist hostility of the USSR toward the capitalist world. He pointed out that the USSR suffered from serious postwar political and economic weaknesses, but emphasized Moscow's willingness to accept short-term losses in its efforts to achieve its long-term objectives of wearing down and defeating its capitalist foes. Kennan did not specify how America's containment of the USSR should be implemented. Neither did he place limits on containment policies or priorities, nor did he distinguish between America's vital or peripheral interests. "Counterforce," he argued had to be applied by the United States against the "constantly shifting geographical and political points" of the Soviet Union as to "promote tendencies which must eventually find their outlet in either the break-up or the mellowing of Soviet power."[8]

Kennan's containment premises convinced the administration's top policymakers that they needed to move quickly to set a foreign policy that firmly could check advances by the USSR in the Eastern Mediterranean and in Western Europe. Truman's message to Congress on March 12, 1947, requesting economic and military assistance to Greece and Turkey, proclaimed what

---

8. For Kennan's concepts of containment in 1947 see "X" (George F. Kennan), "The Sources of Soviet Conduct," *Foreign Affairs* XXV (July 1947): 566–582. Other than Kennan's own works, some of the most recent and insightful studies on Kennan are Walter L. Hixon, *George F. Kennan: Cold War Iconoclast* (New York: Columbia University Press, 1989); David Mayers, *George Kennan and the Dilemmas of US Foreign Policy* (New York: Oxford University Press, 1988); Wilson D. Miscamble, C.S.C., *George F. Kennan and the Making of Foreign Policy, 1947–1950* (Princeton: Princeton University Press, 1992); Anders Stephenson, *Kennan and the Art of Foreign Policy* (Cambridge: Harvard University Press, 1989). An early but very insightful biographical essay that should be consulted is Thomas G. Paterson, "The Search for Meaning: George F. Kennan and American Foreign Policy" in Frank J. Merli and Theodore A. Wilson, eds., *Makers of American Diplomacy: From Benjamin Franklin to Henry Kissinger* (New York: Scribner's, 1974), 249–284. A full-length biography of Kennan is currently in progress by John Lewis Gaddis that will be most useful for historians in the near future.

became known as the Truman Doctrine: the nation's willingness to "assist free peoples" in the polarized world of democracy and totalitarianism "in maintaining their freedoms" from
aggressor powers. Secretary of State George C. Marshall's
Harvard address on June 5, 1947, announcing Department of
State plans for a European Recovery Program, signaled the
administration's hope of developing a long-term assistance program of economic containment.[9]

* * *

Recent studies of the Soviet Union's foreign policies indicate that America's pronouncements of the Truman Doctrine
and the Marshall Plan marked a turning point for Soviet Premier Joseph Stalin. In 1946 and early 1947 the Kremlin's foreign policy seemed to project détente, a cautious but calculated
attempt not to provoke the United States. This would give the
USSR room to establish a security zone within what Stalin
viewed as the Soviet peripheries of Eastern Europe, Iran, and
Turkey, and to seek postwar alliances with Germany and Austria. Stalin became concerned by the Truman administration's
reactions to Soviet pressures on Iran and Turkey, its efforts to
fill a power-vacuum and serve as a surrogate for the British in
Greece, and its attempt through the Marshall Plan to become
the dominant influence in Europe. "For Stalin the Marshall
Plan was a watershed," note the Russian historians Vladislav
Zubok and Constantine Pleshakov.[10]

---

9. For the Truman Doctrine see John Lewis Gaddis, "Was the Truman
Doctrine a Real Turning Point?" *Foreign Affairs* 52 (January 1974): 386–402,
and the indispensable Joseph M. Jones, *The Fifteen Weeks* (New York: Viking
Press, 1965), which covers the bureaucratic origins of both the Truman Doc-
trine and the Marshall Plan. Forrest C. Pogue analyzes Secretary of State
Marshall's association with the proposal in 1947 in his final volume biography
George C. Marshall: Statesman, 1945–1949 (New York: Viking/Penguin, 1987),
197–217.

10. Vladislav Zubok and Constantine Pleshakov, *Inside the Kremlin's Cold
War: From Stalin to Khrushchev* (Cambridge: Harvard University Press, 1996),
50–51. For further reference on this point see David Holloway, *Stalin and the
Bomb: The Soviet Union and Atomic Energy, 1939–1956* (New Haven: Yale Uni-
versity Press, 1994), 254–258; Scott D. Parrish, "The Turn Toward Confronta-
tion: The Soviet Reaction to the Marshall Plan, 1948," Working Paper #9, Cold
War International History Project, Woodrow Wilson International Center for
Scholars, Washington, D.C.

The Marshall Plan reinforced Stalin's xenophobia, eradicated the hope of Soviet policymakers that the United States and Great Britain would become entangled over world markets and resources, and demonstrated that the United States and its Western European allies were working to revive the industrial and military potential of Germany. Until early 1947 Stalin had expected that his former Western Allies, including the United States, would compromise with him on the issue of postwar Germany. The announcement of the Marshall Plan revealed that a separate German policy by the West was probable, and that his plans for relations between Germany and the USSR were being undermined.

Amidst these growing geopolitical and strategic confrontations, Truman's new NSC assumed the task of a complicated foreign policy coordination effort. The thinking that emerged from the NSC was a policy for Truman that by late 1947 emphasized the containment of the Soviet Union, but not the containment of communism. NSC policymakers recognized that communism could become indigenous and those Communists who rejected Stalin's leadership deserved support and even direct assistance from the United States. Despite the anti-Communist rhetoric that President Truman and his administration officials employed to gain domestic political support for the Truman Doctrine and the Marshall Plan, the policies that the NSC coordinated and Truman implemented between late 1947 and late 1949 did not suggest an American effort to contain international communism. NSC policies, moreover, reflected the constraints of America's postwar military power. By 1947 United States military forces had declined significantly and concerns about postwar inflation by the administration and the military services made nearly impossible the prospects for escalated Cold War defense spending. Chapters 2 and 3 assess how the limits of American power forced the NSC to set priorities for the containment policy between vital interests, above all in Western Europe, and peripheral interests such as in China, Japan, Palestine, and Korea.

Within two years the scope of the Cold War changed dramatically. In late 1949 three events tested the confidence of American hegemony as well as the validity of the NSC's containment policies, and that is the focus of Chapter 4. It became clear that neither the Marshall Plan nor American programs designed for the revival of Japan's industry had forged stable monetary environments in Western Europe and Japan. The Communist defeat of Chinese Nationalists was followed by the formation of a new Communist state, the People's Republic of China, and the detonation by the Soviet Union of its first atomic bomb marked the beginning of the end of America's atomic monopoly. These three crises of late 1949, coupled with growing domestic political pressures, hampered the NSC's freedom to distinguish between peripheral and vital interests. In response, the NSC shifted from a previous containment strategy of limited and reactive response to containment policies that were more active.

By the early 1950s the Communist threat to United States hegemonic interests appeared monolithic. This inflamed domestic right-wing anti-Communist political interests that charged Truman's foreign policy and his policymakers with being soft on communism. As rabid anti-Communist ideology even before McCarthyism tightened its grip on political and cultural institutions, Truman responded quickly to the Soviet nuclear challenge with the development of a hydrogen bomb, and the NSC conducted major reevaluations of Cold War policies that called for aggressive military containment strategies worldwide. Chapters 5 and 6 examine the impact that the ensuing Korean War had on the NSC's global policy of countering the hegemonic aspirations of the Soviet Union, increasing America's military spending at home and abroad, and fostering Western economic internationalism.

The history of Cold War foreign and national security policymaking during the Truman presidency is only partly a story of bureaucratic differences, turf battles, and compromises. Understanding the major policy disputes and their leading participants on the NSC makes it clear that the model first suggested by Graham Allison in his study of the Cuban Missile Crisis—"Where you stand depends on where you sit"—does not apply fully to NSC coordination and formulation from 1947 to 1952.[11] Truman's NSC struggled to coordinate appropriate responses to a series of international crises. As a result, the civilian policymakers and the military professionals on the council

---

11. Graham T. Allison, *Essence of Decision: Explaining the Cuban Missile Crisis* (Boston: Little, Brown, 1971), 162–180.

set aside their smaller bureaucratic differences to reach a consensus for President Truman. In general the Departments of State and Defense agreed on the major priorities and commitments of United States containment policy regarding Western Europe, the Middle East, and Asia. On Western Europe, the two argued for continued economic assistance and political countermeasures to thwart long-term Soviet pressures. The Department of Defense also perceived the Soviet military threat to Western Europe as an immediate priority. State and Defense both agreed on a containment policy that limited the American commitment of conventional military forces to peripheral areas such as Greece and Italy to bolster the defense of Western Europe. Furthermore, State and Defense also were concerned about the effects that the instability of the Middle East would have on the nation's access to petroleum resources and its strategic interests in the Eastern Mediterranean. Each sought a policy of measured intervention to contain future conflict as well as chances of Soviet encroachment in the region. This consensus, which Truman understood to work to the Arabs' advantage and against Israel, he overrode when he recognized Israel in 1948. Policy that the NSC coordinated toward Asia aimed at maintaining American credibility in an unpredictable part of the world was another concern of both State and Defense. Each called for circumscribed American economic and political influence in Asia along with limited conventional military forces, to thwart potential political and military collaboration between the People's Republic of China and the USSR throughout the region. The Korean War, of course, widened the nation's involvement.

Five decades have passed since Truman served as president of the United States. Yet, with the demise of the Cold War in the early 1990s and the recognition of Truman's fiftieth anniversary as president, few Americans understand that his NSC served as the central formulator of his administration's foreign and military policies from September 1947 through January 1953. Studies to date by historians and other scholars have either concentrated on the establishment of the NSC or surveyed the organizational development of the council during Truman's presidency. The voluminous literature on the Cold War has produced over the last fifteen years works that often note the subject of the NSC, and provide brief assessments of the council's policy recommendations during the Cold War. Notable among these are the penetrating analyses of United States national security policy provided by Melvyn P. Leffler, a masterful study that examines Cold War containment policy from World War II through the presidency of Richard M. Nixon by John Lewis Gaddis, and the always insightful editions on the Cold War by Walter LaFeber. John Prados has provided an extremely useful historical survey of the NSC from Truman's presidency through the presidency of George W. Bush.[12] Anna Kasten Nelson and Alfred Sander have furthered our understanding of the organizational history of the NSC. And a collection of essays, articles, and documents edited by Loch K. Johnson and Karl F. Inderfurth give us a better grasp of NSC history from the presidencies of Truman through Ronald W. Reagan.[13]

Though this book centers on American foreign policy, it also assesses the influence of other nations and their policymakers on the United States. In recent years, Russian historical archives have opened slowly, but access to the classified Cold War documents of the former Soviet Union that shaped the USSR's policies, and those of other Communist nations, remains difficult at best. The efforts of some American and Russian scholars, however, have produced initial and revealing

---

12. Melvyn P. Leffler, *A Preponderance of Power: National Security, the Truman Administration, and the Cold War* (Stanford: Stanford University Press, 1992) and his *The Specter of Communism: The United States and the Origins of the Cold War, 1917–1953* (New York: Hill and Wang, 1994); John Lewis Gaddis, *Strategies of Containment: A Critical Appraisal of Postwar National Security Policy* (New York: Oxford University Press, 1982); Walter LaFeber, *America, Russia, and the Cold War, 1945–1996* (New York: McGraw-Hill, 1997); John Prados, *Keepers of the Keys: A History of the National Security Council from Truman to Bush* (New York: William Morrow, 1991).

13. Anna Kasten Nelson, "National Security I: Inventing a Process (1945–1960)," in Hugh Helco and Lester Salamon, eds., *The Illusion of the Presidency* (Boulder: Westview Press, 1981), 229–262; idem, "President Truman and the Evolution of the National Security Council," *Journal of American History* 72 (September 1985): 360–378; Alfred Sander, "Truman and the National Security Council, 1945–1947," *Journal of American History* 59 (September 1972): 369–388; Loch K. Johnson and Karl F. Inderfurth, eds., *Decisions of the Highest Order: Perspectives on the National Security Council* (Pacific Grove, CA: Brooks/Cole, 1988).

studies on Soviet, Chinese, and North Korean policies and those have been taken into account where applicable in the book.[14]

This book provides a synthesis of recent studies about the Cold War during Truman's presidency. And its analysis of the NSC's policies and its appraisal of the evolution of the Truman administration's foreign policy coordination processes expands on the themes that this introduction outlines. It reveals that President Truman was a minor participant in the actual coordination of foreign policy, that the NSC served his needs well because it provided a valuable forum for reconciling differences between State and Defense, and that Truman depended on NSC consensus for the formulation of policies. Because of the council's coordinated efforts, the containment doctrine did not dictate the policies of Truman and the NSC; the policy recommendations of the NSC shaped containment.

14. Representing the newest scholarly studies based on Soviet and Chinese documents are Thomas J. Christensen, "A Lost Chance for What? Rethinking the Origins of U.S.-PRC Confrontation," *Journal of American-East Asian Relations* 4 (1995): 249–278; idem, *Useful Adversaries: Grand Strategy, Domestic Mobilization, and Sino-American Conflict, 1947–1958* (Princeton: Princeton University Press, 1996); John W. Garver, "Little Chance," *Diplomatic History* 21 (Winter 1997): 87–94; Sergei N. Goncharov, John W. Lewis, and Xue Litai, *Uncertain Partners: Stalin, Mao, and the Korean War* (Stanford: Stanford University Press, 1993); Chen Jian, *China's Road to the Korean War: The Making of the Sino-Soviet Confrontation* (New York: Columbia University Press, 1994); idem, "The Myth of America's 'Lost Chance' in China: A Chinese Perspective in Light of New Evidence," *Diplomatic History* 21 (Winter 1997): 77–86; Michael Sheng, "The Triumph of Internationalism: CCP-Moscow Relations Before 1949," *Diplomatic History* 21 (Winter 1997): 95–104; Kathryn Weathersby, "Korea, 1949–50: To Attack, or Not to Attack? Stalin, Kim Il Sung, and the Prelude to War," *Bulletin of the Cold War International History Project* 5 (Spring 1995): 1–9; idem, "New Findings on the Korean War," *Bulletin CWIHP* 3 (Fall 1993): 1, 14–18; idem, "The Soviet Role in the Early Phase of the Korean War: New Documentary Evidence," *Journal of American-East Asian Relations* 2 (1993): 425–458; Odd Arne Westad, *Cold War and Revolution: Soviet-American Rivalry and the Origins of the Chinese Civil War* (New York: Columbia University Press, 1993); idem, "Losses, Chances, and Myths: The United States and the Creation of the Sino-Soviet Alliance, 1945–1950," *Diplomatic History* 21 (Winter 1997): 105–115; idem, "Rivals and Allies: Stalin, Mao, and the Chinese Civil War, January 1949," *Bulletin CWIHP* 6–7 (Winter 1995–96): 219, 226–227; Zubok and Pleshakov, *Inside the Cold War*.

Chapter One

Organization of a Policy Instrument

Such a council would introduce fundamental changes in the entire question of foreign relations.
(George C. Marshall, 1947)

As the Cold War intensified during 1947, the passage of the National Security Act on July 26 was a seminal event in the history of the United States. The law established the NSC, and made the council responsible for the formulation of United States foreign and national security policies.[1] Thereafter, the ideas and institutions that governed America's Cold War containment policies for nearly forty-five years were a direct legacy of Truman's NSC.

The NSC helped Truman formulate a national security policy for his administration during the Cold War, and "national security" became synonymous with the Cold War. Preferable to the terms "foreign policy" or "national defense," "national security" reflected a broadened concept along the corporatist line of thinking that called for an organized and perpetual mobilization of national resources in time of world war and cold war. More important, the NSC was to help Truman

---

1. *The National Security Act of 1947, Public Law 253*, 80th Congress, 1st sess., 26 July 1947 (Washington, D.C.: G.P.O., 1947).

shape the containment policy, bringing direct and indirect United States intervention in Europe, the Mediterranean, the Middle East, and Asia. Near international chaos in the years immediately after World War II complicated an already uncertain foreign policy for this administration. So, the NSC emerged at the right time for Truman, and it provided him coordination and direction of both foreign and defense policy during the early and tense years of the Cold War.

Except for a brief period of interdepartmental rivalry and semiparalysis, when Secretary of Defense Louis A. Johnson and Secretary of State Dean G. Acheson were hardly on speaking terms, Truman's NSC functioned quite well. The council provided for the first time in American history an official forum for discussion and debate among advisers and policymakers of superlative abilities in foreign and defense fields. During his presidency Truman benefited from the talents and advice of NSC members such as Acheson, James V. Forrestal, W. Averell Harriman, Robert A. Lovett, W. Stuart Symington, and George C. Marshall.

In its early years, the Department of Defense had four representatives—the secretary of defense and the three military service secretaries—and State only one, its secretary. In 1949 a balance of power was created in the NSC when Congress amended the National Security Act, eliminating the three military service secretaries from membership on the council. That same year the vice-president was made a statutory member, and the NSC became part of the Executive Office of the President. Those changes, combined with placement of the secretary of state on an equality with the secretary of defense, made it the leading arbiter of Cold War policy for Truman.

*   *   *

The National Security Act of 1947, better known for unifying the armed services, created the NSC to serve the president. It was to be "a policy-forming and advisory" body, and assist him "with respect to the integration of domestic, foreign, and military policies related to the national security."[2] Truman advocated the passage of the act. His reasons relate to his early

---

2. Ibid.

presidential years, a time when largely because of demobilization the country had no unified defense.

When Truman became president he was in a tenuous position of power. Since the Democratic Party's nominating convention of 1944, when he was selected the vice-presidential nominee on the Roosevelt ticket, he had been aware of the president's deteriorating health and suspected that Roosevelt could not complete his fourth term. Yet although he had served in Congress, Truman did not know much about Roosevelt's foreign policies or conduct of the war. Much of his knowledge came from nothing more than two informal meetings with Roosevelt. Truman felt quite insecure as the new chief executive.[3] His decisions during his first presidential years came from his Midwestern common sense and the experience he had gained in his years in the United States Senate. He quickly realized that, in order to compensate for his background and to grasp the major problems, he had to establish a structured method of obtaining information about military and foreign policy affairs. He later wrote that the "scattered method of getting information for various departments of the government first struck me as being badly organized when I was in the Senate."[4] As vice-president, Truman had observed that many messages were not relayed to Roosevelt. He concluded: "The President up to that time had to make decisions sometimes 'by guess and by God,' which is not a very satisfactory way to do business."[5]

Truman came to the White House, however, with a strong background in defense organization. He had served as an Army National Guard captain in France during World War I, had

---

3. For thorough accounts of the Democratic party's nomination of Truman in 1944 see Robert H. Ferrell, *Choosing Truman: The Democratic Convention of 1944* (Columbia, MO: University of Missouri Press, 1994); idem, *Harry S. Truman and the Modern American Presidency* (Boston: Little, Brown, 1983), 40–41; idem, *Harry S. Truman: A Life* (Columbia, MO: University of Missouri Press, 1994), 198; David McCullough, *Truman* (New York: Simon & Schuster, 1992), 335–336; Hamby, *Man of the People*, 289–290.

4. Harry S. Truman, *Memoirs of Harry S. Truman 1946–1952: Volume II, Years of Trial and Hope* (Garden City, NY: Doubleday, 1956; reprint, New York: DaCapo Press, 1986), 56.

5. Harry Truman cited in William Hillman, ed., *Harry S. Truman in His Own Words* (New York: Farrar, Straus & Young as *Mr. President*, 1952; reprint, New York: Bonanza Books, 1984), 14–15.

studied military organization, and was an avid reader of American military history. He had served on the Senate Subcommittees of the Appropriations and Military Affairs Committees. During World War II also he had been chairman of the Special Committee to Investigate the National Defense Program (the Truman Committee) concerned with military procurement and industrial mobilization.[6] "One of the strongest convictions which I brought to the office of the President," Truman would recall, "was that the antiquated defense setup of the United States had to be reorganized quickly as a step toward insuring our safety and preserving world peace."[7] Throughout the presidential campaign of 1944, Truman advocated the unification of the army and the navy. The Department of War under Secretary Henry L. Stimson and his successor, Robert P. Patterson, shared Truman's views. But the idea of a coequal air force, encompassing naval aviation, drew opposition to the plan from the Department of Navy. Truman, whose allegiance rested with the Army, supported the Department of War's unification plans.[8]

Soon after Truman became president, two unification bills were introduced in Congress, and hearings on them continued into December 1945. In January 1946 Undersecretary of State Dean Acheson informed Truman that demobilization "was a matter of great embarrassment and concern" to his department in the conduct of foreign policy. Acheson also recognized that the Department of State was lacking "ideas, plans, or methods for the painstaking and exhaustive collection and correlation of foreign intelligence."[9] This type of postwar problem persuaded

---

6. Ferrell, *Choosing Truman*, 6–8, idem, *Harry S. Truman*, 56–71, 124–162; McCullough, *Truman*, 102–135, 213–291; Hamby, *Man of the People*, 57–82, 200–227, 248–273.

7. Truman, *Years of Trial and Hope*, 46.

8. Truman, "Our Armed Forces Must Be United," 63–64; Clark M. Clifford Oral History Interview; George M. Elsey Oral History Interview; Stuart Symington Oral History Interview; Oral History Collection, HSTL, Independence, Missouri; Letter, W. John Kenney to Ferdinand Eberstadt, 27 September 1946, PFE-SGML, Box 3, PU, Princeton, New Jersey.

9. Dean Acheson, *Present at the Creation, My Years in the State Department* (New York: Penguin Books, 1969), 16. Acheson cited in Walter Millis, ed., *The Forrestal Diaries* (New York: Viking Press, 1951), 129.

Secretary of the Navy James V. Forrestal, 1944–1947. *(Courtesy of Harry S. Truman Library)*

Truman to initiate a plan that would coordinate information as well as provide for a highly structured military establishment. Throughout late 1945 and 1946, the administration debated various plans. Secretary of the Navy Forrestal became the most vocal advocate of a more effective coordination within the government, and he approached Truman, other cabinet members, and members of Congress with a proposal.[10] Among all the studies leading to the passage of the National Security Act, Forrestal's proposal, the Eberstadt Report, was the most influential. It recommended a National Security Council that would bring together policy proposals from the Departments of State, Navy, and Army, and an independent Air Force. Eberstadt also recommended forming within the NSC a central intelligence

---

10. Clark M. Clifford Oral History Interview; George M. Elsey Oral History Interview. For a thorough account of the various departmental and agency plans as well as Forrestal's own plan see Sander, "Truman and the National Security Council," 369–388; Nelson, "President Truman and the Evolution of the National Security Council," 361–362; Dorwart, *Eberstadt and Forrestal*, 131–148. For Forrestal's own recollection of work on the National Security Act see Millis, *The Forrestal Diaries*, 59–64, 118–121; Memorandum, James Forrestal to Harry S. Truman, PFE-SGML, Box 61. For Truman's recollections see Harry S. Truman, *Memories of Harry S. Truman 1945:* Volume I, *Year of Decisions* (Garden City, NY: Doubleday, 1955; reprint, New York, DaCapo Press, 1986), 77–78.

group for the purpose of supplying the council with "authoritative information of conditions and developments in the outside." Two years after intense lobbying efforts by Eberstadt and Forrestal, it took form as the National Security Council.[11]

The National Security Act established the NSC and granted the council specific functions and duties. The primary purpose of the NSC would be to advise the president on the integration of national security domestic, foreign, and military policies, "so as to enable the military services and other departments and agencies of the Government to cooperate more effectively in matters involving the national security." Under the direction of the president, the NSC was to: "assess and appraise the objectives, commitments, and risks of the United States" relating to the military and national security interests of the nation; "consider policies on matters of common interest to the departments and agencies of the Government concerned with the national security;" and make policy recommendations and reports "to the President as it deems appropriate or as the President may require."[12] The NSC's statutory membership according to the act of 1947 would consist of the president, secretary of state, secretary of defense, secretary of the army, secretary of the navy, secretary of the air force, and chairman of the National Security Resources Board. The president would chair NSC meetings, or in his absence, appoint another council member to preside in his place. In addition, the act provided for the creation of a career staff for the NSC, headed by an executive secretary appointed by the president.[13]

---

11. Senate, Committee on Naval Affairs, *Unification of the War and Navy Departments and Postwar Organization for National Security*, 20, 42. Until the creation of the National Security Council, President Truman relied on an interim policy-forming group for advice—the National Intelligence Authority (NIA). The NIA was founded by Executive Order on 22 January 1946, and comprised of Truman's Secretaries of State, War, the Navy, and his Chief of Staff. Within the NIA was an intelligence-gathering section known as the Central Intelligence Group (CIG). It was designed to take the place of the Army's dismantled Office of Strategic Services (OSS). Serving as Director of the CIG was Sidney W. Souers (January–June 1946), who later would serve as the Executive Secretary of the NSC from 1947 to 1950. His successor was General Hoyt S. Vandenberg (June 1946–May 1947), who later would serve as the Secretary of the Air Force.

12. *The National Security Act of 1947, Public Law 253.*

13. The NSRB was responsible for the acquisition and stock-piling of scarce metals such as tin, aluminum, and steel. On this point see Stuart Symington Oral History Interview.

After passage of the National Security Act the State-Army-Navy-Air Force Coordination Committee (SANACC) was created for more effective coordination of policy and strategy among the four military services. Recommendations from SANACC were forwarded to the Joint Chiefs of Staff (JCS) and the secretary of state for comment, a practice that Truman's NSC adopted. SANACC functioned until the summer of 1949, and the NSC often consulted the committee on policy issues related to Cold War political and military strategy. Over time, the NSC gradually assumed the major functions of SANACC, the latter became an anachronism, and in 1949 the Department of Defense recommended its dissolution.[14]

For the first executive secretary of the NSC, Truman appointed Rear Admiral Sidney W. Souers. He was sworn in immediately before the NSC's first meeting. From then until his resignation in January 1950, Souers assumed the position he referred to as "a broker of ideas." One observer at the time called Souers "the President's chief informant."[15] A recent scholar has determined that he filled the role of the "custodian-manager" of the NSC.[16] A successful businessman and astute naval intelligence officer during World War II, Souers had learned from the corporate and military worlds how to transmit ideas with a minimum of friction.[17] Less interested in the actual formulation of policy, he instead served as a conciliator

---

14. Kenneth W. Condit, *The History of the Joint Chiefs of Staff: The Joint Chiefs of Staff and National Policy:* Volume II, *1947–1949* (Wilmington, DE: Michael Glazier, 1979), 6; Memorandum, "Clearance of SANACC Papers which will be referred to the National Security Council," 16 June 1948, RG 59-PPS, NA, Washington, D.C.

15. Margaret Truman, *Harry S. Truman* (New York: William Morrow, 1973), 332; Biographical Sketch of Sidney William Souers, PSS-NSC, Box 1, HSTL; Sidney W. Souers, "Policy Formulation for National Security," *American Political Science Review* 43 (June 1949): 537; Cabell Phillips, "Men Around the President," *New York Times Magazine*, 11 September 1949, 69.

16. On the role of the custodian-manager see David K. Hall, "The 'Custodian-Manager' of the Policymaking Process," in Karl F. Inderfurth and Loch K. Johnson, eds., *Decisions of the Highest Order: Perspectives on the National Security Council* (Pacific Grove, CA: Brooks/Cole, 1988), 146–154.

17. Biographical Sketch of Sidney William Souers, PSS-NSC, Box 1; *Current Biography 1949* (New York: The H.W. Wilson Co., 1949), 577–578; David F. Barrett, "Admiral Sidney W. Souers," *The Eastern Underwriter*, 18 December 1959; Thomas Troy, *Donovan and the CIA: A History of the Establishment of the Central Intelligence Agency* (Frederick, MD: University Publications of America, 1981), 250–252.

between the executive departments and the military services represented on the NSC.

Throughout Souers's term he served as Truman's "nonpolitical confidant."[18] He met with the president each morning at 9:30 a.m. to brief him on the council's agenda and discuss NSC recommendations and directives. At that time, Truman signed proposals he wanted implemented as official policy and forwarded his recommendations to the council by Souers.[19] The executive secretary was also an administrative troubleshooter. During the NSC's formative years he helped correct several of its internal weaknesses, a task that he found natural, for he felt responsible for the successful operational mechanisms of the council. When he resigned in 1950, Souers noted that the NSC had become "fully accepted . . . valuable . . . well supported by the authorities . . . and making progress."[20] Truman afforded Souers the time he needed to return to his business interests in 1950 by appointing him Special Consultant on National Security Matters and giving him an office in the White House. War broke out in Korea shortly thereafter, and he became a regular occupant of the White House.[21]

Souers's successor was his former assistant, James S. Lay, Jr. He served as chief administrator over the NSC until the end of the Truman administration. Like Souers, Lay had worked in the intelligence branch of the military during World War II. An army lieutenant colonel by the end of the war, he returned to Washington for an assignment of secretary to the joint intelligence committee of the JCS. After discharge from the army, he became a management analyst in charge of research and intelligence for the Department of State.[22] A young career service

---

18. Memorandum, Sidney Souers to Harry Truman, 17 November 1949, PSS-NSC, Box 1, HSTL, Independence, Missouri; Souers, "Policy Formulation for National Security," 537; "The Security Council at Work," *The Reporter*, 10 May 1949, 9; Joseph and Stewart Alsop, "How Our Foreign Policy Is Made," 116.

19. Stuart Symington Oral History Interview; Phillips, "The Men Around the President," 69; Alsop, "How Our Foreign Policy Is Made," 114.

20. Sidney Souers to Ferdinand Eberstadt, 4 October 1949, PSS-WHC, Box 1, HSTL, Independence, Missouri.

21. Harry Truman to Sidney Souers, 22 December 1949, Ibid.

22. Letter, Sidney Souers to Ferdinand Eberstadt, 20 December 1949, PFE-SGML, Box 112; *The New York Times*, 22 December 1949, 6; 17 January 1950, 29; *Current Biography 1950* (New York: The H.W. Wilson Co., 1950), 329–331; "People of the Week," *U.S. News and World Report*, 30 December 1949, 36–37.

President Truman awards the Distinguished Service Medal to Admiral Sidney W. Souers, December 1951. *(Naval Photo Center; Courtesy of Harry S. Truman Library)*

officer, Lay was thirty-six years old when he accepted Souers's offer to become the chief assistant to the executive secretary of the NSC. Throughout Souers's tenure, he remained Lay's mentor. One associate of Souers observed that he had "served as a sort of informal father-confessor and guardian for Lay . . . present at Lay's daily briefings of the President, confidante to both."[23]

The NSC met every first and third Thursday of the month in the Cabinet Conference Room of the White House. The council's staff, headed by the executive secretary, was housed in the Old State Department Building next to the White House. The staff was organized into three divisions: NSC staff members, a secretariat, and a small group of consultants from other departments and agencies represented on the council.[24]

NSC consideration of policy involved the preparation of a policy paper, either by the NSC staff, the Department of State, or its Policy Planning Staff (PPS); comment and recommenda-

23. Richard E. Neustadt, "Notes on the White House Staff Under President Truman," June 1953, 40, PRN-SF, Box 10, HSTL, Independence, Missouri.

24. Souers, "Policy Formulation for National Security," 537, 539.

tions on the paper by consultants or committees; and formal NSC discussion, with the submission of adopted policy papers to Truman for his consideration.[25] Recommendations by the NSC addressed policy applying to key geographic areas or specific countries; matters bearing on the functional policies of atomic energy, mobilization, and foreign trade; and organizational and procedural matters of NSC operations, foreign intelligence activities, and internal security; as well as basic political, military, psychological, and economic policies concerning security. Each category related to the others, as Souers noted, forming "a basis for a balanced and consistent conduct of foreign, domestic, and military affairs related to our national security."[26] In addition to formulating policy papers, the NSC often became a day-to-day Cold War crisis forum where Truman and the council reached decisions that required immediate action. The Berlin blockade of 1948–1949, the threatened Chinese Communist attack on the United States naval base at Tsingtao, China, in late 1948, and the emergency events during the early months of the Korean War in the summer and fall of 1950, for example, were occurrences when the NSC often convened in special meetings without elaborate briefings or preparations.

*   *   *

The NSC decided early upon the nature of its basic role. It would suggest, not determine, national security policy for Truman, provide the president with policy advice and information, and consider matters that only required Truman's attention. Known as "The Concept of the National Security Council," the role definition was circulated to all council members and NSC staff members. Truman endorsed it in July 1948, because it reassured him that the NSC would not intrude upon the authority of the president.[27] Truman regarded the NSC, one observer was to comment, "with Missourian show-me skepti-

---

25. Ibid., 540; Department of State Memorandum, "Procedures for Preparation of National Security Council Papers," RG 59-PPS, NA; James S. Lay, Jr. cited in Francis H. Heller, ed., *The Truman White House: The Administration of the Presidency 1945–1953* (Lawrence, KS: The Regents Press of Kansas, 1980), 207.

26. Lay cited in Heller, *The Truman White House*, 207.

27. The Concept of the National Security Council, 26 July 1948, in "Current Policies of the Government Relating to National Security, Volume III," Papers of Harry S. Truman, PSF-NSC, Box 195, HSTL.

cism."[28] He did not participate regularly in the NSC's meetings until the Korean War began, attending twelve of the council's sessions from September 26, 1947 to June 28, 1950. His disinclination for presiding over NSC meetings, however, did not signify that he refused to rely upon the council's policy recommendations. In fact, Truman told the NSC at its thirty-eighth meeting in April 1949, it "had proven to be one of the best means available to the President for obtaining coordinated advice as a basis for reaching decisions."[29]

Any reservations Truman had about the NSC may have been due to the wording of the National Security Act of 1947. Concerned that the act might be interpreted to establish a council with powers and responsibilities similar to those of the British War Council cabinet to the diminution of presidential authority, Truman instead remained a distant participant.[30] He also disapproved of the statutory membership within the National Security Act. "He didn't like to be dictated to as to who came to meetings," one former member of the administration has said. Amendments to the act in 1949 making the membership flexible gave Truman some reassurance.[31] Between 1947 and 1950 other factors may have limited his attendance at the council's meetings. According to both Souers and Lay, the president believed that his expressed opinions at sessions might prematurely terminate NSC discussions or influence the members' own deliberations and final decisions on policy.[32] Clark Clifford believes that Truman's usual absence from NSC meetings was simply because he received a briefing from the executive secretary of the council every workday morning.[33] Whatever indifference or caution the president may have felt about NSC meetings began to dissolve after the Berlin blockade

28. Patrick Anderson, *The Presidents' Men: White House Assistants of Franklin D. Roosevelt, Harry S. Truman, Dwight D. Eisenhower, John F. Kennedy and Lyndon B. Johnson* (New York: Doubleday, 1968), 172.
29. Summary of Discussion at the 38th Meeting, 21 April 1949, PSF-NSC, Box 220, HSTL, Independence, Missouri.
30. Truman, *Years of Trial and Hope*, 59–60.
31. Elmer Staats cited in Kenneth W. Thompson, ed., *Portraits of American Presidents*, Volume II. *The Truman Presidency: Intimate Perspectives* (Lanham, MD: University Press of America, 1984), 93.
32. Souers, "Policy Formulation for National Security," 541; Lay, in Heller, *The Truman White House*, 207.
33. Anderson, *The Presidents' Men*, 170.

in 1948 and the outbreak of the Korean War, when he presided over several council meetings. If the policy debates of the council bored him, the crises of Berlin and Korea provided him with urgent issues to focus upon. Truman later conceded that the creation of the NSC "added a badly needed new facility to the government."[34]

Council members discovered as early as 1948 that the service secretaries of the army, navy, and air force outvoted the secretary of defense largely on the basis of parochial determinations. Truman convinced the newly appointed Secretary of Defense Forrestal that the military establishment would be improved if it were converted into a single Department of Defense, and the Departments of the Army, Navy, and Air Force were reduced from executive departments to military departments. Forrestal agreed to produce a report along the lines that Truman suggested. Although the secretaries of the three military departments would no longer be members of the NSC, Forrestal recommended the creation of an office of under secretary of defense, and a chair of the Joint Chiefs of Staff.[35] Forrestal submitted his plan to a newly-formed Task Force on National Security Organization, headed by Eberstadt, his old friend and former author of the National Security Act of 1947. The Task Force began its investigations as part of the first Hoover Commission on Government Reorganization, headed by former President Herbert Hoover, and it took a significant role in the reorganization of the NSC.[36]

---

34. Truman, *Years of Trial and Hope*, 59.
35. Clark M. Clifford Oral History Interview; George M. Elsey Oral History Interview; National Military Establishment, *First Report of the Secretary of Defense* (Washington, D.C.: G.P.O., 1948). This report stemmed largely from interservice fighting for scarce military budget. Forrestal had met with his chiefs at Key West (March 12–14) and Newport (August 20–22) to resolve the differences, but to no avail.
36. The (Hoover) Commission on Organization of the Executive Branch of the Government had been approved July 7, 1947 by the 80th Congress. The Task Force on National Security Organization was but one of many task forces established by the commission. The Hoover Commission's recommendations helped Truman reorganize much of the Executive Branch and its administrative operations. For a thorough examination of the reorganization see William E. Pemberton, *Bureaucratic Politics: Executive Reorganization During the Truman Administration* (Columbia, MO: University of Missouri Press, 1979); *The National Security Organization: A Report to the Congress by the Commission on Organization of the Executive Branch of the Government, February 1949* (Washington, D.C.: G.P.O., 1949), 5, 19.

Truman signs National Security Amendments Bill, August 1949. *(Abbie Rowe; Courtesy of Harry S. Truman Library)*

The Task Force findings for the Hoover Commission produced an immediate reorganization of the NSC and amendments to the National Security Act. In June 1949, Truman responded by submitting Reorganization Plan No. 4 to Congress, which authorized that the NSC be transferred to the Executive Office of the President. This change became effective on August 20, under the Reorganization Act of 1949. Thereafter, the NSC emerged as an "inner cabinet" of the White House.[37] In March 1949, Truman delivered a special message to Congress that requested legislative reforms based upon the Hoover Commission Task Force's recommendations. On August 22, Congress made amendments to the National Security Act of 1947, and Truman signed them into law. The amendments established that the membership of the NSC would include the president, vice-president, secretary of defense, chairman of the National Security Resources Board, and "Secretaries and Under Secretaries of other executive departments

---

37. NSC, "Policies of the Government of the United States of America Relating to the National Security, Volume II, 1949," 117, PSF-NSC, Box 195; Pemberton, *Bureaucratic Politics*, 114; George A. Wyeth, Jr., "The National Security Council," *Journal of International Affairs* (1954): 187. For the role of the Bureau of the Budget in the transfer of the NSC to the Executive Office see Anna Kasten Nelson, "National Security: Inventing a Process (1945–1960)," 234–235.

and of the military departments . . . when appointed by the President." The amendments also created a chair of the Joint Chiefs of Staff, a deputy secretary of defense, three assistant secretaries of defense research, and a development board.[38]

The Korean War motivated additional changes in the NSC. In July 1950, Truman directed that the NSC would meet each Thursday, and that all major national security recommendations would be coordinated through a new Senior NSC Staff, representing each official member of the council and the Joint Chiefs. At this time, moreover, Truman began to preside regularly over NSC meetings.[39] Although the amendments of 1949 removed the military service secretaries as statuatory members of the NSC, for nearly a year thereafter one or more of them often attended the council's meetings on invitation from the secretary of defense. During the initial weeks of the Korean War, numerous other officials attended NSC meetings, particularly representatives from the Joint Chiefs and invited agency and departmental advisers. Larger attendance made policy coordination and consensus more difficult, with discussions rambling and some policy actions taken later by council memorandum action. As a result, Truman limited attendance at the NSC's meetings to the statutory members, the secretary of the treasury, director of the Central Intelligence Agency, chairman of the JCS, Special Consultant to the President Sidney Souers, Special Assistant to the President W. Averell Harriman, and the executive secretary of the NSC.[40] Truman's reorganizational directives of July 1950 greatly improved the NSC policy coordination process during the last two years of his presidency. Requiring weekly NSC meetings with restricted attendance streamlined and gave consistency to the policymaking and deliberation mechanisms of the council. The creation of a Senior NSC Staff made high-level staff support the norm for the formulation of policy recommendations from all political and

---

38. Memorandum, Clark Clifford to Harry Truman, "Revision of the National Security Act," 8 February 1949, PCC-NME, Box 16, HSTL, Independence, Missouri; PPP:HST (Washington, D.C.: G.P.O., 1964), 163–164, 417–418; Truman, *Years of Trial and Hope*, 50; *The National Security Act of 1947, As Amended, Public Law 216*, 81st Congress, 1st sess., 10 August 1949 (Washington, D.C.: G.P.O., 1949).

39. Minutes of the 60th Meeting, July 6, 1950, PSF-NSC, Box 208.

40. Harry Truman to Sidney Souers, 19 July 1950, PSS-WHC, Box 1.

military members of the council. And in presiding over NSC meetings on a regular basis, Truman extended the president's authority to the process of policy coordination. The NSC worked extremely well thereafter, closer than it had under the Forrestal and Eberstadt guidelines established in 1947.

*   *   *

Under the NSC, and reporting directly to it, existed a central intelligence group similar to the one the Eberstadt Report of 1945 had recommended, but without the powers for domestic intelligence. The National Security Act of 1947 established the Central Intelligence Agency (CIA), with a director of central intelligence (DCI), appointed by the president with the advice and consent of the Senate. According to guidelines in the National Security Act, the primary duties of the CIA were to advise the NSC on intelligence activities, make recommendations for coordinating intelligence activities, and correlate, evaluate, and disseminate intelligence. The act also vaguely made reference to certain unspecified intelligence functions when it granted the CIA the duty "to perform such other functions and duties related to intelligence affecting the national security as the National Security Council may from time to time direct."[41] The CIA was a successor to the wartime Office of Strategic Services (OSS), headed by Major General William Donovan, but abolished by Truman in late 1945. The OSS had engaged in subversive activities worldwide during World War II, and the clause of the National Security Act of 1947 allowing the CIA "to perform such other functions and duties related to intelligence," may have been intended to provide the CIA the same privilege. It has been a topic of concern for scholars whether the Truman administration or Congress intended to authorize the CIA the roles of covert actions or the independent production of intelligence.[42] Clifford, who worked on the Central Intel-

---

41. *The National Security Act of 1947, Public Law 253.*

42. For various opinions see U.S. Congress, Senate, Select Committee to Study Governmental Operations with respect to Intelligence Activities, *Supplementary Detailed Staff Reports on Foreign and Military Intelligence* Book IV, Report 94-755, 94th Congress, 2nd sess. (Washington, D.C.: GPO, 1976), 25–31 (Hereafter cited as Church Committee.); Tom Braden, "The Birth of the CIA," *American Heritage* 27 (February 1977): 11–13; John Prados, *Presidents' Secret Wars: CIA and Pentagon Covert Operations Since World War II* (New York: William Morrow, 1986), 27–28; Phillip Knightley, *The Second Oldest Profession:*

ligence portion of the Eberstadt draft of the National Security Act, maintains that by the language of the act, Congress intended for the CIA to engage in covert actions, but for such activities "to be restricted in scope and purpose."[43] By 1948 the NSC had approved covert actions and was establishing the mechanisms for them. The CIA became involved in Italy's elections in 1948, and participated during 1949 and 1950 in the organization of a Free Europe Committee and Radio Free Europe for the Soviet satellite countries.

Truman believed that Pearl Harbor and World War II had taught the United States that we needed to gather intelligence. When he arrived at the White House in the spring of 1945, he "found that the needed intelligence information was not coordinated at any one place."[44] Truman therefore agreed that a central intelligence group would be necessary for a complete coordination in NSC policy. He had Souers and Lay brief him on intelligence matters each morning when they reviewed NSC policy recommendations. And near the end of his presidency, in a speech to a CIA training group, Truman told agency employees: "You are the organization, you are the intelligence arm that keeps the Executive informed so he can make decisions that will always be in the public interest for his own country."[45]

Despite Truman's appreciation and use of CIA intelligence information, he remained ambivalent about the agency's use of covert operations. In later years Truman seemed to be disturbed by some of the subversive activities undertaken by a peacetime CIA. Yet he had authorized the first covert actions in Italy taken by the agency.[46] On one occasion when Truman

---

Spies and Spying in the Twentieth Century (New York: W.W. Norton, 1986), 246; John Ranelagh, The Agency: The Rise and Decline of the CIA (New York: Simon & Schuster, 1987), 112–116; Rhodri Jeffreys-Jones, The CIA and American Democracy (New Haven: Yale University Press, 1989), 41; Arthur B. Darling, The Central Intelligence Agency: An Instrument of Government to 1950 (University Park: The Pennsylvania State University Press, 1990), 249–250.

43. Clark Clifford cited in Harold Honju Kohn, The National Security Constitution: Sharing Power After the Iran-Contra Affair (New Haven: Yale University Press, 1990), 103.

44. Truman, Years of Trial and Hope, 56.

45. Harry Truman cited in Walter Laquer, A World of Secrets: The Uses and Limits of Intelligence (New York: Basic Books, 1985), 72–73.

46. Ibid., 73; Draft Letter, Allen W. Dulles to Harry S. Truman, 29 December 1963, AWD-SGML, Box 117, PU, Princeton, New Jersey; Harry Truman, "Limit CIA Role to Intelligence" The Washington Post, 22 December 1963, Ibid.

criticized the operation of the CIA, Souers wrote him that the agency had indeed drifted "far from the original goal established by you."[47] One scholar of the CIA observes the reluctance of Truman and Souers to employ covert actions.[48] In most cases, Truman and the NSC opposed an excessive reliance on them at the expense of the CIA's intelligence collecting.

Like the NSC, the CIA experienced growing pains during its early years. Rear Admiral Roscoe H. Hillenkoetter, the first director of the agency, lacked the bureaucratic savy to contend with the other older intelligence services within the military branches. Protecting their bureaucratic turf, they often refused to cooperate with the CIA in its collection and reporting of intelligence information. As a result, the agency at times had difficulty predicting events in a timely manner.[49] In an attempt to correct the CIA's problems with intelligence coordination, Souers asked the NSC to approve the creation of a three-member survey group that would make recommendations for improvement of the agency. As chair of the group, the NSC named Allan W. Dulles, a former OSS officer, and as co-members, two former military intelligence officers, William H. Jackson and Mathias F. Correa.[50]

In late January 1949, the committee submitted its final report to the NSC. Along with the recommendations of the Hoover Commission's Task Force on National Security that "vigorous steps be taken" to improve the work of the CIA, the committee survey's criticisms went on the NSC's agenda. By early July, the NSC concurred with the Dulles-Jackson-Correa report.[51] In August, the council voted its approval of the report,

---

47. Sidney Souers to Harry Truman, 27 December 1963, PSS-Correspondence, Box 1. Truman had been critical after the Kennedy administration's Bay of Pigs fiasco.

48. Jones, *The CIA and American Democracy*, 62.

49. Ibid., 45–46.

50. Ibid., 86; Darling, *The Central Intelligence Agency*, 302–303; Survey of the Central Intelligence Agency, NSC, "Policies of the Government of the United States of America Relating to the National Security, Volume I, 1947–1948," 66, PSF-NSC, Box 195.

51. Ludwell Lee Montague, *General Walter Bedell Smith as Director of Central Intelligence October 1950–February 1953* (University Park: The Pennsylvania University Press, 1992), 43–47. The Dulles-Jackson-Correa Report to the National Security Council on the Central Intelligence Agency and National Organization for Intelligence, January 1, 1949, in William M. Leary, ed., *The Central Intelligence Agency: History and Documents* (University, AL: The University

authorizing the establishment of new CIA offices for long-range intelligence studies, the simplifying of the agency's covert and clandestine mechanisms, and the implementation of new scientific and technological operation.[52] Congress also facilitated the agency's reorganization. Congressional approval of the Central Intelligence Agency Act in 1949 authorized special training of CIA personnel, increased appropriations for the agency, and granted the director of the CIA the right to receive and spend funds without submitting to Congress a full account of expenditures.[53]

The Korean War brought about a change for the CIA when Hillenkoetter returned to sea command in October 1950. From then until the end of the Truman presidency, General Walter Bedell Smith served as director of the CIA. Smith had been General Dwight D. Eisenhower's chief of staff during World War II, and in the immediate postwar years the ambassador to the Soviet Union. According to one scholar, Smith "was pugnacious enough to intimidate anyone," and within days after he became DCI he "made mincemeat of CIA bureaucracy."[54] Under his leadership, and with NSC approval, the CIA expanded its activities and further consolidated its internal operation.

When the National Security Council convened its first meeting in early autumn of 1947, the six members of council, its executive secretary, and the director of the CIA who sat at the large mahogany table in the Cabinet Conference Room of the White House contributed to the coordination of complex Cold War policies that began that day. Each step of operational changes for the NSC and the CIA that took place during the

of Alabama Press, 1984), 134–142; NSC 50, "The Central Intelligence Agency and National Organization for Intelligence," NSC, "Policies of the Government of the United States of America Relating to the National Security, Volume II, 1949," 109, PSF-NSC, Box 195.

52. NSC 50, "The Central Intelligence Agency and National Organization for Intelligence," 4 August 1949, NSC, "Policies of the Government, 1949," 109, PSF-NSC, Box 195.

53. Jones, *The CIA and American Democracy*, 59–60; Ranelagh, *The Agency*, 193–195. For the complete text of the Central Intelligence Agency Act of 1949, 20 June 1949, see Michael Warner, ed., *CIA Cold War Records: The CIA Under Harry Truman* (Washington, D.C.: History Staff Center for the Study of Intelligence, Central Intelligence Agency, 1994), 287–294.

54. Prados, *Presidents' Secret Wars*, 82. For the official, and newly released history, of General Smith's tenure see Montague, *General Walter Bedell Smith as Director of Central Intelligence*.

Truman administration helped further the development of the national security state and established the parameters of containment policy. By the end of Truman's presidency the NSC had become a well-integrated and functioning institution. It had held 128 meetings and had taken 697 actions in the form of policy approvals and recommendations, the great majority affecting the course of the Cold War.

Chapter Two

A New Cold War Counteroffensive

U.S. policy toward the U.S.S.R. must be that of a long-term, patient but firm and vigilant containment of Russian expansive tendencies.

(George F. Kennan, 1947)

At the first meeting of the NSC on September 26, 1947, Souers addressed the council and its staff concerning policies and procedures. Perhaps more important was the council's discussion of the first of many monthly reports from the CIA—the "Review of the World Situation as It Relates to the Security of the United States." The CIA maintained that the Soviet Union was intent upon spreading its influence by "deliberately conducting political, economic, and psychological warfare against the United States." The "greatest danger" to the security interest of the United States, the report observed, would be the "possibility of economic collapse in Western Europe" as well as the lack of political "stabilization and recovery in Europe and Asia." This might lead to the "consequent accession to power of Communist elements."[1]

---

1. Minutes of the 1st Meeting, 26 September 1947, PSF-NSC, Box 203; CIA-1, "Review of the World Situation as It Relates to the Security of the United States," Ibid.

The CIA's assessment of the world situation held a telling force particularly for the NSC's agenda during the last months of 1947 and early half of 1948. The council had to consider the nature and extent of American assistance for Greece; an appropriate response on Eastern Europe, over which the Soviet Union continued to tighten its control; a policy on covert political countermeasures and its application in Eastern Europe and in Italy; the pressing need for a reply to Western European proposals for a collective defense organization; and a suitable approach to the initial phase of the Soviet blockade of Berlin. Any of these issues provided enough difficulties to test the ability of the NSC to coordinate political and military objectives, but the council formulated a policy for each one of them, and in doing so provided an early framework for Truman's containment counteroffensive.

Since the end of World War II, Greece had been embroiled in a bloody civil war, wracked by rampant inflation, and ruled by an oligarchic right-wing government. After the war ended, the British restored the Greek monarchy to power, maintained occupying forces, and provided assistance to the beleaguered economy. By 1946 Communists and other leftist resistance groups had formed an insurgency to oust the monarchy. Throughout 1946 and 1947 guerrilla warfare ensued and escalated, largely through aid from Soviet satellite sources such as Yugoslavia, Bulgaria, and Albania. The British government decided that stopping the civil war was too difficult and expensive, and thus in February 1947, it announced that it was terminating all forms of assistance to Greece. By the time the NSC analyzed the situation, the administration had already announced the Truman Doctrine and the Marshall Plan.

In the spring of 1947 when Congress studied the amount of economic aid necessary for the proposed Greek-Turkish Aid Act, it learned from the Department of State that American military personnel might have to provide technical assistance and training for the Greek National Army. Following an intensive inspection, Major General Stephen J. Chamberlin, director of army intelligence, reported that the situation was desperate. Poorly equipped, ill-trained, and demoralized, the Greek National Army, Chamberlin warned, risked losing to the Communist insurgents. He recommended that the United States send a military advisory and planning group, but only for the purpose of offering operational advice.[2] Secretary of State Marshall forwarded Chamberlin's report to the NSC. The council approved his suggestions without debate and recommended "the diversion for military purposes" of portions of the Greek and Turkish aid that had been for the economic reconstruction of Greece.[3] In early November, Marshall transmitted the NSC's request, and Truman followed up by dispatching nearly two hundred military personnel along with financial support.[4] This was the first Cold War military policy to be implemented on the basis of NSC recommendation, and set the stage for a debate later by the NSC whether an expanded American military presence in Greece was warranted if Greek national forces continued to falter.

As Truman and the NSC during the autumn of 1947 directed their attention on the economic and military situation in Greece, questions also arose about the continuance of exports to the Soviet Union. The USSR had withdrawn from the Marshall Plan's program for European recovery, pressured Czechoslovakia, Hungary, and Poland not to participate, and denounced the plan as American interference in the internal affairs of European nations. As the USSR tightened its control over Eastern Europe, the Department of Commerce proposed that Congress consider legislation to place a trade embargo on all American exports to the Soviet Union and its Eastern European satellites.

Secretary of Commerce W. Averell Harriman presented the

---

2. PPS 8, "United States Policy in the Event of the Establishment of Communist Power in Greece," 18 September 1947, in Anna Kasten Nelson, ed., *The State Department Policy Planning Staff Papers 1947* (New York: Garland Publishing, 1983), 76–90; *FRUS: 1947*, V, 226–231; Condit, *History of the JCS*, II, 36–38; Leffler, *A Preponderance of Power*, 194.

3. "Extension of Operational Advice to the Greek Armed Forces," 31 October 1947, PSF-NSC, Box 193. For a detailed account of the debates over military assistance to Greece see Chester J. Pach, Jr., *Arming the Free World: The Origins of the United States Military Assistance Program, 1945–1950* (Chapel Hill: The University of North Carolina Press, 1991), 107–117.

4. Memorandum, George Marshall to Harry Truman, 3 November 1947, Ibid. For the debates and policies that revolved around the establishment of a Joint U.S. Military Advisory and Planning Group for Greece see Howard Jones, *"A New Kind of War": America's Global Strategy and the Truman Doctrine in Greece* (New York: Oxford University Press, 1989), 107–122.

proposal before the NSC at its second meeting. He argued that an embargo was necessary for eliminating Soviet access to Western military and atomic energy technologies, and that it would conserve strategic exports "in short supply for the European recovery plan." Undersecretary of State Robert Lovett thought the proposal viable if export controls were applied only to the USSR, and if the Soviet satellites were exempted from controls. The NSC deferred any decision on the matter until a Department of State study could be made.[5]

The Department of State's study, conducted by George F. Kennan, director of the PPS, proved to be a compromise report that made concessions between Commerce's desire for a trade embargo and those who sought select export controls. This in turn allowed the administration, at its discretion, to cease trade with the Soviet Union, but avoided singling out any Soviet satellite nation. The revised report, "Control of Exports to the USSR and Eastern Europe," had the agreement of the Department of Commerce, and at the fourth meeting of the NSC Lovett suggested that the council accept its new wording. With no further debate, other members concurred in the revisions, and Harriman set out on a time-consuming task that required that the Department of Commerce work with the Department of Defense and negotiate with Europeans in desperate need of American exports.[6] Truman approved the report coordinated by the NSC, and as a result the administration by 1948 had virtually eliminated all trade with the Soviet Union.[7] The only additional export control measures the NSC later considered

5. Minutes of the 4th Meeting, 17 December 1947, PSF-NSC, Box 203. PPS 17, "U.S. Exports to the U.S.S.R. and the Satellite States," 26 November 1947, in Nelson, *PPS Papers 1947*, 152–175; PPS 17, 26 November 1947, *FRUS: 1947*, IV, 489–507; Robert Lovett to Averell Harriman, 8 December 1947, Ibid., 508–509.

6. PPS 17, "U.S. Exports to the U.S.S.R. and the Satellite States," 26 November 1947, in Nelson, *PPS Papers 1947*, 152–175; PPS 17, 26 November 1947, *FRUS: 1947*, IV, 489–507; Robert Lovett to Averell Harriman, 8 December 1947, Ibid., 508–509; "Control of Exports to the USSR and Eastern Europe," nd, PSF-NSC, Box 203; Minutes of the 4th Meeting, 17 December 1947, Ibid.

7. "Control of Exports to the USSR and Eastern Europe," 18 December 1947, NSC, "Policies of the Government, 1947–1948," 28, PSF-NSC, Box 195; Memorandum, Sidney Souers to Harry Truman, 17 December 1947, Ibid., Box 203.

President Truman confers with Undersecretary of State Robert A. Lovett and State Department Officials George F. Kennan and Charles E. Bohlen, November 1947. *(Courtesy of Bettmann Newsphotos, Inc./United Press International)*

concerned a separate policy regarding the elimination of future American aircraft parts to the USSR and its satellites that went into effect in the summer of 1948.[8]

Economic and military measures employed during 1947 were innovative foreign policy methods—methods of a newly-operating national security state. But there was another option that the United States began to employ actively early in 1948— covert action. Commonly referred to by SANACC as psychological warfare, covert action was an instrument designed to frustrate "Soviet ambitions without provoking open conflict."[9] In late 1946 SANACC had proposed covert psychological warfare.[10] One of the weaknesses of the older intelligence services

---

8. NSC 15/2, "U.S. Aviation Policy Toward the USSR and Its Satellites," 13 July 1948, NSC, "Policies of the Government, 1947–1948," 29–30, PSF-NSC, Box 195; PPS 32, "U.S. Civil Aviation Policy Toward the U.S.S.R. and Its Satellites," 11 June 1948, in Anna Kasten Nelson, ed., *The State Department Policy Planning Staff Papers 1948* (New York: Garland Publishing, 1983), 274–280.

9. Church Committee, 26.

10. Ibid., 27–29. Psychological warfare was proposed by the State-Army-Navy-Air Force Coordinating Committee as SANACC 304/11.

had been the lack of any effective covert intelligence capability. SANACC recognized the flaw, and so did the NSC. In late 1947, the council and Truman approved the directive, "Coordination of Foreign Information Measures," which maintained, although vaguely, that the CIA would use "information measures" to influence attitudes in foreign countries in a direction favorable to Washington's objectives.[11] Two weeks later the CIA established a Special Procedures Group (SPG) to carry out the mandate. The SPG's first assignments were to initiate psychological operations in Central and Eastern Europe.[12] In preparation for these and future activities, the NSC approved the SPG's acquisition of a printing plant for clandestine publications, a short-wave radio transmitter for signals across the Iron Curtain, and the first units of a balloon fleet to carry print materials into the Soviet satellite countries of Eastern Europe.[13] Psychological warfare marked the beginning of an early and progressive bureaucratic growth of the NSC and the CIA. By 1947, as one historian of American intelligence writes, the CIA had adopted a secret slogan, "bigger than State by forty-eight." The CIA "was not merely in the business of collecting information about what was happening in the world . . . it saw its duty as making things happen."[14]

In 1948 as tensions between the United States and the Soviet Union intensified, the NSC's influence upon diplomatic, economic, and military containment policy increased. In February 1948 the Communists overthrew the democratic government of Czechoslovakia. The coup d'etat imprisoned political opposition leaders and set up a regime tied to the Soviet Union. Of all the Eastern European countries bordering the USSR, only the Czechoslovak republic had retained its democratic government; now it was gone. During the coup the Czechoslovak Foreign Minister Jan Masaryk died suddenly. The Soviet Union reported that he was murdered. At the same time, growing support of the Communist Party at the polls and within labor organizations threatened Italy and France. One month

---

11. Ibid., 28; NSC 4, "Coordination of Foreign Information Measures," 17 December 1947, PSF-NSC, Box 203.

12. Church Committee, 28–29.

13. Ibid.; NSC Record of Actions, 13 January, 12 February 1948, PSF-NSC, Box 191.

14. Knightley, *The Second Oldest Profession*, 244.

later, the Soviet delegation stormed out of the Four Power Allied Control Council talks in Berlin, worsening tensions in Germany. Shortly thereafter, Truman gave a speech before Congress calling for passage of Marshall Plan appropriations, resumption of the selective service, and the establishment of a universal military training program. Congress responded by restoring selective service and increasing appropriations for the air force, but it rejected Truman's proposal for universal military training. More important for United States foreign policy was the Economic Cooperation Act that set up the European Recovery Program (ERP), or the Marshall Plan.

*   *   *

During the winter and spring of 1948, the NSC concentrated on developments in Greece and Italy. By summer, however, the council had become more concerned with Western Europe, as resistance to American economic reconstruction efforts emerged there and the Soviet Union initiated the blockade of Berlin. Intelligence estimates and reports in early 1948 stressed that although the Soviet Union had not intervened directly in the ongoing Greek civil war, it had provided "moral and material aid" for the insurgents through its satellites. Concluding that the Soviet Union would avoid a "direct conflict with the United States," the CIA warned that an absence of American counteraction in Greece could have "substantiative psychological and political repercussions." Fixing upon geopolitical and economic interests, the intelligence reports advocated an American presence in Greece large enough to prevent Soviet military access to the Mediterranean, the fall of Italy to the Communist Party, and Soviet domination of Iran and the Kurdish area of Iraq. The CIA's most serious concern about the economic consequence of indirect or direct Soviet control of Greece was the possible loss of access to Middle Eastern petroleum resources that provided about forty percent of the world's oil reserves, and was necessary for the economic recovery of Western Europe.[15]

---

15. CIA-4, "Review of the World Situation as it Relates to the Security of the United States," 12 January 1948, PSF-NSC, Box 203; CIA-ORE-69, "Possible Consequences of Communist Control of Greece in the Absence of United States Counteraction," 9 February 1948, PSF-IF, Box 256, HSTL, Independence, Missouri.

Despite intelligence assessments that urged an ever greater American presence in Greece, debate over the application of direct intervention there developed within the administration. It sharpened when in January 1948 the NSC staff presented a report influenced by Loy Henderson, director of the Department of State's Office of Near Eastern and African Affairs, numbered NSC 5. Henderson advocated the deployment of combat troops to Greece if Communist forces from Soviet satellite countries were overtly to intervene. The council discussed the report at length, and the meeting revealed differences within the Department of State on the point of sending American military forces to Greece.[16]

Speaking for Marshall, who was unable to attend the meeting, Lovett told NSC members that the secretary of state felt the whole position paper should be "reworked." Secretary of Defense Forrestal admitted that he was "somewhat puzzled" when he read the paper, and wondered whether it overstepped the legal bounds of the NSC's authority when it suggested "specific actions" such as the use of military force in Greece. Lovett informed Forrestal and the others that the problems involved in formulating a policy toward Greece had been submitted to the NSC because the time had come "to know how far militarily we can afford to go" in Greece. Henderson, Lovett pointed out to the NSC, "believes that if we send in one division we will hear no more from the Communists." A very skeptical Secretary of the Army Kenneth Royall replied that the army's knowledge of the situation in Greece gave it reason to determine that "one division cannot contain the Greek guerrillas." Reacting to the confusion and differences about the premises of the report, the council voted to return it for revision. The NSC recommended that future revisions include comments from the Joint Chiefs and a position paper on Greece from the Department of State's PPS.[17]

The NSC staff's revised report, "The Position of the United States with Respect to Greece" (NSC 5/2), was completed by early February, and the council spent nearly an entire meeting

---

16. Leffler, *A Preponderance of Power*, 195; H. W. Brands, *Inside the Cold War: Loy Henderson and the Rise of the American Empire 1918–1961* (New York: Oxford University Press, 1991), 147–164; Jones, *A New Kind of War*, 130–133; Minutes of the 5th Meeting, 13 January 1948, PSF-NSC, Box 203.

17. Ibid.

deliberating it. Forrestal opened the meeting by reading comments from the JCS that emphasized that further involvement of United States military forces in Greece would make necessary at least partial military mobilization. Concerned about the deployment of substantial American combat forces abroad, and the availability of the forces for the task, the Joint Chiefs did not wholly endorse direct American intervention in Greece. This was the first of several warnings over the next two years that the JCS would send to the NSC when Cold War policies coordinated by the NSC recommended use of combat forces abroad. Kennan and the PPS, like the Joint Chiefs, expressed reservations about dispatching military forces to Greece. In its study for the Department of State, the PPS noted that any immediate application of combat forces in Greece would be premature. As the NSC's discussions continued, Marshall reminded each council member that the use of any American military force in Greece risked leading the administration to react in the same manner in Palestine and China. Forrestal thought that during an election year he could not "politically conceive of the President sending troops" to Greece unless there was "some further provocative action." Marshall agreed with Forrestal that the use of military force in Greece could put Truman "in a bad position," but he believed that the United States "must nonetheless be ready." Marshall concluded: "If we appear to be weakening, we will lose the game and prejudice our whole national position."[18]

Given Marshall's and Forrestal's consensus, all NSC members approved the report. It included previous recommendations made by the JCS, and the Department of State's position that called for "using all feasible means short of the application of United States military power." The next day Truman approved the revised policy paper and directed its implementation. At this point, the NSC had played an important role in not only coordinating but modifying a compromised policy on Greece. By the summer of 1948, the amending efforts of the NSC had become more extensive. The JCS held that the possibility of partial mobilization in the Eastern Mediterranean or the Middle East as outlined in the report required increasing appropriations for the supplemental military budget of 1948.

---

18. Ibid.; Leffler, *The Specter of Communism,* 70.

Truman, however, refused to increase the budget. In the summer, the NSC staff issued a newer position paper, "The Position of the United States with Respect to the Use of Military Power in Greece" (NSC 5/4). It recommended that military action should be made only "in the light of the overall world situation and not primarily as a contribution to the solution of the problem in Greece." Reflecting opinion of the JCS, the report cautioned restraint and the continued application of indirect military tactical advice and supply support to the Greek National Army. The council also amended the report to guarantee reevaluation of United States policy toward Greece should the situation deteriorate. The NSC adopted the report without discussion and sent it to Truman, who approved it as policy.[19]

The first test of the council's ability to coordinate policy arrived in early 1948 when the council and its staff were asked to clarify the premises of United States containment for Greece. The Henderson report of January 1948 that called for the dispatching of American combat troops to Greece represented a worse case scenario. Revised with input from the Department of State's PPS, and including reservations from the JCS, the report was resubmitted and received the council's approval as NSC 5/2. The JCS opposed deployment of combat troops into Greece on grounds that it would require a partial mobilization of forces as well as drain troop strength from Western Europe. The PPS concurred with the JCS because Kennan and his staff believed the application of direct military force in Greece was premature and would set a dangerous precedent for American policy in peripheral regions. Soviet intervention in Greece, moreover, had remained indirect. Until the time that the USSR should directly challenge the United States in Greece, containment of Soviet interests would restrict itself to economic and political measures, primarily in the form of indirect military operational advice and supplies.

Truman's approval greatly reduced the chances of Ameri-

---

19. Minutes of the 6th Meeting, 12 February 1948, PSF-NSC, Box 203; Memorandum, Sidney Souers to Harry Truman, 12 February 1948, Ibid.; NSC 5/2, "The Position of the United States with Respect to Greece," 2, 12 February 1948, *FRUS: 1948*, IV, 2–7, 46–51; NSC 5/2, PSF-NSC, Box 203; PPS 18, "United States Policy with Respect to Greece," 10 January 1948, in Nelson, *PPS Papers 1948*, 1–33; Miscamble, *George F. Kennan and the Making of Foreign Policy*, 87–92.

can troop deployment to Greece, all the while Yugoslavia provided more support for insurgent forces. The Communist guerrillas early in the year conducted several successful raids. With
the help of the Yugoslavian government, assistance was for
naught, for some months later the insurgents suffered major
defeats. The reason was not American intervention but a split
in the Greek Communist Party as a consequence of Yugoslavia's expulsion in June 1948 from the Soviet bloc. Switching
to full-scale conventional warfare in an effort to counter American assistance, insurgent forces allied with Yugoslavia met
with disaster. By the spring of 1949 a cease-fire was implemented, and five months later, on October 16, 1949, the civil
war ended with the Greek national government in control of
the country.[20]

The administration concluded that Greece had strategic
linkage to America's interests in the Mediterranean.[21] It also
determined that the Greek national triumph in 1949 was an
American victory over international communism. Economic
and military containment had succeeded. After 1949, Greece
became the model that the administration followed in its
counterinsurgency efforts, and this success seemed to predict
that anti-Communist guerrilla operations in other parts of the
world would for a long time be a viable option for the United
States.[22]

The cautious position that the NSC took regarding direct
military action in the Greek civil war was partly due to the suc-

---

20. NSC 5/3, NSC 5/4, "The Position of the United States with Respect to
the Use of U.S. Military Power in Greece," 25 May, 25 June 1948, *FRUS: 1948*,
IV, 93–95, 101; NSC, "Politics of the Government, 1947–1948," 9–10, PSF-NSC,
Box 195; Edgar O'Ballance, *The Greek Civil War, 1944–1949* (New York;
Frederick A. Praeger, 1966), 156–157, 212–213. Also see CIA-1-49, "Review of
the World," 19 January 1949, in which the CIA maintained that a reactionary
government or a "dictatorial solution" would be the only possible answer to the
military stalemate and inflated economic situation in Greece.

21. A formal United States policy on the Mediterranean–Middle East region had been approved by the NSC on 12 November 1947, and by Truman on
24 November 1947. The so-called American Paper enunciated that the United
States would "support the security" of the region and "assist in maintaining the
territorial integrity and political independence of Italy, Greece, Turkey, and
Iran." See Memorandum, Robert Lovett to Harry Truman, 24 November 1947,
PSF-NSC, Box 203; "The American Paper," *FRUS: 1947*, V, 575–576, 623–624.

22. For a full account of the origins of the counterinsurgency doctrine and
its application see Douglas S. Blaufarb, *The Counterinsurgency Era: U.S. Doctrine and Performance 1950 to the Present* (New York: The Free Press, 1977).

cessful Communist coup in Czechoslovakia.[23] A flurry of intelligence reports explained that American successes in Europe posed an economic and military threat to the Soviet Union.[24] One widely-circulated estimate of March 1948 issued by the CIA had an especially significant influence. It indicated that the coup in Czechoslovakia had been consistent with the "Soviet intention" to consolidate its control in Eastern Europe "as a vital measure of security." The fall of Czechoslovakia, the CIA maintained, did not reflect "any sudden increase in Soviet capabilities." But if any Soviet military actions took place in Eastern Europe during the year, as warned, it would be as a result of "ongoing American initiatives" in Western Europe. The Communist coup in Czechoslovakia had "created widespread apprehension," the CIA asserted, and Communist "political action committees" in Italy and France posed a serious threat to the security of Western Europe because they were similar to those that had "played so effective a part" in Czechoslovakia. It concluded, "the most serious and immediate danger of an extension of Communist influence in Western Europe is the growing possibility of a Popular Democratic Front victory in the Italian elections of April 8."[25]

Such comments could point in opposite directions. As warnings against provocation of Soviet fears, they encouraged the care that the NSC took in restraining American intervention in Greece. Yet in recognizing that the USSR had already embarked, reactively or not, upon its own aggressive course, they suggested the need for American military vigilance.[26] The NSC responded with a preliminary policy reevaluation of United States political and military strategy. "The Position of the United States with Respect to Soviet-Directed World Communism" (NSC 7), proposed a counteroffensive against communism that included the continuance of "overwhelming U.S. superiority in atomic weapons, the rearming of the United States," and greater assistance to Western Europe as well as a

---

23. Also see Melvyn P. Leffler, "The American Conception of National Security and the Beginnings of the Cold War, 1945–48," *American Historical Review* 89 (April 1984): 373–374.

24. CIA-4, CIA-3–48, CIA-4–48, "Review of the World," 12 January, 10 March, 2 April 1948, PSF-NSC, Box 203.

25. CIA 3–48, "Review of the World," 10 March, Ibid.

26. Ibid.

program to render support to "underground resistance movements" in Eastern Europe. Vague about the implementation of its proposed programs, the study gave some guidelines for future Cold War policy initiatives the NSC was considering. Truman had not yet approved the new policy study when events in Italy turned his attention from Eastern Europe towards the Eastern Mediterranean once again.[27]

A joint American-British occupation of Italy that had existed until the ratification of a peace treaty in September 1947 encountered problems. The terms of the treaty stipulated that the last Allied troops would withdraw by December 1948. Italy would forfeit its colonial empire in North Africa and agree to specific reparations and military restrictions. In addition, the area in and around Trieste, a controversial northern locale with neighboring Yugoslavia, was to become a free territory under a combined Anglo-American peacekeeping operation. The Italians considered the peace treaty humiliating. Complicating matters was an economy suffering from high postwar inflation and unemployment under an unstable government of Christian Democrats and factions of Communists and socialists. In an effort to remove the leftist influence, Premier Alcide de Gasperi in May 1947 dissolved the government. In retaliation, and hoping to remove the de Gasperi leadership, left-wing groups initiated several nationwide strikes.[28]

As the deadline for withdrawal of British and American troops neared and reports of Communist political activity in Italy reached the administration, Truman and Souers put the matter before the NSC for evaluation.[29] The NSC was already alerted to the problem: Lovett and Forrestal had submitted a report by the PPS that predicted a Communist coup, assisted

---

27. NSC 7, "The Position of the United States with Respect to Soviet-Directed World Communism," 30 March 1948, *FRUS: 1948*, I, pt. 2, 546–550; Thomas H. Etzold and John Lewis Gaddis, eds., *Containment: Documents on American Policy and Strategy 1945–1950* (New York: Columbia University Press, 1978), 164–169; PSF-NSC, Box 203.

28. James E. Miller, *The United States and Italy, 1940–1950: The Politics and Diplomacy of Stabilization* (Chapel Hill: The University of North Carolina Press, 1986), 193–210, 213–237. For the context of the treaty see U.S. Congress, *A Decade of American Foreign Policy: Basic Documents, 1941–49* (Washington, D.C.: G.P.O., 1957), 460–465.

29. Memorandum, Sidney Souers to Harry Truman, 12 November 1947, PSF-NSC, Box 203.

by Yugoslav military aid. In it, Kennan suggested that Italy was the "key point" in Europe. If the Communists were to win there, he argued, United States credibility in the Mediterranean and in Europe would "be undermined."[30] Truman began to feel the pressure. In a letter to his wife, three days after receiving Kennan's report, he wrote: "Yesterday was one of the most hectic days. . . . Suppose, for instance, that Italy should fold up and that Tito then would move into the Po Valley. All the Mediterranean coast of France is open to Russian occupation. We withdraw from Greece and Turkey and prepare for war. It must not happen."[31] The NSC concurred with the PPS report and recommended that the United States send technical advisers to the Italian armed forces and actively combat Communist propaganda with psychological warfare, and "by all other practicable means." "The Position of the United States with Respect to Italy" (NSC 1/2) concluded that should "a Communist-dominated government [be] set up in all or part of Italy" prior to the withdrawal of occupational forces, the United States should suspend all original agreements and retain its military presence there.[32]

After the CIA circulated its March intelligence report, Truman approved the recommendation by the NSC for shipment of arms to Italy.[33] With elections there scheduled for April, Truman approved "The Position of the United States with Respect to Italy in the Light of the Possibility of Communist Participation in the Government by Legal Means" (NSC 1/3) that authorized covert political and financial assistance by the CIA to the Italian Christian Democratic and Social Democratic par-

---

30. PPS 9, "Possible Action by the U.S. to Assist the Italian Government in the Event of Communist Seizure of North Italy and the Establishment of an Italian Communist 'Government' in that Area," 24 September 1947, in Nelson, *PPS Papers*, 1948, 102–107; Leffler, *A Preponderance of Power*, 197.

31. Truman cited in Robert H. Ferrell, ed., *Dear Bess: The Letters from Harry to Bess Truman 1910–1950* (New York: W.W. Norton, 1983), 550.

32. NSC 1/1, NSC 1/2, "The Position of the United States with Respect to Italy," 14 November 1947, 12 March 1948, *FRUS: 1948*, III, 724–726, 765–769; Memorandum, Sidney Souers to Harry Truman, 11 March 1948, PSF-NSC, Box 203. Supply of military equipment to the Italian armed forces was approved by SANACC on 16 January 1948, and by Truman 12 February 1948. See SANACC 390/1 and Memorandum, Harry Truman to Sidney Souers (non-letterhead), Ibid.

33. Memorandum, Harry Truman to James Forrestal, 10 March 1948, PSF-CF, Box 285, HSTL, Independence, Missouri.

ties.[34] For several weeks thereafter, the CIA waged a propaganda campaign in Italy that stressed the importance of the Marshall Plan to the recovery of the Italian economy and made clear American support for the de Gasperi government. Italy was saturated with documentary films on American democracy. Hollywood distributors also made available to Italian movie houses copies of the movie "Ninotchka," Greta Garbo's film of 1939 that satirized Soviet life. The Voice of America increased radio broadcasts to Italy featuring Italian-Americans like former boxing champion Rocky Graziano with other famous Americans such as Dinah Shore, Bing Crosby, Eleanor Roosevelt, and Walter Pidgeon. American propaganda influenced the election, helping the Christian Democrats poll nearly forty-nine percent of the popular vote and allowing them to capture a majority of seats in the Italian Parliament.[35]

Encouraged by the success of the CIA's covert political countermeasures in Italy, Kennan responded with a proposal for the expansion of American covert activity from that of psychological and propaganda warfare to covert political action for the specific purpose of lending support to anti-Communist parties within foreign governments.[36] Weeks later, the NSC issued a directive that would increase covert operations against the Soviet Union, and in all "threatened countries of the free world." Titled "Office of Special Projects" (NSC 10/2), it called for expanded covert actions including political, psychological, and economic warfare, sabotage, anti-sabotage, various modes of subversion against hostile states, and limited paramilitary contingency operations. The directive also established within the CIA the Office of Policy Coordination (OPC). It placed only

---

34. NSC 1/3, "The Position of the United States with Respect to Italy in the Light of the Possibility of Communist Participation in the Government by Legal Means," *FRUS: 1948*, III, 775–779, 868–890; PSF-NSC, Box 203; Leffler, *A Preponderance of Power*, 197–198; idem, *The Specter of Communism*, 71.

35. Miller, *The United States and Italy*, 248–249; James E. Miller, "Taking Off the Gloves: The United States and the Italian Elections of 1948," *Diplomatic History* 7 (Winter 1983): 48–49; Alan A. Platt and Robert Leonardi, "American Foreign Policy and the Postwar Italian Left," *Political Science Quarterly* 93 (Summer 1978/1979): 202.

36. Church Committee, 29; Memorandum, George Kennan to Robert Lovett, 16 June 1948, RG 59-PPS, NA; Miscamble, *George F. Kennan and the Making of American Foreign Policy*, 108–109.

a single restriction on the OPC: its operations had to be "planned and conducted so that any U.S. government responsibility for them is not evident to unauthorized persons and that if uncovered the U.S. government can plausibly disclaim any responsibility for them."[37] The NSC placed OPC under the supervision of the secretaries of state and defense. The secretary of state would choose the OPC's director. In August Marshall selected Frank Wisner, a former OSS agent assigned to Romania and then deputy assistant secretary of state for occupied areas. William Colby, one of the agents Wisner recruited into the OPC, was to recall: "Wisner landed like a dynamo, read all the intelligence and set out to form a clandestine force worldwide." Wisner's OPC drew eventually from a large number of Ivy League graduates and OSS veterans. A determined man, Wisner worked to develop an organization that epitomized the can-do attitude characteristic of the old OSS.[38]

The NSC directive and its guidelines differed in one respect from Kennan's original proposal. It placed under the authority of the CIA, not the Department of State, the responsibility for covert actions. In addition, all covert operations were allocated funds from the CIA's budget, and thus escaped congressional oversight. In early 1948 OPC had operated on a budget of $4.7 million with a staff of three hundred intelligence officers and seven field stations. By 1949 its budget and staff had doubled.[39] The official implementation of NSC 10/2 had taken the national security state past a crucial stage in development, and the Cold War had evolved into a reality that Truman and the NSC could manage through a combination of economic and military containment and covert action. What had been a moderate policy

---

37. Church Committee, 29–30; Memorandums, George H. Butler to Robert Lovett, 7, 29 December 1948, RG 59-PPS, NA; Memorandum, Sidney Souers to the NSC, "Establishment of a Special Services Unit in the Central Intelligence Agency," 2 June 1948, PSF-NSC, Box 203; NSC 10/2, "Office of Special Projects," 18 June 1948, Ibid.; Etzold and Gaddis, *Containment*, 125–128; Darling, *The Central Intelligence Agency*, 275.

38. Minutes of the 18th Meeting, 19 August 1948, PSF-NSC, Box 203; Church Committee, 30; William Colby and Peter Forbath, *Honorable Men: My Life in the CIA* (New York: Simon and Schuster, 1978), 73; Darling, *The Central Intelligence Agency*, 276–281.

39. Knightley, *The Second Oldest Profession*, 248.

by the NSC through late 1947 and early 1948, stiffened over the stabilization of Germany and the Berlin blockade of 1948 and 1949.

In the last stage of World War II, the Big Three Powers had met at the Potsdam Conference and agreed that Germany should eventually be reunited. From 1945 through 1947 debates in the administration over German unity shifted to the concept of a Western European third force. The third force, according to one historian of the Cold War, would be "built upon a foundation of European self-confidence." For the United States, it was a way to establish a balance of power in Europe, making Western Europe an economically prosperous center of power around a unified Germany. Through 1946 and 1947, however, German issues such as currency reform and reparations payments created Allied differences with the USSR at the London Conference of the Council of Foreign Ministers. The conference adjourned in December 1947 with no firm resolution on the issues and with no unified Germany.[40]

The failure of the London Foreign Ministers Conference in 1947 doomed the concept of a third force that rested upon a unified Germany. Instead, the administration opted for the second-best chance, the integration of Western Germany under the ERP. By doing so the administration could forestall American military spending and prevent a major commitment to Europe's security. That would not be the case. The Western European nations were dismayed at the failure of the conference, and alarmed by the brutality and swiftness of the Communist coup in Czechoslovakia. As a result, they began negotiations for a mutual defense pact. In March 1948, Britain, France, Belgium, the Netherlands, and Luxembourg signed the Brussels Pact, a collective defense treaty. This pact, called the Western Union, was based upon the ideas of Ernest Bevin, the British Foreign Minister. Bevin hoped it would establish a precedent for a future North Atlantic alliance around which the United States, Canada, Germany, Scandinavia, Greece, Italy, Portugal, and Spain could organize defensive measures. Concerned about the possibility of a Soviet military attack and the future

---

40. John Lewis Gaddis, *The Long Peace: Inquiries into the History of the Cold War* (New York: Oxford University Press, 1987), 64; Leffler, *A Preponderance of Power*, 198–199.

President Truman wishes success to Secretary of State George C. Marshall as he departs for the London Conference of the Council of Foreign Ministers, November 1947. *(Courtesy of Harry S. Truman Library)*

possible reintegration and rearmament of Germany, Britain and France insisted that Western Union defense planning could not ultimately succeed without a firm American commitment to Europe's security.[41]

After consulting with Truman, Secretary Marshall told the British that the United States was "prepared to proceed at once in the joint discussions on the establishment of an Atlantic se-

---

41. Memorandum, Sidney Souers to the NSC, "Paraphrase of a Recent Telegram From Mr. Bevin," 23 April 1948, PSF-NSC, Box 203. For a thorough analysis of the British initiative in the formation of NATO see Timothy P. Ireland, *Creating the Entangling Alliance: The Origins of the North Atlantic Treaty Organization* (Westport: Greenwood Press, 1981), 48–79; Geir Lundestad, "Empire by Invitation? The United States and Western Europe, 1945–1952," *SHAFR Newsletter* 15 (September 1984): 5; Martin H. Folly, "Breaking the Vicious Circle: Britain, the United States, and the Genesis of the North Atlantic Treaty," *Diplomatic History* 12 (Winter 1988): 59–77; Leffler, *A Preponderance of Power*, 202–203; idem, *The Specter of Communism*, 74.

curity system."[42] On March 20, the NSC called for a "world-wide counter-offensive" against the Soviet Union, including American military assistance to the Western Union. Shortly thereafter, secret consultations on American participation in a mutual defense alliance began at the Pentagon between American, British, and Canadian representatives.[43] At the same time, Marshall, Lovett, and other officials of the Department of State initiated exploratory meetings with the Senate Foreign Relations Committee and its Republican chair, Senator Arthur Vandenberg, a proponent of bipartisanship in foreign policy.[44]

Anticipating the creation of a North Atlantic alliance that would replace the Western Union, the Department of State informed the NSC with a subject paper titled "The Position of the United States with Respect to Support for Western Union and Other Related Free Countries" (NSC 9). Lovett presented the paper in brief but also noted that it had already become outdated. He assured NSC members, however, that the Department of State would provide an updated and revised version, and that NSC 9 called for the United States to support, but not join, the Western Union. NSC 9 also recommended American military assistance to the potential North Atlantic alliance. It requested that Truman call a conference to draft a collective security treaty, modeled after the Rio Treaty of 1947 with Latin American nations.[45] According to Forrestal, the presentation by Lovett: "Outlined tentative proposals . . . a statement that we were willing to consider under Article 51 of the United Nations

42. George Marshall to Lord Inverchapel, 12 March 1948, *FRUS: 1948*, III, 48; PPP:HST, 182–186.

43. Sidney Souers to the NSC, NSC 7, 20 March 1949, *FRUS: 1948*, I, pt. 2 548–550. The Pentagon Talks concluded with a recommendation that the Western Union include eventually the Scandinavian countries, Austria, Germany, and Spain. See minutes of 6th Meeting of Pentagon Talks, 1 April 1948, *FRUS: 1948*, III, pt. 3, 71–75.

44. George F. Kennan PPS 27/1, *Memoirs*, Volume I (Boston: Little, Brown, 1967), 405–407; Leffler, *A Preponderance of Power*, 211–212.

45. Minutes of the 10th Meeting, 22 April 1948, PSF-NSC, Box 203; PPS 27/1, "Western Union and Related Problems," 6 April 1948, in Nelson, *PPS Papers 1948*, 165–171; PPS 27/2, "The Position of the United States with Respect to Support for Western Union and Other Related Free Countries," 24 June 1948, in Nelson, *PPS Papers 1948*, 171–174; NSC 9, "The Position of the United States with Respect to Support for Western Union and other Related Free Countries," 13 April 1948, *FRUS: 1948*, III, 85–88.

[Charter], steps looking to the construction of a regional agreement."[46]

Vandenberg and Lovett met several times, and worked to draft a Senate resolution that would pledge the administration's partnership with the Western European nations in creating a collective security agreement. Meanwhile, the JCS requested that the NSC clarify the military objectives of the proposed policy. Before the council could do so, the Department of State submitted NSC 9/2, a revised version, which contained a draft of Senate Resolution 239, better known as the Vandenberg Resolution. Recently approved by the Senate Foreign Relations Committee, it repeated verbatim the Department of State's recommendation presented earlier to the NSC, that the United States sanction "the progressive development of regional or other collective arrangements for individual and collective self-defense." The resolution recommended as well that prior to any military assistance European members demonstrate a willingness for self-help. Instead of specifying details of a treaty, NSC 9/2 proposed that Congress be consulted before any action on a formal treaty.[47]

During their meeting in late May, NSC members spent considerable time examining NSC 9/2. After Lovett read the Senate version of the Vandenberg Resolution, Marshall noted that he had received a request from Bevin asking that the administration initiate negotiations for the creation of a North Atlantic pact. Marshall agreed with Bevin's opinion that "what is needed is evidence of the U.S. willingness to accept obligations." Secretary of the Army Royall reported the suggestion of the JCS that in addition to embracing the charter nations of the Western Union, negotiations for a North Atlantic pact "leave

46. Millis, *The Forrestal Diaries*, 423, 434. For Forrestal's initiatives that called for changes in the administration's military assistance policies see Pach, *Arming the Free World*, 152–155.

47. Memorandum, George Kennan to Robert Lovett, 7 May 1948, w/encs (NSC 9/2), *FRUS: 1948*, III, 116–119; Minutes of the 11th Meeting, 20 May 1948, PSF-NSC, Box 203; George F. Kennan, *Memoirs*, Volume I (Boston: Little, Brown, 1967), 405–407; Senate Resolution 239, 11 June 1948, *FRUS: 1948*, III, 135–136. For a history of the formulation and ratification of the treaty see Ireland, *Creating the Entangling Alliance*, 80–151. For the context of the North Atlantic Treaty, 4 April 1949 see *A Decade of American Foreign Policy*, 81st Congress, 1st sess. (Washington, D.C.: G.P.O., 1957), 1339–1356.

the way open to include Spain, Germany and Austria." At that point, Forrestal added that the JCS had informed him they were concerned a North Atlantic collective security alliance might compete for congressional appropriations earmarked for the armed forces. Lovett, however, dismissed JCS concerns on the grounds that Congress at that time would not grant Truman "open-ended authority" to make a "substantial shipment of military equipment except in an emergency." Secretary of the Air Force Stuart Symington, Lovett, and Royall jointly reassured Forrestal that first priority was the improvement of American military strength. Lovett turned the NSC's attention again to the issue of a collective security treaty. He informed the NSC that "the general feeling" in Congress was that the United States should not formally associate with the Western Union. Lovett reminded the council that the Vandenberg Resolution represented only "a minimum" form of assistance to the Western Union countries. For that reason, and because of the Joint Chiefs' fears, Lovett suggested deferring any action on NSC 9/2 until the Senate formally took up the Vandenberg Resolution. The other members agreed.[48]

On June 11 the Senate approved the resolution. It assured American membership and participation in the North Atlantic Treaty Organization (NATO) by April 4, 1949. Three days after Senate approval, the NSC staff released "The Position of the United States with Respect to Providing Military Assistance to Nations of the Non-Soviet World" (NSC 14). It addressed the concerns of the Joint Chiefs regarding United States military assistance to future allies of a mutual collective security pact, and asserted that "excessive" assistance would be prohibited if it jeopardized "the minimum material requirements of the United States armed forces." NSC 14 insisted that military assistance to non-Communist countries "should not be inconsistent with strategic concepts approved by the Joint Chiefs of Staff." By early July the JCS, satisfied with these provisions, dropped their objections to NSC 9/2. Without further debate, the NSC adopted a new version of NSC 9/2 that contained the Vandenberg Resolution approved by the Senate, and adopted with only minor changes NSC 14, then forwarded both to Truman. The president gave his approval and ordered that they

---

48. Minutes of the 11th Meeting, 20 May 1948, PSF-NSC, Box 203.

Robert A. Lovett, Undersecretary of State from 1947 to 1949, and Secretary of Defense from 1951 to 1953. *(U.S. Army Photo Center; Courtesy of Harry S. Truman Library)*

become policy.[49] With Truman's endorsements Congress, the Department of State, and the military moved the creation of NATO into its final phase. Again the NSC had provided the forum and coordination process necessary for reconciling differences between State and the JCS.

*   *   *

The London Conference of the Council of Foreign Ministers reconvened from February through June of 1948 without inviting the Soviet Union. During that time France, Great Britain, and the United States proposed a constitutional convention to establish a West German state, and worked to institute currency reform. In late March the Soviet Union, alarmed by the steps taken at the London Conference, particularly the proposal to create a West German state, walked out of the Allied Control Council meeting in Berlin, and moved to impose a mini-blockade of the city of West Berlin, refusing mail and

---

49. NSC 9/3, "The Position of the United States with Respect to Support for Western Union and other Related Free Countries," 28 June 1949, *FRUS: 1948*, III, 140–141; NSC 14/1, "The Position of the United States with Respect to Providing Military Assistance to Nations of the Non-Soviet World," 1 July 1948, Ibid., 585–588; Minutes of the 14th Meeting, 1 July 1948, PSF-NSC, Box 204. For official approval by Truman see NSC, "Policies of the Government, 1947–1948," 37–39.

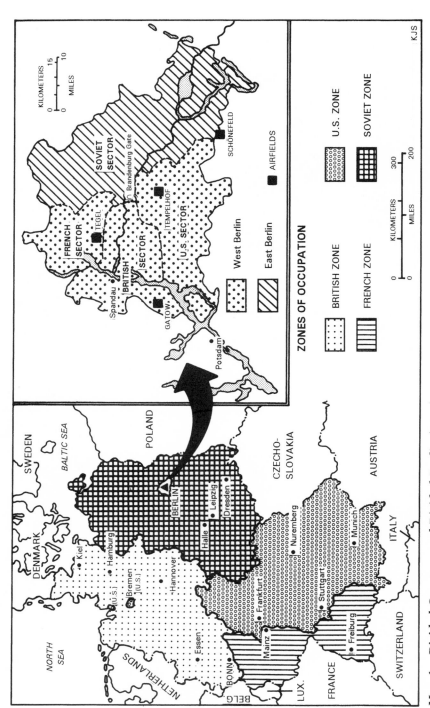

Map 1. Divided Germany and Divided Berlin (1948)

54

freight shipments to and from the west sector of the capital. On June 24, one day after American, British, and French occupation authorities issued the new German currency, the USSR blocked all overland routes between the Western Allied sectors of Germany and West Berlin.

Stalin reasoned that Britain, France, and the United States were violating their agreements with the Soviet Union, made at the Yalta and Potsdam Conferences at the end of World War II, for the zonal division of Germany under military occupation. Stalin deduced that since his former allies violated the Yalta and Potsdam accords by merging their occupation zones into a separate West Germany, he could do the same by squeezing them out of Berlin. The Soviet encirclement of Berlin was the beginning of the Berlin blockade, or the first Berlin crisis of the Cold War.[50]

The CIA had warned the administration that the Soviet Union might "undertake a program of intensified obstructionism and calculated insult" to force the United States and the other Allied powers to withdraw from Berlin. It concluded that the USSR would apply "every means short of armed force" and devices such as "obstruction to transport and travel to and within the city."[51] In spite of warnings months prior to the blockade, the NSC took no initiatives regarding military and diplomatic commitments to Berlin. During that period, "the initiative, the impetus, the guide, the force of anything that was done," Assistant Secretary of State for Occupied Areas Charles Saltzman was to recall, came from General Lucius Clay, head of American occupation forces in Germany, more so than from Truman and the NSC.[52] In January 1948 the army conducted a study of possible courses of action should the Soviets force the United States out of Berlin. Secretary Royall circulated the report for information only. Later the CIA warned: "Not intend-

---

50. Zubok and Pleshakov, *Inside the Kremlin's Cold War*, 50–51; Leffler, *The Specter of Communism*, 82.

51. CIA-Special Evaluation No. 23, "Possible Soviet Action in Berlin as a Result of the CMF Breakdown," 23 December 1947, PHT-NSC, Box 2, HSTL, Independence, Missouri.

52. Charles Saltzman Oral History Interview, Oral History Collection, HSTL, Independence, Missouri. For a thorough treatment of Clay's role in the infamous war scare of 1948 and its impact on the Soviet's decision to blockade Berlin, see Frank Kofsky, *Harry S. Truman and the War Scare of 1948* (New York: St. Martin's Press, 1993).

ing an actual resort to force . . . the USSR will probably resume its efforts to force a Western withdrawal from Berlin." In a special intelligence estimate on April 2, the CIA and an ad hoc committee made up of the intelligence agencies of the Department of State, and army, navy, and air force observed that the Soviet forces had the capability of "overrunning" all of Western Europe and the Middle East, but it concluded that the USSR would not resort to "direct military action throughout the rest of the year."[53]

At a cabinet meeting on June 25, Truman reviewed the situation. He understood that the Soviet military greatly outnumbered Allied forces in Berlin, moreover, that during the course of the blockade, negotiations between the United States and the Soviet Union could endanger the creation of a new West German government. Seeking a reaction that would counter Moscow's blockade efforts without raising the ante, Truman adopted a British suggestion that an Anglo-American airlift deliver critical supplies into West Berlin. "We are going to stay period," Truman asserted, approving a massive airlift of food and medical supplies that began the following day as C-47 cargo planes took off with provisions destined for West Berlin. On June 25, Truman ordered that the airlift be organized full-scale and that every plane in the European Command be pressed into service. By August, C-47 and larger C-54 cargo planes were carrying nearly three thousand tons of supplies a day; by September, the average daily airlift had reached four thousand tons.[54]

Despite the early accomplishments of the airlift, Clay believed that further measures were needed in case the airlift failed. On June 27, the general called for the use of overland armed convoys to break the blockade and endorsed a recommendation from the British government that the United States deploy B-29 atomic bombers to Germany and England. At a White House meeting the next day Truman met with advisers and approved the bomber deployment. On July 2, the Strategic

53. CIA-4-48, "Review of the World," 2 April 1948; CIA, "Possibility of Direct Soviet Military Action During 1948," 2 April 1948, PSF-NSC, Box 203; Millis, *The Forrestal Diaries*, 409.

54. Millis, *The Forrestal Diaries*, 452–455; Condit, *History of the JCS*, II, 133–134; Truman, *Years of Trial and Hope*, 123–124.

Air Command (SAC) went on alert, and a SAC bombardment group moved to western Germany.[55] Thereafter, the NSC and Truman considered several approaches to the Berlin crisis: withdraw from Berlin, stay and run the risk of military confrontation with Moscow, or delay in hopes of negotiating a settlement. At the same time much discussion centered on whether to begin a complete deployment of B-29 squadrons to the British Isles. The administration hoped that their arrival in Western Europe would force the Soviet Union to the negotiating table.[56]

The Berlin crisis dominated the NSC's meeting of July 15, 1948. With Truman presiding, the council debated the escalation of the airlift, the American public's reaction to events in Germany, and the deployment of B-29 squadrons to the British Isles. Forrestal warned the NSC that the services were facing an October 15 deadline. The Soviet authorities, he observed, were well aware that flying weather would be too poor for the airlift to continue beyond October. A decision was therefore needed whether armed convoys should be sent to Berlin. Royall agreed that the airlift probably could not carry through the winter, but he had no doubt that the operation could continue until October.[57] Lovett told the NSC that the Department of State had received a formal invitation from the British government for the B-29 squadrons. Marshall pointed out one advantage of sending the planes; it would be a further indication of America's resolve to contain Soviet expansionism. The more important effect of such a decision, he pointed out, was that it would stiffen the determination of the French and the British and might offset any tendency on their part toward an appeasement. Forrestal said that he feared "the American people were not aware of the seriousness of the Berlin crisis either."[58]

All NSC members agreed to reserve a decision regarding an

---

55. Millis, *The Forrestal Diaries*, 452–453.

56. Summary of Discussion at the 15th Meeting, 16 July 1948, PSF-NSC, Box 220. For the USSR's reaction to the airlift and the deployment of B-29 bombers see Holloway, *Stalin and the Bomb*, 260–261.

57. Summary of Discussion at the 15th Meeting, 16 July 1948, PSF-NSC, Box 220.

58. Ibid.; NSC Action 77, "Dispatch of B-29 Bombers to the British Isles," 15 July 1948, NSC, "Policies of the Government, 1947–1948," 133, PSF-NSC, Box 195.

increase in the airlift until the air force and JCS could provide more information. The council recommended, and Truman approved, the deployment of two B-29 groups, but it provided no specific directions for their use. The Berlin B-29 deployment intended to make a show of security in order to make up for the lack of capability.[59] The NSC had suggested the first application of the deterrence doctrine in Cold War history. No doubt the deployment of the B-29s was more symbolic than a threat of nuclear retaliation. The NSC did not want to provoke war with the Soviet Union; nor did the Joint Chiefs believe that ground forces were adequate for breaking the blockade at that time. Truman, the underdog in the upcoming presidential election, preferred a strong yet moderate approach to Berlin.

The most important decision of the Berlin crisis was made at the sixteenth meeting of the NSC on July 22. Truman as chair focused discussion on the future course of action on Berlin. General Clay, whom the president had called to Washington days earlier, explained existing options for the United States. The Joint Chiefs of Staff and high-ranking service officers and advisers also attended.[60] Clay told the NSC: "Abandonment of Berlin would have a disastrous effect upon our plans for Western Germany." He said that Berliners were "determined to stand firm," and that the United States should "remain in Berlin in any event." Clay recommended adding to the airlift seventy-five C-54 cargo planes, and suggested completing the construction of a new airdome in Berlin. Following his report, Air Force Chief of Staff General Hoyt Vandenberg objected to the proposed escalation of the airlift. Should war break out, Vandenberg observed, the air force could lose many of its planes. This would greatly hamper strategic warfare, he warned, as well as the "ability to reinforce outlying garrisons." Marshall then asked Clay what opinion he had concerning the use of armed convoys. Clay pointed out that the initial Soviet reaction would be to set up road blocks. The final reaction to armed convoys, said Clay, might be a military attack by the USSR. This prompted Truman to ask Clay whether he thought

59. Condit, *History of the JCS*, II, 139; Gaddis, *The Long Peace*, 110; Leffler, *The Specter of Communism*, 83–84.

60. General Lucius D. Clay Oral History Interview, Oral History Collection, HSTL, Independence, Missouri; Minutes of the 16th Meeting, 22 July 1948, PSF-NSC, Box 204.

the Soviet officials would go to war. The general replied that they would not interfere with the airlift "unless they mean to go to war." He told Truman that the USSR was "operating with great care" and that there were no other signs that it was preparing for a war. The president then concluded decisively that the airlift, in his words, "involved less risks than the armed convoys," and left the meeting.[61] Following Truman's departure the NSC adopted all of Clay's report, agreed that American dependents in Berlin should be evacuated by the end of August, added a directive that specified that all B-29 bombers be based in Great Britain, and noted that the United States should seek a direct diplomatic approach to Moscow.[62] After considering NSC recommendations, Truman committed the United States to defending Berlin.

In nearly one year since the NSC began its operations, the council had formulated Cold War policies for Truman on Greece, Eastern Europe, Italy, participation in the North Atlantic collective security alliance, and the initial strategies in dealing with the Berlin blockade. Each presented a different situation for Truman and the NSC. Throughout the year, no coherent or tested method existed for the implementation of containment, and policies were formulated in a somewhat haphazard manner. Several times the Department of State's PPS served as the sole formulator of policy approved by the NSC. It was the council, or at any rate the debates within it, that gave strength and coherence to containment.

---

61. Summary of Discussion at the 16th Meeting, 23 July 1948, PSF-NSC, Box 220.

62. NSC Decisions, "The Situation in Germany," Minutes of the 16th Meeting, 22 July 1948, PSF-NSC, Box 204. For a thorough analysis of the precrisis and post-crisis periods of the Berlin blockade see Avi Shlaim, *The United States and the Berlin Blockade, 1948–1949: A Study in Crisis Decision-Making* (Berkeley: University of California Press, 1983).

Chapter Three

Establishing Cold War Parameters

Our position has not changed. All we want is peace in the world.

(Harry S. Truman, 1948)

The uncertainties of the Cold War plagued Truman and the NSC throughout the rest of 1948, but by the end of the year the president and his council had set some new parameters for United States foreign and national security policies. In addition to the ongoing Berlin blockade, many older and newer Cold War developments concerned the NSC—the location of custody for atomic weapons, along with formation of a rudimentary system of atomic air bases; examination of military preparedness; an appropriate policy for the Middle East, largely with regard to Palestine; and measures that redirected the administration's attention from Europe and the Middle East to East Asia. All the while, American credibility in Western Europe, the problem of forming a West German nation, and the economic, military, and political components of containment remained beseiged by the Berlin crisis.

Throughout most of August and early September of 1948 several meetings took place between American and Soviet diplomatic representatives but with no breakthrough regarding a settlement on Berlin. It soon became apparent that the talks had stalled. Frustrated, Truman called a second special meet-

ing of the NSC for the purpose of considering the Berlin negotiations.

The meeting opened on September 9 with Marshall and
Lovett reporting that diplomatic endeavors had deteriorated to
the point that "the negotiations may blow up shortly." Marshall
declared that he regarded as extremely remote the prospect of
a negotiated settlement on Berlin. The situation he defined as
"discouraging and serious." Lovett proposed a course of action
that the Department of State had suggested: resuming talks in
Moscow and, if no satisfactory conclusions could be reached,
refer the Berlin situation to the United Nations (UN) Security
Council. The NSC and Truman concurred in this recommendation.[1] The meeting heard from Air Force Secretary Symington
a progress report on the airlift. Pointing out that the United
States had been averaging four thousand tons of supplies during most of August, he recommended increasing the average to
five thousand tons with the addition of more C-54 cargo planes.
Symington and Lovett questioned whether the council should
consider plans in the event an emergency or military conflict
broke out in Berlin. After further discussion, the NSC concluded that it would be preferable to explore any war plans first
with the JCS and at the same time with the president.[2]

The next day the service secretaries, the Joint Chiefs,
Marshall, and Forrestal held a meeting to reach a decision
on the use, plans, and targets for American atomic air operations out of Great Britain. Three days later, Forrestal, Royall,
and army and air force representatives outlined for Truman
the Pentagon's plans. "Forrestal, Bradley, Vandenberg, Symington briefed me on bases, bombs, Moscow, Leningrad, etc.,"
Truman recorded in his diary. "I have a terrible feeling after-
wards that we are very close to war. I hope not . . . Berlin is a
mess."[3]

In late September, the United States, Britain, and France
petitioned the UN Security Council to investigate the Soviet

1. Summary of Discussion at the 20th Meeting, 9 September 1948, PSF-
NSC, Box 220; Minutes of the 20th Meeting 7 September 1948, Ibid., Box 204.
2. Ibid.
3. Truman cited in Robert H. Ferrell, ed., *Off the Record: The Private Papers of Harry S. Truman* (New York: Harper & Row, 1980), 148–149. For the
HALFMOON Short Range Emergency War Plan see Etzold and Gaddis, *Containment*, 315–323.

Union's blockade of Berlin. Meanwhile, the airlift along with negotiations with Soviet officials went on. The JCS, however, produced two reports that assessed the risks involved with the airlift. Both were especially critical of the administration for allowing foreign policy initiatives to outrun military capabilities. One argued that an alternative plan was needed in case an outbreak of sudden hostilities threatened the United States presence in Berlin or the airlift itself. The other concluded that to continue the airlift beyond March 1949 would require additional military budget supplements.[4]

The NSC held a third special meeting on October 14. Concerned about a possible Soviet interruption of the Berlin airlift, the council heard both reports from the Joint Chiefs. Major General A. M. Gruenther, director of staff of the JCS, read the comments. He stressed that the airlift had drained the finances and personnel of the military services. For the airlift to continue, Gruenther pointed out, the military needed additional appropriations soon. Army Chief of Staff General Omar N. Bradley made it a point to attend the meeting with Gruenther and pressed for additional money. Bradley emphasized that the airlift made it mandatory that for the military services the "presently authorized strength should be maintained" and that the JCS were concerned that they might have to cut the armed forces' capabilities. Lovett reassured the generals that funding needed for the airlift would be provided quickly.[5]

Symington pointed out that the primary purpose of the NSC meeting that day was to consider what the administration would do in the event the USSR took military action against the airlift. Lovett replied that he preferred that the council defer any discussion on the subject until it consider a position paper that the Department of State had been preparing on policy toward Germany. He informed the NSC that the Department of State's study would "express a series of guesses" about Soviet actions against Berlin or the airlift. Symington suggested that the NSC send Truman the JCS report on military budget supplements. Without further discussion all members concurred and forwarded to Truman four recommendations: aug-

4. Condit, *History of the JCS*, II, 151–154.
5. Summary of Discussion at the 24th Meeting, 15 October 1948, PSF-NSC, Box 220; Minutes of the 24th Meeting, 14 October 1948, Ibid., Box 204.

ment the airlift by sixty-six C-54 planes; review requirements for stockpiling aviation fuel; authorize $25 million in supplemental funding for the air force, with future personnel ceilings increased for the fiscal year 1949; and grant the air force authority to procure additional transport planes offsetting depreciation and attrition from the airlift. After consulting with the Bureau of the Budget (BOB), Truman approved the NSC's recommendations for sixty-six more C-54 planes, and a review of gasoline stockpiles, and announced that "steps would be taken to insure adequate personnel and financial support" for the airlift. He left, though, the finer points of budget supplements for the BOB, and after some delay it consented to the council's requests.[6] The NSC and Truman had provided for the continuation of the airlift, if necessary, through 1949.

The blockade of Berlin proved that the NSC could take a larger part in the process of collecting and centralizing information from many bureaucratic sources, and that the council provided the institutional and ad hoc forum necessary for making decisions during a crisis. The mechanisms set up under the National Security Act of 1947 greatly assisted Truman during the crisis, but problems also appeared. Most noticeably, the NSC before the blockade had made no recommendations to Truman on Berlin, nor had it established a long-range policy proposal for military strategic planning during an emergency. Forrestal was aware of the dearth of strategic planning, particularly for the use of atomic weapons. When B-29 aircraft were deployed to Great Britain, he had called for an independent NSC review that would serve his department and the JCS by procuring from the NSC and the president a stated policy that would address atomic weapons, the application of conventional forces, and the expansion of the military services within a tighter proposed budget for fiscal year 1950. In a memorandum to the council and Truman, Forrestal stated that a "national policy" responding to danger from the USSR was imperative.[7]

6. Ibid.; Memorandum, Harry Truman to Sidney Souers, 22 October 1948, PSF-NSC, Box 204.

7. James Forrestal to Sidney Souers, 10 July 1948, in NSC 20, "Appraisal of the Degree and Character of Military Preparedness Required by the World Situation," 12 July 1948, PSF-NSC, Box 204; *FRUS: 1948*, I, pt. 2, 589–592. For insightful assessments of Forrestal's initiative and the NSC 20 Series see

Since 1945 members of the administration had debated whether the military or civilian branches of the government should retain custody of atomic weapons. During World War II the Manhattan District Project under the Department of War had supervised the development of the atomic bomb. In early 1946 Truman requested that Congress place custody of the atomic energy program in civilian hands, and Congress passed the Atomic Energy Act of 1946. It established a five-member Atomic Energy Commission (AEC) along with various subordinate civilian and military committees that guaranteed consultation regarding atomic energy matters before the commission. The act also provided for presidential authorization over the transfer of atomic weapons and materials.[8] In spite of the confusion that resulted from the B-29 deployment during the Berlin crisis, Truman refused to surrender civilian custody of the atomic bomb. Pragmatic reasoning, coupled with political strategy, apparently affected Truman's decision. In late July, the president told Forrestal that "political considerations" made the transfer of custody moot, but he added that he might "take another look at the picture" after the November election.[9]

The issues of for what objectives, and at what targets atomic weapons would be used, concerned Truman. "Lack of high level policy guidance, aggravated by extreme secrecy," points out one historian of nuclear planning, "retarded coordinated planning for nuclear war."[10] The Department of Defense's concerns were partly alleviated when Truman and Forrestal discussed the issue earlier in July. Both concluded that a flexible policy should be adopted. The president argued, however, that due to the Berlin crisis and the custody dispute between the military and the AEC he wanted his options open and civilian custody secure. Truman told Forrestal that the decision to use the atomic bomb should be the president's and not that of

---

Joseph M. Siracusa, "NSC 68: A Reappraisal," *Naval War College Review* 33 (1980): 6–7.

8. *The Atomic Energy Act of 1946, Public Law 585,* 79th Congress, 1st sess., 1 August 1946 (Washington, D.C.: G.P.O., 1946).

9. Truman cited in Millis, *The Forrestal Diaries*, 461.

10. David Alan Rosenberg, "The Origins of Overkill: Nuclear Weapons and American Strategy," in Norman Graebner, ed., *The National Security: Its Theory and Practice, 1945–1960* (New York: Oxford University Press, 1986), 129.

President Truman and Secretary of Defense James V. Forrestal, 1949.
(Courtesy of Harry S. Truman Library)

"some dashing lieutenant colonel."[11] But after consulting with the chair of the AEC, David Lilienthal, he notified the secretary of defense of his discomfort with a flexible policy. "I do not feel justified in exercising my authority under the provisions of the Atomic Energy Act," Truman stated, "to order the transfer of the stock piles to the Armed Services." Truman concluded that "national security will be both safeguarded and promoted" if the military and the AEC collaborated "by refining the existing arrangements."[12]

By mid-September the NSC had completed a long-awaited policy statement, "United States Policy on Atomic Warfare" (NSC 30), and at the same time resolved the old custody dispute. It suggested that "in the event of hostilities" the military services must "utilize promptly and effectively" all appropriate means of warfare, including the atomic bomb. NSC 30 clari-

---

11. Millis, *The Forrestal Diaries*, 458.
12. Harry Truman to James Forrestal, 6 August 1948, PSF-CF, Box 285.

fied, though, that the decision to use atomic weapons would be the president's.[13] In NSC 30, the council issued a broad policy statement leaving unresolved the question of when and how atomic weapons should be used but settling the earlier issues about the custodianship of atomic weapons and whether the United States would use them in the event of a war. Because nothing was specific about how atomic weapons would be applied, Truman never approved NSC 30. The report, however, reflected his opinion on atomic weapons and nuclear policy. Three days before the council adopted it, he met with Forrestal and other members of his administration. Truman, by Forrestal's account, "said that he prayed that he would never have to make such a decision, but that if it became necessary, no one need to have a misgiving but what he would do."[14]

Throughout the rest of Truman's presidency military planners and nuclear strategists initiated research and development projects that created various atomic and thermonuclear weapons. As knowledge and application of nuclear energy increased during those few short years, the likelihood of restrictions on the use of nuclear weapons decreased. This became even more apparent after the Soviet Union detonated its first atomic bomb in the fall of 1949, and its first hydrogen bomb in 1953. The NSC, however, offered no additional policy statements on the use of atomic or thermonuclear weapons.[15] But as events of the nuclear age unfolded amid Cold War tensions, Truman often asked the NSC for political and military coordination of the less general but more complicated issues of fissionable materials and the nuclear arms race.

As the military prepared atomic air strategies, the administration moved to add Greenland and Iceland to the American air base system. In late 1947 the NSC had facilitated the development when it affirmed, with Truman's concurrence, the "strategic importance" of the two base areas, and authorized

---

13. NSC 30, "United States Policy on Atomic Warfare," *FRUS: 1948*, I, pt. 2, 624–628; Etzold and Gaddis, *Containment*, 339–357; PSF-NSC, Box 204; Minutes of the 21st Meeting, 16 September 1948, Ibid., Box 220.

14. Millis, *The Forrestal Diaries*, 458.

15. According to David Alan Rosenberg, NSC 30 would be the single American policy statement "for atomic welfare approved by the NSC until 1960." See Rosenberg, "The Origins of Overkill," 130.

negotiations for retaining postwar installations on each.[16] The addition of Greenland and Iceland would not only enhance the defense of a strategic polar atomic air defense and communication route but thwart any immediate Soviet efforts to establish military installations on Norway's Spitzbergen archipelago and Bear Island.[17] Soon after the USSR invited Finland to sign a mutual assistance pact in February 1948, the Scandinavian countries of Norway, Denmark, and Sweden became of strategic concern to Truman and the NSC. In the course of the council's discussions over the authorized strength of the armed forces, Marshall insisted that the administration had to determine what could be done to deter Soviet advances in Scandinavia. He wanted a policy that would "have a maximum of encouraging effect" on the rest of Western Europe. The administration needed "to give the Russians pause" in their efforts in Norway, Denmark, and Greece, but without a general mobilization. With this in mind, and yet concerned that all of Scandinavia might fall to Soviet control as had Czechoslovakia days earlier, the NSC recommended that the region be integrated into a future North Atlantic defense alliance.[18]

In early September the council adopted, and Truman approved, "The Position of the United States With Respect to Scandinavia" (NSC 28/1). Observing that the region "lies astride the great circle air route" that existed between North America and western Russia, the NSC recommended that the United States extend to Norway and Denmark economic aid and more favorable trade policies, provide the two with military equipment, combat Soviet propaganda in Scandinavia

---

16. NSC 2/1, "Base Rights in Greenland, Iceland, and the Azores," 25 November 1947, PSF-NSC, Box 203; Minutes of the 2nd Meeting, 14 November 1947, Ibid.

17. By 1948 the President's Air Policy Commission and strategic planners such as Bernard Brodie argued that a Soviet nuclear attack could come by way of the polar region, especially since it represented the shortest and least defended distance. For elements of the polar strategy see *Survival in the Air Age: A Report by the President's Air Policy Commission* (Washington, D.C.: G.P.O., 1948), 10–19.

18. Minutes and Summary of Meeting Discussion at the 8th Meeting, 23 March 1948, PSF-NSC, Box 203; Senate Resolution 239, 11 June 1948 (Vandenberg Resolution), *FRUS: 1948*, III, 135–136. For details of the NATO negotiations see Geir Lundestad, *America, Scandinavia, and the Cold War 1945–1949* (New York: Columbia University Press, 1980), 290–328.

with an "intensified U.S. information program," and influence
Sweden to abandon its "subjective neutrality and look toward
eventual alignment" with the Western powers.[19] In April 1949,
Norway, Denmark, and Iceland joined NATO; Sweden, however, remained uncommitted. Military containment denied the
USSR base sites in Scandinavia and the North Atlantic and
helped promote the concept of polar strategy for the air force.
Economic containment ensured that much of Scandinavia remained tied to Western Europe.

*   *   *

As the NSC formulated policy on Scandinavia and on custody of atomic weapons, its staff began work on reviewing
Forrestal's earlier request for an evaluation of the nation's military preparedness and a policy towards the Soviet Union. In
early August the council received the secretary of defense's initial recommendations, "Appraisal of the Degree and Character
of Military Preparedness Required by the World Situation"
(NSC 20). Forrestal told the NSC that the Joint Chiefs were
"very anxious" to have a broad policy statement concerning
military objectives "beyond the point of war with the USSR,"
adding a somewhat premature observation that the JCS had inquired "what we propose to do with Russia after we may have
defeated her." If the United States had provided similar objectives during the course of World War II, he concluded, the
Truman administration "would be in better shape today," both
diplomatically and militarily. No discussion followed the secretary of defense's presentation of NSC 20. Instead, council members voted to send it to the Department of State for comment,
asking State as well to define the department's objectives for
safeguarding the national security of the United States.[20]

19. NSC 28/1, "The Position of the United States with Respect to Scandinavia," 2 September 1948; Summary of Discussion at the 19th Meeting, 3
September 1948, PSF-NSC, Box 220; Minutes of the 19th Meeting, 2 September 1948, Ibid., Box 204. On 3 December 1948, the NSC recommended that
the Department of State continue negotiations with Denmark for base-rights
in Greenland, but discontinue negotiations with Norway for base-rights in
Spitzbergen. NSC 32/1, "Current Position of the United States Respecting Base
Negotiations with Denmark and Norway," 2 December 1948, concurred in by
the President on 3 December 1948, NSC, "Policies of the Government, 1947–
1948," 27, Ibid., Box 195.

20. Minutes of the 17th Meeting, 5 August 1948, PSF-NSC, Box 204;
Leffler, *A Preponderance of Power*, 264–265.

Later that month, the Department of State's PPS completed a lengthy study paper that resembled closely what Forrestal had in mind. Kennan wrote the paper. Although he concentrated on the administration's military strategy and objectives, he questioned that the Soviet Union had plans in place for a war of aggression. The massive destruction the USSR had suffered in World War II and the sluggishness of its recovery, he believed, would restrain Soviet military action. Nevertheless, he did not discount the possibility that a full-scale military conflict could result from the escalation of a minor incident, or from Moscow's miscalculations of American interests. He recommended, therefore, that the United States steadily develop permanent military preparedness over an indefinite period of the Cold War. [21]

The NSC staff made some minor revisions to Kennan's study and recommendations for a military preparedness program, then in late November presented the whole to the council for full consideration as "U.S. Objectives with Respect to the USSR to Counter Soviet Threats to U.S. Security" (NSC 20/3).[22] Forrestal, Marshall, and Royall stated they had no objections to the paper and its guidelines. Souers mentioned that the PPS had proposed one correction to the report, that the word "Communist" be made "bolshevik." This change would "make it clear that only Russian Communists were referred to." Without debate, NSC members voted unanimously to adopt the amended version as NSC 20/4. In doing so, the United States set the very first guidelines for its Cold War policy toward the Soviet Union. NSC 20/4 declared that the administration had to "develop a level of military readiness . . . maintained as long as necessary as a deterrent to Soviet aggression." The nation must proceed immediately so to empower its peacetime economy as to establish and maintain "essential reserves readily available

---

21. PPS 38 (NSC 20/1), "United States Objectives with Respect to Russia," 18 August 1948, in Etzold and Gaddis, *Containment*, 173–203; Nelson, *PPS Papers 1948*, 372–411; PPS 33 (NSC 20/2), "Factors Affecting the Nature of the U.S. Defense Arrangements in the Light of Soviet Policies," 23 June, 25 August 1948, Ibid., 281–292; *FRUS: 1948*, I, 621–623. For a thorough analysis of the PPS proposals see Gaddis, *Strategies of Containment*, 48–51.

22. NSC 20/3 was prepared on the basis of NSC 20/1 and NSC 20/2, and CIA-ORE 60–48, "Threats to the Security of the United States," 18 September 1948, and submitted to the council in November as NSC 20/3.

in the event of war." The country must make a concerted effort to "strengthen the orientation" toward the interests of the United States of all nations outside the USSR. NSC 20/4 stressed that the primary efforts of the United States in the world beyond the Soviet Union would concentrate upon economic and political stability and military capability. In addition to making recommendations for securing national interests worldwide preparatory to confrontation or war with the USSR, NSC 20/4 reasserted the primary principles of American national security and the containment doctrine. Moscow's political, economic, and psychological warfare, it declared, threatened "the relative world position of the United States" and disrupted its "traditional institutions." It concluded that any Soviet domination of "the potential power of Eurasia," by either military, political, or subversive actions, "would be strategically and politically unacceptable to the United States."[23]

While Kennan had taken seriously Forrestal's request for a "comprehensive statement of national policy" and the PPS had incorporated the recommendations of Defense and the Joint Chiefs for continual military preparedness, NSC 20/4 clarified that the nation's objectives for containment of the Soviet Union would concentrate on all means short of actual military conflict. NSC 20/4 as approved by the council reflected the effectiveness of the PPS in the coordination of policy, not that of the NSC. And it signaled that by the end of 1948 Kennan and the Department of State had begun to assume more control of the council's power and influence in the formulation of Truman's foreign policy. Yet, Forrestal along with Truman, Marshall, and other members of the NSC recognized the need for a definitive containment policy statement toward the USSR as well as clearer national security objectives in the event of war. NSC 20/4 provided both until it was superseded two years later by NSC 68.

---

23. NSC 20/4, "U.S. Objectives to Counter Soviet Threats to U.S. Security," 23 November 1948; Minutes of the 27th Meeting, 23 November 1948; PSF-NSC, Box 204; *FRUS: 1948*, I, pt. 2, 663–669; Etzold and Gaddis, *Containment*, 203–223.

*   *   *

The Middle East, including Palestine and many of the Arab states, had been under Great Britain's sphere of influence since the 1920s, and by 1947, the British were seeking greater influence and security in the region. Of particular sensitivity for the Truman administration was the Holy Land, where Jewish and Arab nationalists began to fight over the creation of a Jewish homeland in Palestine. Just as important was the security of Middle Eastern petroleum reserves, for the economic recovery of Western Europe made critical American access to Persian Gulf oil supplies.[24] Palestine was the historical homeland of the Jews and of Palestinian Arabs. Since the founding of the World Zionist Organization in 1897, efforts had been sustained to reestablish a Jewish state. After World War II hundreds of thousands of Jewish immigrants, many of them survivors of the Nazi holocaust, sought refuge in Palestine. As Jewish pressure to establish a national homeland there intensified, Arab hostilities increased, and violence swept the area. In early 1947 Great Britain petitioned the UN for relief from its earlier mandate in Palestine. In late November 1947, the UN voted to partition Palestine and recognized a Jewish claim to part of the region.[25]

Although the Roosevelt administration had pursued a policy of neutrality and nonintervention in the Middle East, Truman supported the UN partition of Palestine and the creation of a Jewish state. He did so for humanitarian and political reasons. The holocaust in Europe had touched Truman. He believed that the Jewish refugees deserved a homeland. As Truman was to recall: "The fate of the Jewish victims of Hitlerism was a matter of deep personal concern to me."[26]

---

24. For a thorough background see David S. Painter, *Oil and the American Century: The Political Economy of U.S. Foreign Oil Policy, 1941–1954* (Baltimore: Johns Hopkins University Press, 1986); Michael B. Stoff, *Oil, War, and American Security: The Search for a National Policy on Foreign Oil, 1941–1947* (New Haven: Yale University Press, 1980).

25. Ben Halpern, "The Idea of the Jewish State," in Robert Silverberg, *If I Forget Thee O Jerusalem: American Jews and the State of Israel* (New York: William Morrow, 1970); U.S. Congress, *A Decade of American Foreign Policy*, 820–839.

26. Truman, *Years of Trial and Hope*, 132; Michael J. Cohen, *Truman and Israel* (Berkeley: University of California Press, 1990), 44–56; Dean Rusk Oral History Interview, DLHP, Durham, North Carolina.

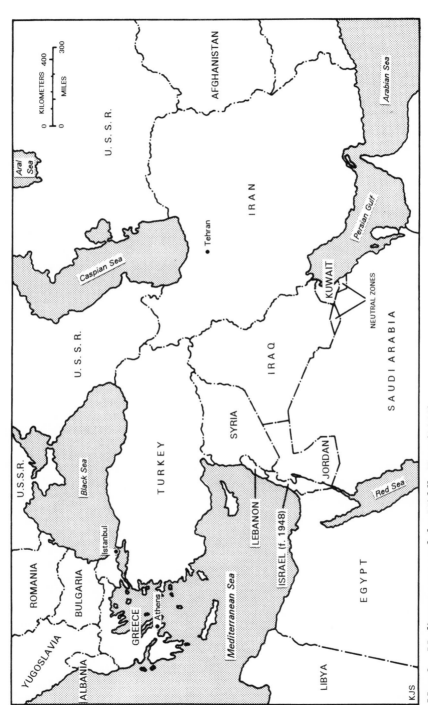

Map 2. Mediterranean and the Middle East (1948)

72

American domestic politics also affected Truman's sympathy toward Zionism. He faced a very tough battle to win the presidential election in 1948. His most formidable challenger in the 1948 presidential campaign, Republican Party candidate Thomas E. Dewey of New York, waged a pro-Zionist campaign and throughout early 1948, Truman's political advisers constantly reminded him of the importance of the Jewish vote and of Dewey's efforts to secure it.[27]

Truman never sought the NSC's coordination or recommendation for his decision to support the partition of Palestine and the creation of a Jewish state, and it went on record as the first of two policy decisions that he made without consulting the council. The Department of State, the military services, and the intelligence community were opposed to partition of Palestine. Marshall, Lovett, Kennan, Forrestal, Royall, and the JCS were not willing to risk alienation of the Arab states rich in oil. The region was, in addition, a strategic locale for future American military bases. Forrestal seemed to be most concerned about not offending the Arabs, so much so that Truman wondered whether his secretary of defense was anti-semitic. Kennan and the PPS hoped they could reverse the president's support of the partition and recommended that instead the United States support a provisional UN trusteeship over Palestine. Even though the USSR also supported the UN partition plan, the Department of State's alternative concerned Truman, because any reversal of partition in favor of trusteeship would allow for greater involvement of the Soviet Union in the Middle East.[28]

The opposition to partition by the Department of State, the military services, and the intelligence community began in late 1947, when Royall requested that the NSC "assess the implications of current United Nations discussion of the problem of Palestine on the security interests of the United States." Of par-

---

27. George M. Elsey Oral History Interview; Cohen, *Truman and Israel*, 240–256; Alonzo L. Hamby, *Beyond the New Deal: Harry S. Truman and American Liberalism* (New York: Columbia University Press, 1973), 209–212; idem, *Man of the People*, 461–462; Robert A. Divine, "The Cold War and the Election of 1948," *Journal of American History* 59 (June 1972): 90–110; Ferrell, *Harry S. Truman*, 309–312; McCullough, *Truman*, 613–619.

28. George F. Kennan, "Palestine Problem (1948)," GKP-SGML, PU, Princeton, New Jersey; Millis, *Forrestal Diaries*, 323–324, 356–357; Brands, *Inside the Cold War*, 165–192; Miscamble, *George F. Kennan and the Making of American Foreign Policy*, 93–102.

ticular concern to Royall and Forrestal was the prospect that the United States might be requested to contribute troops under a UN trusteeship. In response, the council recommended that the Department of State initiate a comprehensive review of policy on Palestine.[29] Throughout late 1947 and early 1948 the CIA and the Department of State both cautioned against the administration's support of partition. Both feared that a UN military contingent to enforce the partition would require the use not only of American, but also Soviet troops. The CIA warned that a Soviet military force "will undoubtedly seek to include elements specially trained in Soviet subversive activities," and concluded that the USSR would "make every effort . . . to increase the anti-U.S. sentiment that is already strong among the Arabs."[30] By spring of 1948 Clifford had become convinced that UN trusteeship, not partition, was in the best interest of the United States. He urged his conviction upon Truman. On March 19, American representatives placed the trusteeship proposal before the UN Security Council. Days later, Truman issued a public statement in which he announced support of a provisional trusteeship plan, pending the orderly permanent settlement of a Jewish state.[31] On May 14, 1948, Jewish leaders in Palestine declared the creation of the new state of Israel. Ten minutes later Truman announced United States recognition of Israel. In doing so he made it clear that foreign policy decisions rested with the chief executive.[32]

As soon as Israel announced independence, armed forces of the Arab League attacked, and the first Arab-Israeli War began. During the first six months of the war, Forrestal received requests from the Department of State for additional military personnel to protect the United States consulate in Jerusalem

---

29. Kenneth Royall to Sidney Souers, 24 November 1947, *FRUS: 1947*, V, 1283.

30. PPS 19, "Position of the United States with Respect to Palestine," 20 January 1948; PPS 19/1, "Mr. Rusk's memorandum of January 26, 1948 Concerning PPS 19," 29 January 1948; PPS 21, "The Problem of Palestine," 11 February 1948, in Nelson, *PPS Papers 1948*, 34–77, 80–88; CIA-3, "Review of the World," 17 December 1947, PSF-NSC, Box 203.

31. Dean Rusk Oral History Interview; George M. Elsey Oral History Interview; Clark M. Clifford Oral History Interview; Clifford, *Council to the President*, 3–24; PPP:HST, 190–193; U.S. Congress, *A Decade of American Foreign Policy*, 839–841.

32. U.S. Congress, *A Decade of American Foreign Policy*, 843–844; PPP: HST, 258.

and to increase logistical support for the UN peace-keeping mission. The JCS feared that repeated UN requests would cause the deployment of combat troops in Palestine and lead to the possibility that Soviet or Soviet bloc forces might also intervene.[33] In the summer of 1948 the CIA warned that Czechoslovakian clandestine air operations to Palestine had been confirmed, and that the USSR had made arms shipments both to Arab nationalists and to the Israelis.[34] The reports of Soviet intervention in Palestine coupled with the military services' concerns about the risk of confrontation there prompted Forrestal to ask the NSC for advice. In mid-August, the council noted that the attempt to establish peace in Palestine with American forces could deplete troop strength around the world and risk military confrontation with the USSR in Palestine. The NSC, though, referred the report to the Department of State for further study.[35] At its next meeting the NSC again discussed this problem and the Department of State's report on the situation in Palestine, but reached no conclusion. Forrestal pointed out that from the military perspective the whole Middle East "was like a piece of flypaper. Getting stuck on one part would get us stuck on all." Lovett argued that the administration could not stop Moscow from sending troops "in response to a plea for help" from Israel. And the Department of State, he concluded, "was not willing to make a commitment not to send U.S. troops to Palestine."[36] After Truman's victory in the presidential election, the council adopted an NSC staff report, "Provision of a Police Force for Jerusalem" (NSC 27/3), that recommended that "in any event the United States should not accept any proposal for a Jerusalem police force," particularly if such an armed contingency included the United States, the USSR, or any Soviet satellites. Truman approved the policy report the following day on the premise that no American

33. Condit, *History of the JCS*, II, 100–108.
34. ORE 38–48, 27 July 1948, *FRUS: 1948*, V, pt. 2, 1240–1248; Memorandum, Roscoe Hillenkoetter to Harry Truman, 20 July 1948, 5 August 1948, PSF-IF, Box 249.
35. NSC 27, "U.S. Military Point of View for the Eventuality of United Nations Decision to Introduce Military Forces into Palestine," Summary of Discussion at the 18th Meeting, 20 August 1948, PSF-NSC, Box 220; Leffler, *A Preponderance of Power*, 242–243.
36. NSC 27, NSC 27/1, PSF-NSC, Box 204; Summary of Discussion at the 19th Meeting, 3 September 1948, Ibid., Box 220.

troops would be deployed to Palestine throughout his presidency.[37]

Neither the NSC nor the Department of State had taken part in determining Truman's decision to recognize Israel. The NSC nevertheless helped resolve the ongoing debate between the Departments of State and Defense about whether American troops would be sent to the Middle East as a peace-keeping force. In the coordination of policy regarding the protection of petroleum resources in the Middle East, the council's role was far greater. As American connections to Israel strengthened and tension increased in the Middle East, the defense of Western oil reserves became important to the NSC, and it requested that the military examine the feasibility of defending oil fields in the Persian Gulf region.[38] Of particular interest was the ability of United States forces to protect American and British investments in Saudi Arabia, Iran, and Iraq, especially a trans-Arabian pipeline constructed by the American oil firm Arabian American Oil Company (ARAMCO), designed to transport Persian Gulf oil to Mediterranean port cities in Lebanon. Because of conflicts among strategies offered by the JCS, the report was assigned to SANACC.[39] It designed an Anglo-American contingency strategy that concluded that in the event of a general war with the USSR, Soviet military forces would probably overrun the oil fields. To prevent Soviet control or burning of Middle East petroleum reserves during a wartime situation, it maintained, American and British forces would have to plug or obstruct the oil wells and remove all refineries and storage tanks. Warning that such action could seriously jeopardize the economies of the Western European nations and of the Arab oil-producing states for an extended period, SANACC concluded that the measures recommended should "only be taken as a last resort."[40] In the fall of 1948 the NSC staff circulated a report that adopted the SANACC study's findings. Soon thereafter, the

---

37. NSC 27/3, "Provision of a Police Force for Jerusalem," 23 November 1948, NSC, "Policies of the Government, 1947–1948," 25–26, PSF-NSC, Box 195; Minutes of the 27th Meeting, 23 November 1948, Ibid., Box 204.

38. Memorandum, James Forrestal to Sidney Souers, 21 May 1948, PSF-NSC, Box 203.

39. For American investments in the ARAMCO pipeline see Painter, *Oil and the American Century*, 117–119.

40. SANACC 398/4, 20 May 1948, *FRUS: 1948*, V, 2–3.

Department of State consulted with American corporate oil representatives, obtained written approvals from the military services and the intelligence agencies, and Truman and the NSC adopted a report in January 1949 that established a policy for the takeover of Middle East oil production should war erupt between the United States and the USSR.[41]

*   *   *

A confrontation that might have confined itself between the Soviet Union and the West was on its way to becoming global. As conflict threatened in Europe and the Middle East, the Far East also became a theater of the Cold War, beginning with China.

China had become a republic in 1911 under the rule of Sun Yat-sen, a Nationalist who promised China progressive economic and social modernization. His death in 1925 initiated a civil war between the Nationalists, under Jiang Jieshi, and the Communists, led by Mao Zedong. When Japan invaded China in 1937 the two factions declared a temporary truce. Yet for most Americans during World War II, Jiang's government became the symbol of Chinese resistance to Japanese aggression, and Americans viewed him as the rightful successor of the modernization movement launched by Sun. After Japan's surrender the Nationalist government, although corrupt and inept, received continued strong American support, financially and militarily. This occurred partially as a consequence of the lobbying efforts of Madame Jiang, who cultivated close ties with a loosely knit group of American political and business leaders known as the China bloc. While Truman despised Jiang's corruption, he reluctantly promised military assistance as the civil war between Nationalists and Communists renewed in the immediate postwar years. The Soviet Union responded as well by providing Mao's forces with captured Japanese weapons. The United States countered by airlifting and sealifting Jiang's troops to northern China and landing nearly fifty thousand Marines in the Beijing-Tsingtao area to help block Mao's forces. In an effort to mediate a cease-fire and form an eventual coalition government, Truman then sent Army Chief of Staff George C.

---

41. Summary of Discussion at the 19th Meeting, 3 September 1948, PSF-NSC, Box 220; NSC, "Policies of the Government, 1949," Appendix E, Annotated List of NSC Reports, 124–125, Ibid., Box 195.

Marshall to China in December 1945. Marshall returned to Washington in January 1947 to assume the position of secretary of state, writing off his mission as a failure and declaring that neither the Nationalists nor the Communists wanted to cooperate.[42]

By 1947 China had become a subject of congressional attention, especially among conservative Republicans favorable towards Jiang. Lieutenant General Albert C. Wedemeyer, United States commander in the China Theatre from 1944 to 1946, headed Marshall's request for a fact-finding mission to China and Korea. In September 1947 Wedemeyer presented a report to Truman and Marshall. It indicated that China faced a rapid political, military, and economic deterioration together with a well-organized and very determined Communist revolution. Wedemeyer recommended increased military and economic assistance to the Nationalists, as well as aid in the form of military and technical advisers. He further proposed that the UN establish a trusteeship of Manchuria and inaugurate a five-year economic recovery program. Largely because a call for a UN trusteeship might suggest that the Nationalist government was unable to govern China, the administration did not make the report public. Only Truman and Marshall, Forrestal, and Lovett got a copy of the report.[43] The administration, however, did act upon some of Wedemeyer's suggestions. In the fall of 1947, Marshall and Forrestal approved munitions shipments to Jiang's forces and granted permission to an army advisory group left in China to advise the Nationalists and train new recruits.[44]

---

42. For a thorough analysis of the civil war between the Nationalists and the Communists see Michael Schaller, *The U.S. Crusade in China, 1938–1945* (New York: Columbia University Press, 1979); William Whitney Stueck, Jr., *The Road to Confrontation: American Policy Toward China and Korea, 1947–1950* (Chapel Hill: University of North Carolina Press, 1981); Westad, *Cold War and Revolution*.

43. Leffler, *A Preponderance of Power*, 246–247; Stueck, *The Road to Confrontation*, 46–52; U.S. Congress, *A Decade of American Foreign Policy*, 703–713. For the most complete history see William Stueck, *The Wedemeyer Mission: American Politics and Foreign Policy During the Cold War* (Athens: University of Georgia Press, 1984). For the dilemmas involved in providing military aid to Jiang see Pach, *Arming the Free World*, 174–195.

44. Minutes, Meeting of Committee of Two, 3 November 1947, *FRUS: 1947*, VII, 908–912. The Wedemeyer Report was released as part of the *China*

General George C. Marshall, 1946. *(Defense Department Photo Center; Courtesy of Harry S. Truman Library)*

During the winter of 1947 and 1948 the issue of extending economic and military aid persisted. As escalation in fighting occurred, it became increasingly apparent that Jiang's military position, especially in Manchuria, was deteriorating. The administration feared that a Communist victory would have serious implications for American interests in East Asia, but State and Defense disagreed as to what should be done. Jiang's unwillingness to establish an honest and competent government convinced the Department of State that there was little hope of defeating the Communists, and it began to advocate a policy of gradual disengagement. The Department of Defense and the JCS maintained that the Department of State was underestimating the consequence of a Communist victory in China, and instead advocated continued and increased assistance to the Nationalists.[45]

White Paper in 1949, see Department of State, *United States Relations with China: With Special Reference to the Period 1944–1949* (Washington, D.C.: G.P.O., 1949), 764–814.

45. Memorandum, George Kennan to Robert Lovett, 2 November 1948, RG 59, Records of the PPS, NA; PPS 39, PPS 39/1, "United States Policy Toward China," 15 September, 24 November 1948, in Nelson, *PPS Papers, 1948*, 412–451; George F. Kennan, "Notes on China (1948)," GKP-SGML, Box 23; Stueck, *The Road to Confrontation*, 58–61.

In January and February of 1948 the NSC began work on a long-term policy for China. Marshall announced that he would ask Congress for $500 million in additional nonmilitary assistance. He told the NSC that he would oppose further military aid because any military solution would obligate the United States to take over the Nationalist government. In late March, the NSC staff presented its view of assistance to China, but a final policy statement would not be issued until completion of a comprehensive study by the Department of State. The tentative report recommended that the administration provide only short-term assistance to China.[46] Congress quickly passed the China Aid Act of 1948, authorizing $436 million for one year, and the NSC abandoned its suggestions. Truman signed the act, but assistance was too little and too late to reverse the deterioration of Jiang's forces. In May, as Mao's armies closed in on the Shantung peninsula, the prospect of a Communist victory seemed strong. The administration recognized the need for a consensus regarding the reduction or deployment of American military forces in China.[47]

Admiral Oscar C. Badger, commander of naval operations, cabled his superiors that the Marine base at Tsingtao, as well as its personnel and dependents, might be in imminent danger of an attack from Mao's forces. The situation in Tsingtao was referred to Forrestal, who recommended that the NSC study the problem.[48] The JCS ordered Badger to evacuate only when attacked. The Department of State requested an immediate withdrawal of all American forces. Before the NSC could reconcile the differences, the USSR imposed the Berlin blockade.[49] By July, however, the council had become concerned that an

---

46. Minutes and Summary of Discussion at the 6th Meeting, 12 February 1948, PSF-NSC, Box 203; Millis, *The Forrestal Diaries*, 372; *China White Paper*, 380–384; NSC 6, "The Position of the U.S. Regarding Short-Term Assistance to China," 26 March 1949, *FRUS: 1948*, VIII, 44–60.

47. U.S. Congress, *A Decade of American Foreign Policy*, 713–715; Record of NSC Actions, 9th Meeting, 2 April 1948, PSF-NSC Subject File, Box 191; Stueck, *The Road to Confrontation*, 61–65; Leffler, *A Preponderance of Power*, 249–250.

48. Cable, Admiral Badger to CNA, 3 May 1949, *FRUS: 1949*, VIII, 310–311, 316–318; NSC 11, "Action by U.S. Forces at Tsingtao in Defense of U.S. Lives and Property," 24 May 1949, *FRUS: 1949*, VIII, 314–316.

49. James Forrestal to George Marshall, 17 June 1949, *FRUS: 1948*, VIII, 319–312; Condit, *History of the JCS*, II, 456–457.

immediate evacuation from Tsingtao might damage American credibility and make it more difficult to convince the Soviet Union that the United States would stand firm in Berlin. The NSC therefore decided to defer action on Tsingtao for thirty days.[50] Truman decided to delay evacuation of United States forces from Tsingtao until after the November election. In late October, the NSC agreed that Badger should stay in the city.[51] In a special meeting the day after Truman's victory in the presidential election, the NSC reexamined Badger's orders. The PPS proposed a new report, which the council and Truman adopted, recommending the orderly withdrawal of American civilian dependents as well as the provision of Marine reinforcements and the strengthening of the naval defenses at Tsingtao.[52] Within a month, Jiang had retreated from the Shantung peninsula and relocated on the island of Taiwan, then known as Formosa.

In "U.S. Armed Forces at Tsingtao" (NSC 11/2), the Department of State suggested the immediate evacuation of all forces from Tsingtao, and it opposed any establishment of naval facilities on Taiwan.[53] Five days later, the JCS concurred. In late December Truman approved the recommendations, formally initiating the gradual evacuation of the last American forces from China. The withdrawal was completed by the following spring.[54]

The United States had narrowly avoided becoming embroiled in the Chinese civil war. "The magnitude of the tasks of establishing order and of repulsing the Communist challenge," contends historian William Whitney Stueck, "was far greater

---

50. Summary of Discussion at the 15th Meeting, 16 July 1948, PSF-NSC, Box 220.

51. Memorandum, Harry Truman to James Forrestal, 18 October 1948, *FRUS: 1948*, VIII, 326–328; NSC Record of Actions, 25th Meeting, 21 October, PSF-NSC Subject File, Box 191.

52. PPS 45, "United States Policy Toward China in the Light of the Current Situation," 26 November 1948, in Nelson, *PPS Papers 1948*, 509–517; NSC 11/1, "U.S. Armed Forces at Tsingtao," 19 October 1948, PSF-NSC, Box 204; Minutes of the 26th Meeting, 2 November 1948, Ibid.; Memorandum, Sidney Souers to Harry Truman, 3 November 1948, Ibid., Box 220.

53. NSC 11/2, "U.S. Armed Forces at Tsingtao" 15 December 1948, PSF-NSC, Box 205; Minutes of the 13th Meeting, 16 December 1948, Ibid.

54. Memorandum, William Leahy to James Forrestal, 20 December 1948, PHT-NSC, Box 9; NSC 11/3, "U.S. Armed Forces at Tsingtao," 24 December 1948, NSC, "Policies of the Government, 1947–1948," 2, PSF-NSC, Box 195.

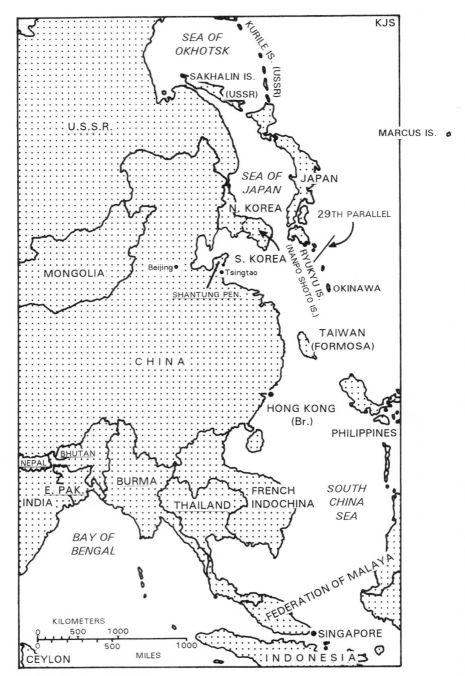

Map 3. East Asia (1948)

than in Greece."[55] A lack of confidence in the Nationalists' ability to succeed, the priority of military commitments in the Mediterranean, and the demands of economic assistance to Western Europe, justified for Truman and the NSC a lesser concern for Jiang's situation. But by early 1949, as the collapse of the Nationalists approached rapidly, Truman and the NSC found it imperative to proceed with a long-range containment policy for China and all of Asia.

*   *   *

As containment strategies and programs for Europe and the Middle East proceeded, and China was left to Mao's impending control, the NSC and Truman determined that Japan, like Germany, must serve as an economic and democratic bulwark against Soviet expansionism, vital to the administration's defensive perimeter in East Asia. The concept, as one historian points out, maintained "the safeguarding of selected island strong points," including Japan, the Philippines, and Okinawa, "while avoiding potentially debilitating commitments on the mainland."[56]

The United States had insisted on a free hand in Japan's postwar administration, with executive powers granted to General MacArthur. In early 1947 MacArthur had stated that he believed Japan was ready for an end to military occupation and that the administration should proceed with a permanent Japanese peace treaty. In March 1948 the PPS finalized a study concerning a treaty with Japan. It summarized a Kennan fact-finding mission conducted earlier in the year, and was forwarded to the NSC in June 1948.[57] Looking to developing a more stable postwar Japan and thereby containing potential Soviet intervention in East Asia's defensive perimeter, Kennan proposed a new policy for Japan. It advised that the United States concentrate on Japan's economic rehabilitation. Kennan

---

55. Stueck, *The Road to Confrontation*, 56.

56. Gaddis, *Strategies of Containment*, 41. On this point see Michael Schaller, *The American Occupation of Japan: The Origins of the Cold War in Asia* (New York: Oxford University Press, 1985), 77–106.

57. PPS 28/2, "Recommendations with Respect to United States Policy Toward Japan" (A Revision of PPS 28 and PPS 28/1), in Nelson, *PPS Papers 1948*, 175–243; Kennan, *Memoirs*, Volume I, 382–391; PPS 28, 25 March 1948, *FRUS: 1948*, VI, 691–696. The paper was referred to the NSC Staff and reissued as NSC 13 on 2 June 1948, PSF-NSC, Box 204.

also urged instead of pursuing reforms imposed by MacArthur's military occupation, that the administration not negotiate a peace treaty at the time, but strengthen Japan's economy and lift postwar reparations to prepare for an end of military occupation. He recommended that the United States meanwhile gradually turn over to the Japanese responsibility for their government and their internal security; that the United States transfer naval operations from Tokyo Bay to Okinawa; and that American strategic control over Japan's islands stop at the 29th parallel.[58] A reverse in course for Japan had been of interest to other Americans for nearly a year, when an influential pro-Japan corporate lobby group called the American Council on Japan began publicly to criticize MacArthur's purge of Japan's business interests and his dissolving of the Japanese Zaibatsu. Their dissatisfactions came to the attention of Forrestal, Harriman, Royall, and Under Secretary of the Army William Draper. Influenced by the Council's charges against MacArthur's policies, Draper and a group of American businessmen, including chair of Chemical Bank Percy H. Johnson, investigated conditions in Japan in early 1948. They concluded that MacArthur's occupation measures contributed to economic uncertainty and discouraged foreign investment in Japan. They submitted to Secretary Royall a report written by Johnson and Draper that provided details similar to Kennan's PPS policy recommendations. The report specified the lifting of Japan's reparations and stimulating industrial recovery with the help of American assistance programs.[59]

The NSC staff issued Kennan's report on Japan for the council's consideration as "Recommendations with Respect to U.S. Policy Toward Japan" (NSC 13/1). Forrestal submitted the policy's recommendations to the JCS, and objections were raised to setting the 29th parallel as the limit of American strategic control. The Joint Chiefs believed that islands south of the 29th parallel, primarily Marcus Island, the Nanpo Shoto Is-

---

58. Ibid.; Leffler, *A Preponderance of Power*, 255–257.

59. Miscamble, *George F. Kennan and the Making of American Foreign Policy*, 256–258. For treatments concerning the American Council on Japan and the Draper-Johnson mission see Howard Schonberger, "The Japan Lobby in American Diplomacy, 1947–1952," *Pacific Historical Review* 46 (August 1977): 327–359; idem, *Aftermath of War: Americans and the Remaking of Japan, 1945–1952* (Kent: Kent State University Press, 1989).

lands, and the Ryukyu Islands, needed to fall within the strategic sphere of the United States.[60]

In late September 1948 the council discussed NSC 13/1. On the issues of Japan's reparations and its economy, the Department of State expressed some differences with army. Influenced by the Draper-Johnson report, Royall pointed out that the Department of the Army's position was one concerned primarily with Japan's industrial levels. Walton Butterworth, representing State's position, added that Japan's reparations had been accepted "because it was what the other governments desired" at the end of World War II. The Department of State, Butterworth observed, believed "that the level of industry problem . . . was the other side of the coin of which reparations was one side."[61] He informed the NSC that the Department of State was prepared to push for lifting reparations in future negotiations. Royall made it clear that the army wanted to "make certain" that after reparations were removed "there would be no other limits to Japanese productivity." The council offered no definite decision on NSC 13/1, but it did recognize that all reparations issues had to wait until negotiations on a final peace treaty with Japan took place.[62]

One week later, NSC 13/1 returned to the council, and Lovett informed it that the Chinese had made before the UN their own proposals for a peace treaty with Japan. Lovett requested that the NSC avoid delay and asked that any points of dispute "be laid aside" in order for the rest of NSC 13/1 to move forward. The council wasted no time, and after minor revisions, adopted the policy as NSC 13/2. Truman approved it, opening the way for the Department of State's preliminary preparations for negotiations. Truman also sent a special emissary to oversee the reconstruction of Japan's economy, but recovery was a slow process, as were the treaty negotiations.[63]

---

60. NSC 13/1, "Recommendations with Respect to U.S. Policy Toward Japan," 24 September 1948, PSF-NSC, Box 204; Memorandum, Joint Chiefs of Staff to James Forrestal, 29 September 1948, Ibid.; Summary of Discussion at the 22nd Meeting, 1 October 1948, Ibid.

61. Minutes of the 22nd Meeting, September 30, 1948, PSF-NSC, Box 220.

62. Ibid.

63. Minutes of the 23rd Meeting, October 7, 1948, PSF-NSC, Box 220. Truman also approved paragraph 5 of NSC 13/2 on 5 November 1948, stating the United States intended to maintain long-term military facilities at

In crafting a policy of detachment from China and presenting a reverse-course policy for Japan, Kennan's PPS had successfully deflected the concerns of Defense and the Joint Chiefs. Under pressure to evacuate Americans from China as Nationalist forces fell to defeat, and rushing to counter a potential Sino-Japanese peace treaty, the Department of State at the right moment in the process of coordinating policy placed before the NSC the policies for China and Japan formulated by the PPS. When Truman and the NSC approved the State's policy agenda they began a shift in American containment to the defensive perimeter of Asia, albeit with a gradual reduction of direct military support for both Nationalist China and Japan.

Like China and Japan, Korea became a dilemma for Truman and the NSC. An impoverished country under Japanese imperial rule from 1905 through 1945, Korea lacked the indigenous self-government and stability of Japan. At the end of World War II the Allied powers placed Korea under the temporary administration of the United States and the USSR. Divided at the 38th parallel, Korea was occupied by American forces in the South and Soviet troops in the North. Both the United States and the USSR had advocated a peaceful reunification of Korea, but the Cold War prohibited any such prospect. The Soviet Union recommended that all occupation of Korea be withdrawn by early 1948, yet refused to allow the UN to sponsor elections in the North. As the United States was faced with a shortage of troops to meet requirements elsewhere, the problem of prolonged military occupation in Korea became a concern for Truman and the NSC. The military services advised that all efforts be made for a withdrawal of forces from Korea by December 1948, but the Department of State opposed setting a firm date and argued for a stronger commitment.[64]

Okinawa, Memorandum, Sidney Souers to Harry Truman, 27 October 1948, Ibid., Box 204.
    64. Dean Rusk Oral History Interview; Leffler, *A Preponderance of Power*, 251–253. For a detailed background see William Stueck, *The Korean War: An International History* (Princeton: Princeton University Press, 1995), 13–27; idem, *The Road to Confrontation*, 19–28. Necessary for a thorough understanding of the civil war in Korea that precipitated the Korean War is Bruce Cummings, *The Origins of the Korean War*: Volume I, *Liberation and the Emergence of Separate Regimes, 1945–1947* (Princeton: Princeton University Press, 1981).

A few months prior to the elections sanctioned by the UN in the South, the NSC examined a SANACC policy statement on Korea that the JCS had approved. "The Position of the U.S. with Respect to Korea" (NSC 8) recommended withdrawal of all American forces by the end of 1948, and endorsed continued economic and military aid to the anti-Communist South Korean government of Syngman Rhee. Forrestal asked the NSC how much "credibility" the administration might lose by withdrawing from Korea. Lovett conceded that such action would be "the best we can expect to do." The strongest objection came from Royall, who argued that the administration's conditions for withdrawal should not make "an adequate internal security force a prior condition." The rest of the council agreed and amended the paper to reflect Royall's view.[65] Truman also agreed and American military withdrawal from South Korea seemed probable. NSC 8 suggested that by the end of 1948 South Korean military forces should be strong enough to provide, "so far as practicable, effective protection for the security of South Korea against any but an overt act of aggression." It observed that a victory by forces under Soviet domination would have a harmful psychological impact upon much of East Asia. Recognizing the inability of the United States to protect South Korea from outside attack, NSC 8 nevertheless urged efforts, including full cooperation with the UN, to prevent Communist control of the country.[66]

By the fall of 1948 rumors circulated in South Korea that the North was planning an invasion to reunify the country. At the urging of the Department of State and the American ambassador to South Korea John Muccio, the army delayed its schedule for withdrawal until early 1949, and agreed to leave one combat team of seventy-five hundred men in place.[67] Con-

---

65. SANACC 176/39, NSC Record of Actions, 9th Meeting, 2 April 1948, PSF-NSC, Box 191; Summary of Discussion at the 9th Meeting, 2 April 1948, Ibid., Box 220; NSC 8, "The Position of the U.S. with Respect to Korea," Ibid., Box 203. For a fuller analysis of SANACC's report see James F. Schnabel and Robert J. Watson, *The History of the Joint Chiefs of Staff: The Joint Chiefs of Staff and National Policy: Volume III, The Korean War* (Wilmington, DE: Michael Glazier, 1979), 15–17.

66. NSC 8, "The Position of the U.S. with Respect to Korea," PSF-NSC, Box 203. Portions are printed in *FRUS: 1948*, VI, 1168–1169.

67. Condit, *History of the JCS*, II, 515–516; Schnabel and Watson, *History of the JCS*, III, 19–21.

cerned about the potential effect of Communist control of the Korean peninsula upon the administration's position in Japan, the Department of State recommended in December that the NSC reconsider a policy for Korea. But the request for a change occurred at a time when Marshall had arranged to retire and Lovett had planned to resign. It would be many months before the NSC could make a thorough review of the situation. Nevertheless, the stage was prepared for continued debate about Korea. As Truman began a full term as president, divisions within the administration, and priorities in other parts of the world, made most unlikely any early coordinated strategy toward Korea.[68]

As the difficult year of 1948 ended, the NSC's workload increased and many of the policy dilemmas were left largely unresolved. Europe remained vulnerable because the Berlin blockade continued, but it had forced Truman and the NSC to address the issue of custody for atomic weapons, initiate guidelines for the nation's military preparedness, and formulate a new strategy toward the Soviet Union. As a result, the parameters of the nation's containment policy were better defined. The Department of State emerged at the end of the year as the primary initiator of ideas approved by the NSC, and its PPS under Kennan's direction alone formulated policies for China and Japan as well as NSC 20/4. The military service secretaries submitted for SANACC's coordination their strategic concerns on Korea and the defense of Middle East petroleum reserves. Consequently, the political and military policy capabilities of the NSC were impeded. President Truman and the Task Force on National Security Organization recognized the problem, and by early 1949 had initiated reform measures that streamlined the council's organization and restored its ability to formulate policy. The reforms were in place at the right time, for the next year of the Cold War presented Truman and the NSC several crises that demanded immediate attention and superior policy coordination.

***

68. Stueck, *The Road to Confrontation*, 105. A superlative earlier work that assesses U.S. political and military policymaking regarding Korea during the Korean War is Rosemary Foot, *The Wrong War: American Policy and the Dimensions of the Korean Conflict, 1950–1953* (Ithaca: Cornell University Press, 1985).

Chapter Four

Crises and Reassessments

To squeeze the capitalist orders. That's the Cold War.
(Viacheslav M. Molotov, 1949)

The first nine months of 1949 gave Truman and the NSC optimism. The CIA reported that containment policies had "checked the Soviet-Communist activities that were seeking to break down Western Europe."[1] A few months after Truman began his new term in the White House, American and Soviet negotiators announced an end to the Berlin blockade, the West concluded the major aspects of the NATO pact, the Greek civil war wound down, the Arab-Israeli War ended, and the administration reorganized the NSC and the CIA. Early in the year, Secretaries Marshall, Forrestal, and Royall resigned from the council, and Truman replaced them with Secretary of State Dean G. Acheson, Secretary of Defense Louis A. Johnson, and Secretary of the Army Gordon Gray. Then in the fall of 1949 officials realized that a dollar gap had appeared in Great Britain after implementation of the Marshall Plan, the United States discovered that the Soviet Union had exploded an atomic bomb, and Mao's Communist forces proclaimed the creation of the People's Republic of China. The American public and Congress questioned why the administration had allowed China to fall to communism and how the USSR acquired highly classified atomic secrets. Was it, asked the political

---

1. CIA-4–49, "Review of the World," 20 April 1949, PSF-NSC, Box 220.

right, because the administration had been soft on communism? Under growing anti-Communist pressure at home and threats to containment policies abroad, Truman and the NSC responded by gradually shifting its strategy from a limited and reactive response to an active and tough defensive confrontation.

The blockade of Berlin continued for the first six months of 1949. So did the airlift, in contradiction to earlier doubts in the military about its ability to persist. During the winter, West Berliners endured a shortage of fuel supplies and suffered food rationing. Truman and the NSC did not know how long, in spite of the airlift, West Berlin could manage the hardships. Although no agreements to end the blockade were reached through the UN, other diplomatic channels opened by spring. American and Soviet representatives engaged in secret negotiations, and by April were working on a final settlement. To universal relief, it recognized that the blockade would end on May 12, and that the Council of Foreign Ministers would convene in Paris for the purpose of resolving the problem of Germany.[2]

Prior to the Paris Conference of the Council of Foreign Ministers, the NSC met in mid-May to consider the administration's plans as well as what action might be needed should the conference adjourn without a settlement on Germany. Acheson told the council that " 'Germany' had become only a geographical expression, a word, with no government and no state." He noted that the priority for the Council of Foreign Ministers would be to proceed with plans for a West German government, with hopes that "any unification of Germany as a whole should grow out of that." The NSC questioned Acheson whether the Department of State had an alternative plan should the Soviet Union attempt a second blockade. Acheson reviewed several options, but concluded that the "best we could hope for" would be a West German government and police force that "could initiate steps to get the Soviets back as far as we could." Truman, presiding over the meeting, declared that he would decide whenever the occasion arose but suggested that Symington "keep the airlift handy." After further discussion the NSC decided that a study would be needed of possible

---

2. Acheson, *Present at the Creation*, 267–274. For text of the negotiations see *FRUS: 1949*, III, 643–817.

United States courses of action in case the USSR reimposed the blockade.[3]

One week after the NSC meeting the Council of Foreign Ministers convened, and in early April it approved a trizonal fusion accord that established a provisional German government in the three western zones, and granted the civilian Allied High Commission in Bonn the authority to replace the tripartite military governors. Five months later military occupation ended and a parliamentary council declared the creation of the Federal Republic of West Germany.[4] The NSC followed up with a plan in the event the blockade was reimposed. It suggested that the administration take two actions: establish another airlift at full capacity, and implement a counter-blockade on East Berlin. The council called for "interim measures," particularly the maintenance of aircraft and continued stockpiling in Berlin.[5] The NSC convened to consider contingency plans by the Joint Chiefs for stand-by airlift operations, but the Council of Foreign Ministers adjourned without a new blockade materializing.[6] Later, Acheson told the council that the work of the conference would discourage the Soviet Union from trying to reimpose a blockade.[7] The JCS reviewed the airlift and reported to Secretary Johnson that a gradual phase-out could begin by August 1. In late July, the NSC recommended ending the airlift as soon as possible. It suggested that should events render necessary a second airlift, one could be resumed within ninety days. Truman sanctioned the report, and on September 30, the United States concluded all airlift operations.[8]

---

3. Summary of Discussion at the 40th Meeting, 18 May 1949, PSF-NSC, Box 220.

4. For the text of the Council of Foreign Ministers Paris Accords regarding Germany and the provisional West German government see *FRUS: 1949*, III, 177–183.

5. NSC 24/2, NSC 24/3, "Possible U.S. Courses of Action in the Event the USSR Reimposes the Berlin Blockade," 2 June 1949, PSF-NSC, Box 206; NSC Memorandum Approval, 14 June 1949, Ibid., Box 191.

6. Minutes of the 42nd Meeting, 16 June 1949, PSF-NSC, Box 206; Condit, *History of the JCS*, II, 160–161.

7. Summary of Discussion at the 43rd Meeting, 8 July 1949, PSF-NSC, Box 220.

8. Condit, *History of the JCS*, II, 159; NSC 24/4, "Phase-Out of the Berlin Airlift," 27 July 1949, PSF-NSC, Box 193; NSC Memorandum Approval, NSC Record of Action, Ibid., Box 191; Memorandum, Sidney Souers to Harry Truman, 28 July 1949, Ibid., Box 193.

The first Berlin crisis had ended, but a Cold War between the United States and the Soviet Union continued. In October a People's Congress met in East Berlin and declared the formation of the German Democratic Republic under Soviet sponsorship. By that time Stalin had "recognized the de facto permanent Western political rights in Berlin," point out Russian scholars, and he conceded defeat by signing a protocol that divided the city of Berlin into a West and an East sector. Stalin had not planned to initiate a war over Berlin. Instead, he hoped that the blockade would force Western Europe and the United States to accept a quid pro quo regarding the settlement of Germany. During the course of the Berlin crisis, the Department of State had considered a proposal for Germany's reunification. Known as Program A, and written by Kennan and the PPS, it recommended complete military withdrawal from Germany and eventual unification of the country under renewed negotiations with the Soviet Union. Both Marshall and Acheson as secretaries of state had given Program A their serious attention and prepared to submit it to the NSC for consideration. When the Council of Foreign Ministers met in Paris, however, British and French opposition to German reunification persuaded Acheson to adopt their alternate plan as the American program for the division of Germany.[9]

After the settlement of the question of Germany, Kennan became professionally disillusioned with Acheson's considering him as merely one of many policy advisers, and expressed concern that the PPS might not serve, in his words, "as the ideological inspirer and coordinator of policy."[10] Although the PPS remained an important policy facilitator for the Department of State through much of 1949, Kennan's assessment of its diminishing influence was correct. A reorganization of the NSC in late August that removed the three military service secretaries

---

9. Nikita Sergeyevich Khrushchev, *Khrushchev Remembers: The Glasnost Tapes* (Boston: Little, Brown, 1990), 165–166; Holloway, *Stalin and the Bomb*, 258–260; Zubok and Pleshakov, *Inside the Kremlin's Cold War*, 52; Melvyn P. Leffler, "Negotiating from Strength: Acheson, the Russians and American Power," in Douglas Brinkley, ed., *Dean Acheson and the Making of U.S. Foreign Policy* (London: Macmillan, 1993), 176–210; idem, *A Preponderance of Power*, 279–285; Miscamble, *George F. Kennan and the Making of American Foreign Policy*, 141–177.

10. Kennan, *Memoirs*, Volume I, 427.

as statutory members made the secretary of state's position on the council equal to the Defense establishment's, and for policy recommendations and assessments Acheson began to rely on other advisers from State's executive secretariat as well as the PPS.

*   *   *

As the Berlin crisis ended, Truman and the NSC were presented with an unexpected Cold War demarche in Eastern Europe. In June 1948 the USSR expelled Yugoslavia from its Cominform, and the Kremlin called for the removal of its leader, Josef Tito. A Yugoslav resistance commander during World War II who turned Communist, Tito had risen to power as dictator in the immediate postwar years. Yet he pursued and maintained independent political, economic, and military controls that soon prompted a falling out with the Soviet Union. After Yugoslavia's break with Moscow, the NSC recommended that the administration encourage Tito's defection from the Soviet bloc by moving very gradually to provide Yugoslavia with economic and military assistance.[11]

In early 1949 the Soviet Union placed an economic blockade on Yugoslavia, and Washington became concerned that Tito might not achieve economic independence from the USSR. The PPS suggested that the administration relax export controls on Yugoslavia. The NSC approved the report with minor revisions and submitted it to Truman as "Economic Relations Between the United States and Yugoslavia" (NSC 18/2). It stated: "Tito has successfully defied the Kremlin myth and effectively destroyed the legend of the infallibility of Stalin." Believing that Yugoslavia might serve as an example to other Soviet satellite states, NSC 18/2 recommended that the United States assist Tito's break, but with an understanding that Yugoslavia withdraw any future support for the Greek insurgency movement. It urged that the administration extend American commercial credits, license for export American material goods not in short supply, and remove the export prohibitions on the

---

11. Gaddis, *Strategies of Containment*, 67–68; Leffler, *A Preponderance of Power*, 236–237; NSC 18, "The Attitude of This Government Toward Events in Yugoslavia," 2 September 1948, Minutes of the 19th Meeting, 2 September 1948, PSF-NSC, Box 204. For PPS 35 see Etzold and Gaddis, *Containment*, 169–172.

shipment of materials required for production of munitions. NSC 18/2 stressed that export controls should be lifted in a "quiet and routine manner," with no public announcement. This approach, it maintained, would prevent any public conclusion that the administration was "making a radical change" in policy.[12]

The next day, Truman approved the report. The NSC thereupon established a special ad hoc committee consisting of representatives from the Departments of State, Defense, Commerce, and the AEC. The committee reviewed all Yugoslav export license applications and advised the secretary of commerce on changes.[13] In March, Yugoslavia requested an export license for a steel mill. The ad hoc committee and the Departments of State and Commerce favored license approval, but Johnson opposed acceptance of the application, pointing out that the steel mill had a "war potential." After several months of debate, the Departments of State and Commerce prevailed and announced the steel mill deal in September. Because members of Congress were charging that the administration had been soft on communism the administration did not publicize its trade relationship with Yugoslavia.[14]

As the details of the steel mill export were being completed, the NSC proposed, and Truman approved, excluding Yugoslavia from restrictions on aviation exports, and allowing export licenses for American aircraft, spare parts, and aviation fuel.[15] The Export-Import Board approved a $20 million loan to Yugoslavia, and the administration supported a loan from the Inter-

---

12. PPS 49, "Economic Relations Between the United States and Yugoslavia," 10 February 1949, in Anna Kasten Nelson, ed., *The State Department Policy Planning Staff Papers 1949* (New York: Garland Publishing, 1983), 14–25; NSC 18/1, NSC 18/2, "Economic Relations Between the United States and Yugoslavia," 18 February 1949, PSF-NSC, Box 205; Summary of Discussion at the 34th Meeting, 18 February 1949, PSF-NSC, Box 205; Summary of Discussion at the 34th Meeting, 18 February 1949, PSF-NSC, Box 220.

13. NSC Progress Report on NSC 18/2, 11 April 1949, PSF-NSC, Box 205.

14. NSC Progress Report on NSC 18/2, 27 May 1949, Ibid. For a fuller analysis of the steel mill deal and its publicity see Lorraine M. Lees, "The American Decision to Assist Tito, 1948–1949," *Diplomatic History* 2 (Fall 1978): 415–418.

15. NSC 15/1, "U.S. Civil Aviation Policy Toward the USSR and its Satellites," 15 August 1949, NSC Memorandum Approval, PSF-NSC, Box 191.

national Monetary Fund of $3 million.[16] American economic assistance helped stabilize the Yugoslav currency and stimulated trade opportunities, and by the fall of 1949 the nation had achieved economic independence from Moscow and gained admittance to the UN Security Council. The success of Tito's break, however, led to renewed Soviet military pressure. In November the CIA reported that the USSR had taken paramilitary and clandestine measures to undermine Tito's regime, and noted that the Yugoslavs were preparing defensive measures in the event of any "large-scale guerrilla infiltration or direct military action."[17] Concerned that Tito might not withstand a Soviet attack, Truman approved the council's recommendation that the administration provide Yugoslavia "quiet" non-grant military assistance should it become necessary.[18] Tito was not informed of the decision, and no military aid was sent to Yugoslavia in 1949 and 1950. NSC recommendations for Yugoslavia, however, provided Truman an alternative approach to Cold War policy.

What came to be known as Titoism, or the defection of a Soviet satellite, Truman and the NSC regarded as an important precedent.[19] Thereafter, policy the council coordinated toward Eastern Europe would go beyond containment, seeking to undermine and fragment Soviet control in Eastern Europe. The CIA reported in the fall of 1949: "Nationalist sentiment embodied in the Yugoslav-Communist doctrine" had attracted followers from "Communist ranks, including some of the satellite states." Tito, the CIA observed, had proven that international communism was not monolithic. Believing that Yugoslavia's defection emphasized an "unresolved strain" in the Communist doctrine and its political organization, the agency suggested

---

16. NSC Progress Report on NSC 18/2, 9 November 1949, PSF-NSC, Box 205.

17. CIA-11-49, "Review of the World," 16 November 1949, PSF-NSC, Box 207.

18. PPS 60, "Yugoslav-Moscow Controversy as Related to U.S. Foreign Policy Objectives," 10 September 1949, in Nelson, *PPS Papers 1949*, 139–150; NSC 18/4, "United States Policy Toward the Conflict Between the USSR and Yugoslavia," 17 November 1949, PSF-NSC, Box 207.

19. Gaddis, *Long Peace*, 68.

that Titoism "may develop into a means of pulling together an anti-Soviet opposition."[20]

As early as 1948, the Department of State had prepared a similar plan for Eastern Europe, though it would follow an armed victory over the USSR. Issued as NSC 7, it recommended the "de-Communization" of a defeated Soviet Union by cultivating, particularly among the White Russians, Ukrainians, and the Baltic states, several ethnic-national independent republics friendly to the United States.[21] The emergence of Titoism by 1949 led the NSC to develop further the argument for encouraging traditional nationalistic identity. In "United States Policy Toward the Soviet Satellite States in Eastern Europe" (NSC 58/2), the council revised a PPS study and adopted it in September 1949. Truman approved the new policy, aiming ultimately at "the appearance in Eastern Europe of non-totalitarian administrations willing to accommodate themselves to, and participate in, the free world community."[22]

Noting cultural and nationalistic possibilities in Eastern Europe, NSC 58/2 advocated that the United States "foster a heretical drifting-away process" from Moscow by the satellite states, and the development of "two opposing blocs in the Communist world—a Stalinist group and a non-conformist faction." NSC 58/2 proposed that the administration disrupt the relationship between the USSR and its Eastern European satellites with American psychological warfare, and encourage nationalism with a pro-West "offensive" that would be "maintained not only on the overt but also the covert plane."[23] Soon thereafter, the NSC stepped up psychological warfare plans for Eastern Europe and authorized a number of CIA operations, and others funded by the agency.

In early 1949 the NSC placed within the Department of

---

20. CIA-10–49, "Review of the World," PSF-NSC, Box 206; CIA-11–49, Ibid., Box 207.

21. NSC 7, "The Position of the United States with Respect to Soviet-Directed World Communism," 30 March 1949, Etzold and Gaddis, *Containment*, 164–169; NSC 20/1, "U.S. Objectives with Respect to Russia," 18 August 1949, Ibid., 173–203.

22. PPS 59, "United States Policy Toward the Soviet Satellite States in Eastern Europe," 25 August 1949, in Nelson, *PPS Papers 1949*, 124–138; NSC 58/2, "United States Policy Toward the Soviet Satellite States in Eastern Europe," PSF-NSC, Box 207; *FRUS: 1949*, V, 50–51.

23. Ibid.

State the responsibility for coordination of overt propaganda activities. The department achieved some success by August when measures were taken against Soviet jamming of Voice of America broadcasts from the United States and Great Britain.[24] After early 1950 the NSC proposed with Truman's approval that the Department of State would be responsible for the coordination of both overt information programs and covert psychological warfare. The operations included all covert and broadcasting monitoring services of the CIA, all foreign information services of the Department of State, and all armed forces' overt informational services. These changes broadened the Department of State's propaganda capabilities, particularly in Europe.[25]

The CIA's covert operations also expanded in 1949. In June the OPC, under director Wisner, helped establish Radio Free Europe with clandestine funding from the CIA. The true coordinating agency of Radio Free Europe was the National Committee for a Free Europe (NCFE), a private organization set up by former Department of State and former OSS officials and advised by Wisner, Kennan, and Allen Dulles. The NCFE was committed to liberating Eastern Europe from Soviet control and assisting refugees from Soviet bloc countries who had made their way to the United States. It hired emigrés as translators, writers, and foreign language broadcasters for Radio Free Europe. In early 1950, shortly after it received its first shortwave radio transmitter donation from the OPC, Radio Free Europe began beaming programs over the Iron Curtain. By the end of the Truman presidency, it had broadcast facilities throughout Germany, North Africa, and the Iberian Peninsula, and was receiving as much as $30 million a year through

---

24. Under Secretary's Meeting, "Planning for Wartime Conduct of Overt Psychological Warfare," 27 May 1949, RG 59-RSS, NA, Washington, D.C.; NSC 43, "Planning for Wartime Conduct of Overt Psychological Warfare," 23 March 1949, PSF-NSC, Box 193; NSC Progress Report on NSC 43, 1 August 1949, Ibid., Box 198.

25. NSC 59, "The Foreign Information Program and Psychological Warfare Planning," 10 March 1950, NSC "Policies of the Government of the United States of America Relating to the National Security, Volume III, 1950," 37–39, PSF-NSC, Box 195. Under Secretary's Meeting, "The Department's Responsibility for Psychological Warfare Policy and Planning," 10 February 1949, RG 59-RSS, NA.

the OPC.[26] CIA-OPC operators organized a large network of agents in Germany, France, Austria, Italy, and Scandinavia, and they provided contacts and potential agents from a growing Soviet bloc refugee population in displaced persons camps throughout Western Europe. Many emigrés trained by the CIA returned to their native countries to gather intelligence. Hundreds of others parachuted home to assist national anti-Soviet groups form paramilitary destabilization fronts in Poland, the Baltic states, and Albania.[27]

The demands for intelligence information and the recruitment and training of large numbers of Eastern European emigrés led the CIA and the United States Army's Intelligence Corps to develop the first contact with Nazis. Many former Nazi officers were vehement anti-Communists, and American intelligence agencies secretly accepted their services. The most notorious Nazi the CIA employed was Klaus Barbie, "the butcher of Lyon." Before American officials assisted his escape in 1951 to South America, the CIA used Barbie for his connection to a ring of anti-Communist Nazi agents.[28] One of the most successful ex-Nazi agents for the CIA was Reinhard Gehlen. A former head of Hitler's military intelligence in the East, Gehlen offered the CIA his assistance and his files on Soviet operations. Gehlen's organization and contacts in East Germany and Eastern Europe provided many intelligence emigré agents in 1949 and later years.[29]

---

26. PPS 54, "Policy Relating to Defection and Defectors from Soviet Power," 29 June 1949, in Nelson, *PPS Papers 1949*, 75–81; Under Secretary's Meeting, "Policy Relating to Defections from Soviet Control," 9 December 1949, RG 59-RSS, NA; Sig Mickelson, *America's Other Voice: The Story of Radio Free Europe and Radio Liberty* (New York: Praeger, 1983), 17–22, 29–30; Harry Rositzke, *The CIA's Secret Operations: Espionage, Counterespionage, and Covert Operations* (New York: Readers Digest Press, 1977), 156–159; Prados, *The Presidents' Secret Wars*, 34.

27. Rositzke, *The CIA's Secret Operations*, 27–29, 41–45, 166–173; Thomas Powers, *The Man Who Kept Secrets: Richard Helms and the CIA* (New York: Knopf, 1979), 38–40; Prados, *The Presidents' Secret Wars*, 41–44. For a careful analysis on Albania see Nicholas Bethell, *Betrayed* (New York: Times Books, 1984).

28. Jones, *The CIA and American Democracy*, 103–104. Recent documentation on the CIA-Barbie connection is cited in Allan A. Ryan, Jr., *Klaus Barbie and the United States Government: The Report, with Documentary Appendix, to the Attorney General of the United States* (Frederick, MD: University Publications of America, 1984).

29. Jones, *The CIA and American Democracy*, 104–105; Prados, *The Presidents' Secret Wars*, 36–37, 40–41; Ranelagh, *The Agency*, 137–138, 770. For

In spite of all the time and work involved in the CIA-OPC Eastern European operations, significant obstacles blocked the successful emergence of another Tito. The CIA could not verify information from inside the Soviet bloc provided by emigré agents. Soviet agents often penetrated emigré resistance and destabilization fronts. By 1950 Moscow's tightening of its security controls on Eastern Europe had made resistance extremely difficult. Nevertheless, the NSC and the CIA continued to wage a costly covert counteroffensive until the end of the Truman presidency, when all major resistance groups had disbanded or been eliminated, and the OPC abandoned as unproductive its activities behind the Iron Curtain.[30]

*   *   *

The strained relations between Yugoslavia and the USSR adversely affected the Communist insurgency movement in Greece, and Tito gradually refused support to the guerrillas. As a result, in early January 1949 the NSC suggested that the development of the Greek civil war was insufficient to justify sending United States armed forces. By summer Tito was ordering the Greek insurgents to pledge their loyalty to him rather than the Soviet Union, the guerrilla leadership refused, and Yugoslavia shut off further support and closed its borders. In October the weakened Greek insurgency declared a cease-fire.[31]

For Truman and the NSC, the Greek civil war emphasized the strategic importance of Turkey to the Eastern Mediterranean region's security. Located on the Dardanelles Strait and striding the Black Sea and the Mediterranean Sea southwest of the USSR, Turkey was valuable as a possible jump-off point for United States air operations.

The Soviet Union had threatened Turkey in August of 1946, when the USSR pressed for rights to establish naval stations

---

other CIA-Army-Nazi connections investigated see Office of Special Investigations, *Robert Jan Verbelen and the United States Government: A Report to the Assistant Attorney General, Criminal Division, U.S. Department of Justice, June 1988*, Neal M. Sher, Aron A. Golberg, and Elizabeth B. White (Washington, D.C.: U.S. Department of Justice, 1988).

30. Rostizke, *The CIA's Secret Operations*, 168–173; Powers, *The Man Who Kept Secrets*, 40–43.

31. NSC Memorandum Approval, NSC 5/4 (Conclusions), NSC Record of Actions, 10 January 1949, PSF-NSC, Box 191; O'Ballance, *The Greek Civil War*, 179–202; Jones, *A New Kind of War*, 191–215.

along the straits, withdrawing its demands after several months of a war of nerves. Congress, under the Greek-Turkish Aid Act of 1947 and an amended version in 1948, voted to provide Turkey military and economic assistance. Under their support Turkey received over two hundred American bombers and eighty-one cargo planes.[32] In December 1948 Symington submitted a report to the council requesting the construction of several airfields in Turkey. The NSC agreed to consider the proposal and directed the NSC staff to use it in an overall policy on Greece and Turkey. Throughout 1948 and 1949 the Turkish government requested a military alliance with the United States. Turkey did not join NATO until 1952, but the Department of State and the JCS recommended that the administration provide it with sufficient support until that time.[33]

In March 1949 the NSC staff declared that it was imperative that neither "Greece nor Turkey fall under Communist domination." In "U.S. Objectives with Respect to Greece and Turkey to Counter Soviet Threats to United States Security" (NSC 42), the council recommended that the United States continue to strengthen the Greek military establishment until it was "capable of maintaining internal security"; provide increased support to Turkey in order to develop the "combat effectiveness" of its armed forces; and construct air bases in Turkey, under congressional funding, and with a provision that allowed American peacetime use of the airfields.[34] NSC 42 observed that Turkey was "strategically more important than Greece," and cautioned that should it fall under Communist influence, United States "security interests" would be "critically affected." Acheson questioned the recommendation for air bases in Turkey and

32. For the 1946 USSR-Turkey incident see Bruce R. Kuniholm, *The Origins of the Cold War in the Near East: Great Power Conflict and Diplomacy in Iran, Turkey, and Greece* (Princeton: Princeton University Press, 1980), 255–270, 358–378. For U.S. air supplies to Turkey in 1948 see Leffler, "The American Conception of National Security," 372–373.

33. NSC 36, "The U.S. Position with Respect to Turkey in the Light of U.S. Security Interests in the Middle East, Particularly as Respects Air Power and the Greek and Turkish Aid Program," 1 December 1948, NSC, "Policies of the Government, 1947–1948," 88, PSF-NSC, Box 195; Leffler, *A Preponderance of Power*, 238–239.

34. NSC 42, "U.S. Objectives with Respect to Greece and Turkey to Counter Soviet Threats to United States Security," 4 March 1949, PSF-NSC, Box 205.

warned that the Soviet Union might perceive that the administration was "encircling the USSR with a lot of jumping-off places." Royall argued that the bases were necessary. Acheson replied that in light of the North Atlantic alliance the Department of State should study the "whole matter of peripheral bases." On that point the NSC agreed to drop references to air base construction. Truman approved the policy report the next day.[35] In accordance with the council's recommendations, he requested that Congress provide additional funding for both Greece and Turkey. The Mutual Defense Assistance Act of that October, creating the Mutual Defense Assistance Program (MDAP), earmarked the two to receive $211 million in aid through 1950.[36]

Meanwhile, the JCS recommended that the United States stockpile twelve thousand barrels of aviation fuel in Turkey for Western European air base reserves. Johnson requested that Souers place the matter before the NSC in conjunction with the pending proposal for Turkish airfields.[37] At its April 21 meeting, with Truman presiding, the council heard the Department of State's claim that arranging with the Turkish government for stockpiling petroleum or for construction of airfields would be inadvisable at the time. Johnson told the NSC that the military services were still in favor of both proposals. He concurred, however, in the Department of State's opposition, but added that Joint Chiefs and the services might later reopen the matter. Truman told the council that he had discussed the question with Acheson, and he endorsed the idea that the Department of State should keep reviewing the issue. The NSC agreed.[38]

---

35. Summary of Discussion at the 36th Meeting, 23 March 1949, PSF-NSC, Box 220; NSC 42/1, "U.S. Construction of Airfields and Stockpiling of Aviation Gasoline in Turkey," Appendix E. Annotated List of NSC Reports, NSC, "Policies of the Government, 1949," 128, Ibid., Box 195.

36. For the complete text of the Mutual Defense Assistance Act, 6 October 1949, see U.S. Congress, *A Decade of American Foreign Policy*, 1356–1365. For a thorough assessment of the Mutual Defense Assistance Programs, including the military aid offered to Greece and Turkey in 1949, see Pach, *Arming the Free World*, 198–226.

37. Memorandum, Louis Johnson to Sidney Souers, 2 April 1949, PSF-NSC, Box 206; Leffler, *A Preponderance of Power*, 287–289.

38. Under Secretary's Meeting, "U.S. Construction of Airfields and Stockpiling of Aviation Gasoline in Turkey," 7 April 1949, RG 59-RSS, NA; NSC 36/1, "Construction of Airfields and Stockpiling of Aviation Gasoline in Turkey,"

Apparently the matter of the Turkish airfields seemed premature. But because the objection of Truman and the NSC was on the basis of timing, the air force proceeded with its plans. Within months, support for Turkey from MDAP allowed work on five air bases to proceed by 1950.[39] In addition to obtaining the bases in Turkey, the United States expanded its strategic air capability with the acquisition of base rights in the United Kingdom and the Cairo-Suez area of Egypt. The secretary of defense submitted this proposal to the NSC. Lieutenant General Lauris Norstad of the air force told the council that coastal bases in the United Kingdom would subject B-29 bombers to much exposure. Norstad also pointed out that the Suez bases were more urgent. The British had negotiated concerning critical materials with the Egyptian government, and if these were not used in the construction soon, he said, "they might be lost." Convinced by Norstad's argument, the council authorized negotiations with the British regarding joint funding, and endorsed the construction of four new airfields in the United Kingdom and one in Cairo-Suez. Truman approved the recommendation.[40] The new airfields in Turkey and Egypt provided the United States greater future military containment options and the NSC established a revised containment policy for Greece and Turkey. NSC 42 merged the military's strategic concerns with the Department of State's recommendations that Greece and Turkey receive continued American military assistance.

With the conclusion of the Greek civil war, containment strategy centered on Turkey and defense of the Suez Canal, then under British control. The military services made it clear to Truman and the NSC that the Eastern Mediterranean's close proximity to the Soviet Union made the region vulnerable to military pressure from Moscow, but the expanding capabilities

---

15 April 1949, NSC, "Policies of the Government, 1949," 19, PSF-NSC, Box 195; Summary of Discussion at the 38th Meeting, 21 April 1949, Ibid., Box 220.

39. Memorandum, John Ohly to General Lemnitzer, 28 February, 26 April 1950, *FRUS: 1950*, V, 1234–1235, 1250–1251.

40. NSC 45, "Airfield Construction," 17 March 1949, PSF-NSC, Box 205; Summary of Discussion at the 36th Meeting, 23 March 1949, Ibid., Box 220; NSC 45/1, "Airfield Construction in the United Kingdom and the Cairo-Suez Area," 15 April 1949, NSC Memoranda Approvals, Box 193; NSC 45/1, Memorandum Approval 15 April 1949, NSC Record of Action, PSF-NSC, Box 191.

of the air force could thwart Soviet expansion and thereby protect America's hegemonic interests and strategic resources.

* * *

For much of early 1949 few major differences existed between the State and Defense Departments regarding the administration's containment policy toward Europe and the Eastern Mediterranean. Yet personal tensions emerged between Acheson and Johnson, and the Cold War in Asia intensified. Beginning in 1949 the advance of the Communists in China forced a reevaluation. While the Department of State pressed for a wait-and-see policy towards China, hoping to exploit any ideological conflict of interest between Beijing and Moscow, the Department of Defense sought greater military assistance to non-Communist forces. The NSC became the prime mediator of these broad policy differences.

On New Year's Day of 1949, Jiang offered to step down as leader of Nationalist China and proposed peace negotiations with Mao's Communists. Several days later the CIA reported that the "final collapse" of Jiang's government would be imminent and that "no realistic means is presently at hand to prevent the establishment of a Communist-dominated regime."[41] As Jiang's forces struggled toward Taiwan, the NSC staff and the Department of State began work on a reevaluation of policy. In February the NSC adopted a paper by Kennan and the PPS titled "United States Policy Toward China" (NSC 34) which recommended that the United States maintain flexibility toward the Communists, while "avoiding irrevocable commitments to any one course of action or to any one faction."[42] The NSC believed that further United States military aid to China could not be "used effectively." With the China Aid Act of 1948 nearing expiration, it proposed that Truman advise Congress that he considered it "in the interest of national security to

---

41. Stueck, *The Road to Confrontation*, 115; CIA-1–49, "Review of the World," PSF-IF, Box 250.

42. PPS 39, PPS 39/1, "United States Policy Toward China," 15 September, 23 November 1948, in Nelson, *PPS Papers 1948*, 412–452; NSC 34/1, "United States Policy Toward China," 11 January 1949, Minutes of the 34th Meeting, 3 February 1949, PSF-NSC, Box 205; *FRUS: 1949*, IX, 474–475, 484–485; Etzold and Gaddis, *Containment*, 247–251.

suspend further shipments."[43] Truman consulted with congressional leaders and found them opposed to the recommendation. Believing that stopping military aid would be a betrayal of Jiang, Senator Vandenberg said that the United States would be accused of giving China "the final push into disaster."[44] Shipments "should not be suspended nor terminated," Truman informed the NSC, but "no effort should be made to expedite deliveries." Although he believed the United States had been wasting money with military aid to Nationalist China, he vacillated between the NSC's recommendation to cut it and political pressures from Jiang's long-time supporters in Congress. Truman's approval of the NSC report, however, showed his willingness to consider an alternative policy toward Jiang as well as toward Mao.[45]

Within the Department of State many, including Acheson, Kennan, and the Sino specialist John Paton Davies, believed that the United States might benefit from the nationalism of the Communists and from Mao's Titoistic tendencies. Davies and the others pointed out that Mao could be more of a heretic because he had been in power much longer. He maintained that after Chinese Communists acquired control they would assert their independence from the Soviet Union.[46] In early March the council and Truman adopted a policy paper to that effect, entitled "United States Policy Toward China" (NSC 34/2). It noted that "eventually most or all of China will come under Communist rule." That "the full force of nationalism" had not been released, it observed, and that the administration needed to exploit, politically and economically, "any rifts" between the Chinese Communists and the Soviet Union. The administration, moreover, had to "nourish and bring to power a new revo-

---

43. Memorandum, Sidney Souers to Harry Truman, 3 February 1949, PSF-NSC, Box 205; Minutes of the 34th Meeting, 3 February 1949, Ibid.; NSC 22/3, "Current Position of the United States Respecting Delivery of Aid to China," 2 February 1949, Ibid.

44. Arthur H. Vandenberg, Jr., *The Private Papers of Senator Vandenberg* (Boston: Houghton Mifflin, 1952), 531.

45. NSC, "Policies of the Government, 1949," 11, PSF-NSC, Box 195; Leffler, *A Preponderance of Power*, 292.

46. PPS 39/2, "United States Policy Toward China," 25 February 1949, in Nelson, *PPS Papers 1949–1950*, 25–28; Nancy Bernkopf Tucker, "China's Place in the Cold War: The Acheson Plan," in Douglas Brinkley, ed., *Dean Acheson and the Making of U.S. Foreign Policy* (London: Macmillan, 1993), 109–132.

lution" that would "modify the composition and character of the Chinese Communists." NSC 34/2 cautioned restraint and patience: the USSR "waited twenty-five years for the fulfillment of its revolution in China. We may have to persevere as long or longer."[47]

The NSC offered one suggestion as to how the administration could encourage a Communist Chinese break with the Soviet Union. It adopted "United States Policy Regarding Trade with China" (NSC 41) that suggested the Communists would eventually need Western and Japanese commerce and technology. NSC 41 recommended that the administration allow controlled trade between China, Japan, and the West. Strategic items would not be shipped to China, while civilian goods would be allowed. According to NSC 41, a "fear and favor" trade policy would slow or prevent Soviet economic influence as well as discourage shipment of items to the Soviet bloc. The result would be that trade with China would benefit Japan's economy and production, allow Japan access to the raw materials and resources of Northeast China, and further its emergence as the hub of East Asian regional stability.[48]

New historical research into Chinese documents discount the possibility that a modicum of comity, much less formal contacts, could have existed between the United States and the Communist Chinese in 1949. Scholars generally agree that because of extreme ideological convictions it was impossible for either side to reach an accommodation.[49] Truman and the NSC hoped that the nationalistic tendencies of the Chinese revolution would result in an eventual split between Mao and Stalin. In turn, the effects of the policies outlined by NSC 34/2 and NSC 41 they felt assured would help drive a wedge between

---

47. Summary of Discussion at the 35th meeting, 4 March 1949, PSF-NSC, Box 220; NSC 34/2, "United States Policy Toward China," 28 February 1949, *FRUS: 1949*, IX, 492–495. This policy had been articulated earlier by George Kennan and the PPS in PPS 28/2, "Recommendations with Respect to United States Policy Toward Japan (A Revision of PPS 28 and PPS 28/1)," 26 May 1948, in Nelson, *PPS Papers 1948*, 175–243.

48. NSC 41, "United States Policy Regarding Trade with China," 28 February 1949, *FRUS: 1949*, IX, 826–834; Minutes of the 35th Meeting, 3 March 1949, PSF-NSC, Box 205; Stueck, *The Road to Confrontation*, 120.

49. New research of Chinese historical sources refutes the "Lost Chance" thesis of earlier years by scholars such as Warren I. Cohen and Nancy Bernkopf Tucker.

Beijing and Moscow, offering peaceful political and economic rapproachments to Mao. The basic premises of NSC 34/2 and NSC 41, however, were erroneous from the beginning. Recent studies based on Chinese sources reveal that Mao consistently sought a new formal alliance of friendship and defense with Stalin in 1948 and 1949. Because of their close communiques no chance existed for the United States to "win over" the Chinese Communists as allies against the Soviet Union.[50] Not knowing of Mao's true intentions the council formulated and Truman approved as policy NSC 34/2 and NSC 41. Soon after the administration sought to divert Congress from another China Aid Act. The Department of State requested only an extension of military aid to Jiang that would last until February 1950, and Congress approved. By spring Mao's military forces launched a major offensive, capturing Nanking and Shanghai. On October 1 the Communist troops seized the last Nationalist provinces, proclaimed the People's Republic, and thousands of Nationalists, including Jiang, took refuge on Taiwan.[51]

In late 1948 the Joint Chiefs had advised the NSC on the importance of Taiwan, and its place in the defensive perimeter with Japan, the Ryukyus, and the Philippines.[52] In February 1949 the JCS again emphasized that Taiwan's strategic importance was great. The report recommended "some form of military support" to Taiwan, limited to "the stationing of minor numbers" of American naval units at Taiwanese ports.[53] Hoping to avoid any impasse with the People's Republic of China, the Department of State took exception to the report by the JCS regarding military support to Taiwan. At the NSC's March 4 meeting, Acheson said that the administration could not "af-

---

50. Garver, "Little Chance," 94; Sheng, "The Triumph of Internationalism," 95; Westad, "Losses, Chances, and Myths," 115; Christensen, "A Lost Chance for What?" 249–278; idem, *Useful Adversaries*, 138–191. For a fuller understanding of the impact that the Cold War had on the Chinese civil war see Westad, *Cold War and Revolution*.

51. Leffler, *A Preponderance of Power*, 293–294; Stueck, *The Road to Confrontation*, 120. Formosa is the Republic of Taiwan, and during the Cold War often referred to as Nationalist China.

52. NSC 37, "The Strategic Importance of Formosa," 1 December 1948, PSF-NSC, Box 205; JCS to James Forrestal, 24 November 1948, *FRUS: 1949*, IX, 261–262.

53. NSC 37/3, "The Strategic Importance of Formosa," 11 February 1949, PSF-NSC, Box 205; *FRUS: 1949*, IX, 285.

ford to compromise an emerging new U.S. position in China" by overtly indicating an interest in Taiwan. If America were to intervene militarily in Taiwan, Acheson pointed out, "we shall, in all probability, do so in concert with like-minded powers."[54] He complained that the JCS had not answered whether they recommended "overt military action." Royall suggested that the Joint Chiefs might disagree among themselves as to whether Taiwan was "more important" than Japan to the defense of the Philippines and Okinawa. Acheson proposed that the NSC support a policy rejecting deployment of United States naval units off the coastal ports of Taiwan.[55] Truman agreed with this change. Weeks later, Johnson asked for a reevaluation by the JCS. They reconsidered and informed the NSC that Taiwan's strategic significance did not justify "overt military action . . . so long as the present disparity exists between our military strength and our global obligations."[56]

The Department of State's continuing efforts to pursue a policy of benign neglect toward the Nationalists received NSC approval a few weeks after Jiang arrived in Taiwan, and the council ratified a strong message to him advising that the United States would not commit any armed forces to the defense of the island.[57] The message also reflected disapproval of Jiang's former inept governance. It observed that economic assistance would be provided "under existing legislation," but warned Jiang that additional aid depended on his "future performance" and the Nationalist administration of Taiwan.[58] On similar JCS views concerning the colonies of British Hong Kong and Portuguese Macao, the NSC judged that contributing

---

54. PPS 53, "United States Policy Toward Formosa and the Pescadores," 6 July 1949, in Nelson, *PPS Papers 1949*, 63–74; Statement by the Secretary of State at the 35th Meeting of the National Security Council on the Formosan Problem, 4 March 1949, PSF-NSC, Box 205.

55. Summary of Discussion at the 35th Meeting, 4 March 1949, PSF-NSC, Box 220; NSC 37/5, "Supplementary Measures with Respect to Formosa, 1 March 1949, *FRUS: 1949*, IX, 290–292.

56. Memorandum, Louis Johnson to Sidney Souers, 2 April 1949, PSF-NSC, Box 205.

57. NSC 37/2, "The Current Position of the United States with Respect to Formosa," 3 February 1949; NSC, "Policies of the Government, 1949," PSF-NSC, Box 195; *FRUS: 1949*, IX, 281–282.

58. NSC, "Policies of the Government, 1949," 16–17, PSF-NSC, Box 195; Summary of Discussion at the 47th Meeting, 20 October 1949, PSF-NSC, Box 220.

military forces for the defense of the two foreign colonies would "risk major military involvement in China and possibly global war." The NSC noted Acheson's comment that the JCS recommendations "would not be affected by U.S. moral support of a British appeal to the United Nations" should a Communist offensive be made on Hong Kong, "since the USSR would certainly veto" any UN Security Council deployment of armed forces. With minor revisions the report was forwarded to Truman as only a recommendation that did not require his policy approval.[59]

*   *   *

The NSC concentrated on forming and coordinating containment policies for China, Taiwan, Hong Kong, and Macao, but reevaluation of the administration's policies toward Japan, Korea, and French Indochina required its attention as well.

By the spring of 1949 the administration had slightly revised its policy toward Japan. Although MacArthur supported an immediate negotiation of a treaty, the NSC circulated a new policy report that held that the administration would not seek a treaty until the Japanese economy showed signs of recovery and the government regained political self-confidence. NSC 13/3 recommended that "all industrial facilities, including so-called 'primary war facilities' designed for reparations to the U.S.," be used for economic recovery. It also directed that the United States reduce its occupation forces gradually, reduce involvement in Japan's internal affairs, and help strengthen Japan's internal security forces. The defensive security of Japan would be established by retention "on a long-term basis" of American base facilities on Okinawa, the Ryukyu Islands, and Marcus and Nanpo Shoto Islands. Truman carefully considered NSC 13/3, and accepted the NSC's recommendations. Growing anti-American sentiment in Japan prevented implementation of the policy, at least complete implementation.[60]

---

59. NSC 55, "Implications of a Possible Chinese Communist Attack on the Foreign Colonies in South China," 26 July 1949, PSF-NSC, Box 206; NSC 55/1, "British Views Respecting Hong Kong," 17 October 1949, Summary of Discussion at the 47th Meeting, 20 October 1949, Ibid., Box 220.

60. NSC 13/3, "Recommendations with Respect to United States Policy Toward Japan," 6 May 1949, NSC Memorandum Approval, NSC Record of Ac-

Soon after they had approved NSC 13/3, council members heard that the Japanese were becoming hostile toward military occupation. The CIA had warned that the Japanese Communist factions were encouraged and non-Communist groups alarmed by reports "that U.S. policy is 'writing-off' Japan."[61] In the summer, Japanese unrest erupted in a series of strikes, and citizens affiliated with American military forces were subject to terrorist actions. At the same time a rift emerged in the administration over occupation policy.[62] For some time the Department of State had supported MacArthur's insistence on signing an early treaty. When Acheson learned of the local unrest in Japan he argued for an immediate treaty to assure continuing Japanese friendship and American security in Asia. The Department of Defense and the JCS believed that a treaty would be premature. Hoping to diffuse the Department of State's efforts, the Joint Chiefs submitted a report that recommended a continuing military presence in Japan and new requirements for an American naval base at Tokyo Bay, and suggested that any future treaty negotiations include the USSR as well as the "de facto Government of China."[63] But, faced with mounting policy decisions on China and Taiwan and an encompassing policy recommendation on Asia, the NSC would not provide until early 1950 a solution to the differences between State and Defense on Japan.

As preparations for evacuating remaining American occupation forces from South Korea continued on schedule, the Department of the Army requested MacArthur's advice on the withdrawal. Reflecting some doubt, MacArthur stated that the United States could not develop Korean security forces "capable of meeting successfully a full-scale invasion from North Korea." Nevertheless, he added, the best time for final troop withdrawals would be May 10, 1949, the first anniversary of

---

tion, PSF-NSC, Box 191; NSC, "Policies of the Government, 1949," 26–28, Ibid., Box 195; Leffler, *A Preponderance of Power*, 334–335.

    61. CIA-3–49, "Review of the World," 16 March 1949, PSF-NSC, Box 205.
    62. Schaller, *The American Occupation of Japan*, 136.
    63. Ibid., 164–177; Leffler, *A Preponderance of Power*, 302–304; NSC 49, "Current Strategic Evaluation of U.S. Security Needs in Japan," 15 June 1949, *FRUS: 1949*, VII, pt. 2, 774–777; Etzold and Gaddis, *Containment*, 231–233. Also see, George F. Kennan, "Department of State Comments on Current Strategic Evaluation of U.S. Security Needs in Japan (NSC 49)," 30 September 1949, in Nelson, *PPS Papers 1949*, 183–186.

South Korea's elections. Should further training assistance of South Korean forces be needed, MacArthur pointed out, a military mission could do the work.[64] In response, the NSC staff prepared a revised policy on Korea for 1949. It concurred with MacArthur's recommendations for a prompt withdrawal and training assistance under an American military mission. NSC 8/1 specified that all American troops should evacuate South Korea at about June 30, 1949, when a sixty-five-thousand-man army of the Republic of South Korea (ROK) had been established and exhibited itself "capable of maintaining internal order . . . and of assuring border security." Furthermore, the administration should transfer to the ROK six months worth of military equipment and supplies. Following withdrawal, the United States would continue economic and political support to the ROK as well as technical and military training to its army, police, and coast guard under a United States Korean Military Advisory Group.[65]

The JCS recommended that NSC 8/1 be revised to ensure that the United States would not have a future obligation to provide ROK forces with air or naval support.[66] The NSC considered the Joint Chiefs' revision requests for NSC 8/1. Acheson remarked that the Department of State accepted the changes. Royall commented that the Joint Chiefs had provided "an excellent solution of a tough problem." Ambassador Muccio, who attended the meeting while in Washington, agreed with Royall. Asked about the internal condition of South Korea, Muccio replied that "there were still many question marks," but added that support of the ROK military "constituted a calculated risk that had to be taken." After some further discussion, the NSC adopted the revisions.[67]

On April 20, less than a month after Truman approved NSC 8/1, the United States extended official recognition to the new Republic of South Korea. In accordance with the NSC's recommendations, American troops withdrew on June 29. A new

64. MacArthur cited in Schnabel and Watson, *History of the JCS*, III, 27.
65. NSC 8/1, "The Position of the United States with Respect to Korea," 16 March 1949, PSF-NSC, Box 205.
66. Memorandum, JCS to James Forrestal, 23 March 1949, Ibid.
67. Summary of Discussion at the 36th Meeting, 23 March 1949, PSF-NSC, Box 220; Dean Rusk Oral History Interview.

phase of American relations with South Korea had begun. Although fully independent, South Korea remained dependent on
the administration for military and economic assistance.[68]

On July 1, a five-hundred-man force of the United States
Korean Military Advisory Group became permanent under the
command of Brigadier General William L. Roberts, and part
of the American administration of Ambassador Muccio. In
July, Truman requested assistance to the ROK for fiscal year
1950 under MDAP. By October, Congress complied with the
president's request. After a bilateral treaty had been completed
between the United States and the ROK in early 1950, $10 mil-
lion in military aid was earmarked for South Korea. Reports of
a North Korean military buildup and a series of clashes along
the 38th parallel between North Korean and ROK troops convinced Roberts and Muccio that this would not be enough
should a North Korean attack occur. But by the fall of 1949 the
course of the Cold War changed dramatically in Asia with the
Communist victory in China.[69] The revolution's success caused
the administration to leave more troops in Korea than had
originally been planned, and it prompted the arming, albeit
lightly, of ROK regular army troops.

Unlike Korea and Japan, where the United States had
greater security interests, Indochina had been a colonial out-
post of France since the mid-1800s. From 1941 through 1945,
Japan occupied Indochina. The French returned there after
World War II to find they were challenged by a well-organized
anti-colonial movement led by Ho Chi Minh. A Communist
revolutionary and leader of a Communist faction called the
Vietminh, he established the Democratic Republic of Vietnam.
Negotiations were conducted briefly between the French and
the Vietminh, but war broke out in 1946 that slowly engulfed
the whole country.[70] In order to ensure a non-Communist

68. Schnabel and Watson, *History of the JSC,* II, 27.

69. U.S. Department of the Army, *Military Advisors in Korea: KMAG in
Peace and War,* by Robert K. Sawyer (Washington, D.C.: Office of the Chief of
Military History, 1962), 44–47; Schanbel and Watson, *History of the JCS,* III,
28, 42–43; John Muccio to Dean Acheson, 16 September 1949, *FRUS: 1949,*
VII, 1079–1080.

70. W. Averell Harriman Oral History Interview, DLHP, Durham, North
Carolina. For a thorough analysis of the early history of Indochina see Edgar
O'Ballance, *The Indochina War, 1945–1954: A Study in Guerilla Warfare* (Lon-
don: Faber and Faber, 1964). Stanley Karnow, *Vietnam: A History* (New York:

Indochina the administration backed France's so-called Bao Dai solution in 1949. A former emperor of the Annam region in Indochina under the French and Japanese colonial regimes, Bao Dai was placed back on the throne as the Nationalist ruler of the country. But Ho's Vietminh quickly perceived Bao Dai as a mere French puppet.[71]

Until the summer of 1949, Truman and the NSC avoided direct involvement in the French effort to retain Indochina.[72] But as French colonial controls eroded, they began to worry that costs would ruin France's economy and seriously hinder its contribution to European recovery. In mid-year the PPS had constructed a thorough study on all of Southeast Asia that suggested encouraging the French to "adapt their policies to the realities of the current situation." It criticized France for squandering resources in a battle between "a native regime" and nineteenth-century imperialism. The report's larger objective was to initiate a new containment concept for Asia. Describing as the "great crescent" the area extending from Japan through Southeast Asia and on to India and Australia, it emphasized that if Japan was to become the economic bulwark for the region, it would need Indochina as a source for raw materials and as a market for its manufactured goods. Acheson submitted the report to the NSC staff for consideration.[73]

Viking, 1983); Gabriel Kolko, *Anatomy of a War* (New York: Pantheon, 1985); Ellen Hammer, *The Struggle for Indo-China, 1940–1954* (Stanford: Stanford University Press, 1966); George C. Herring, *America's Longest War: The United States and Vietnam, 1950–1975* (New York: McGraw-Hill, 1996); Lloyd C. Gardner, *Approaching Vietnam: From World War II Through Dienbienphu 1941–1954* (New York: W.W. Norton, 1988).

71. Leffler, *A Preponderance of Power*, 300–302. For a more thorough treatment of the Bao Dai solution see Gary R. Hess, "The First American Commitment in Indochina: The Acceptance of the 'Bao Dai Solution,' 1950," *Diplomatic History* 2 (Fall 1978): 331–350; The best reference for the 1945–1949 attitudes of the Truman administration toward Indochina is U.S. Department of Defense, *United States–Vietnam Relations 1945–1967*, Book 8 (Washington, D.C.: G.P.O., 1971), 1–151.

72. Clark M. Clifford Oral History Interview; Acheson, *Present at the Creation*, 671–672.

73. PPS 51, "United States Policy toward Southeast Asia," 19 May 1949, in Nelson, *PPS Papers 1949*, 32–59; NSC 51, "United States Policy Toward Southeast Asia," 1 July 1949, NSC, "Policies of the Government, 1949," 130. For the Great Crescent concept see Michael Schaller, "Securing the Great Crescent: Occupied Japan and the Origins of Containment in Southeast Asia," *Journal of American History* 69 (September 1982): 392–414.

Map 4. French Indochina (1949)

113

The PPS had initiated a rather comprehensive report on Southeast Asia, but it was set aside by the NSC because the rapidly changing course of events in East Asia stimied the administration's policy directions. Noting that a "major objective" of United States policy was the containment of communism, Secretary of Defense Johnson made a June request that chastised the NSC for not producing a broad policy for Asia that furthered that objective. Critical of the Department of State's "day-by-day, country-by-country approach," Johnson urged that the NSC begin work on a long-range study that would rethink existing policies as well as "appraise the commitments and risks" of various courses of action in Asia.[74]

The NSC heeded Johnson's request, and in late October it recommended for Asia measures similar to the proposals for containing communism in Western Europe. In "United States Policy Toward Asia" (NSC 48), the council urged increased economic assistance to non-Communist countries and a regional or Pacific association defense pact of non-Communist Asian nations, together with a peace treaty with Japan and the establishment of a strategic defense line from Japan to the Ryukyus, Taiwan, and the Philippines.[75] The council took no further action on NSC 48 until after the Taiwanese problem had been decided, and Johnson urged the JCS to reappraise their views on the importance of Taiwan. In early December they submitted their report to the NSC, which after some study recommended that the United States provide Taiwan with a "closely supervised program of military aid" under the MDAP.[76] At the same time the NSC staff consulted with the Department of State on its long-range policy toward Asia and issued a revised version, NSC 48/1, with the department's ideas.[77]

On December 29 a special NSC meeting convened for con-

---

74. NSC 48, "United States Policy Toward Asia," 10 June 1949, PSF-NSC, Box 206; Memorandum, Louis Johnson to the NSC, 10 June 1949, *United States–Vietnam Relations*, 217–218.

75. Ibid.; Memorandum, Charlton Ogburn, Jr. to State Bureau of Far Eastern Affairs, 2 November 1949, *FRUS: 1949*, IX, 160–161.

76. NSC 37/9, "Possible United States Military Action Toward Taiwan Not Involving Major Military Forces," 27 December 1949, PSF-NSC, Box 206; *FRUS: 1949*, IX, 460–461.

77. NSC 48/1, "The Position of the United States with Respect to Asia," 23 December 1949, *United States–Vietnam Relations*, 226–264; Etzold and Gaddis, *Containment*, 252–269.

sideration of that report. It also provided a forum for confrontation between the two quarreling departments. Before the meeting, Johnson and Acheson had both lobbied Truman. The president told Johnson that he would not argue about the "military considerations": he would side with the Department of State's position. Realizing that Truman had made his decision, Johnson left the following day for a vacation and remained out of town until after the NSC meeting on the matter.[78] At the council, Acheson declared the Department of State's agreement with Defense and the JCS that the military position in Japan, the Ryukyus, and the Philippines should be strengthened "on the understanding" that the position did not change "present policy." Truman concurred, and told the NSC it should not recommend a peace treaty with Japan. At the Potsdam Conference, he observed, "the United States, Britain, and China had suggested surrender terms to Japan." The administration's position on Japan therefore "was a partnership affair" with Great Britain and China, and should not include the involvement of the USSR that the Joint Chiefs had advised. Bradley, presenting the views of the JCS, said that the Department of Defense's position regarding Taiwan was preferable from the military point of view. Acheson questioned the general why the Joint Chiefs' recommendations on Taiwan had changed. Bradley retorted that the military aid and advisers the JCS had requested for Taiwan had changed in October after Communist China's success on the mainland. He explained that without additional funding the new proposals were "based on the existence of funds under Section 303 of the Mutual Defense Assistance Act." After the exchange between Bradley and Acheson, the council made some minor revisions, and reissued the policy report.[79]

Policy toward Asia as NSC 48/2 redefined it aimed not only to effect "gradual reduction and eventual elimination of the power and influence of the USSR in Asia," but also to develop "the nations and peoples of Asia on a stable and self-sustaining

78. Lewis Johnson Testimony, 14 June 1951, U.S. Congress. Committee on Armed Services and Committee on Foreign Relations. *Military Situation in the Far East*. Joint Hearings. 82nd Congress, 1st sess., 1951.

79. Summary of Discussion at the 50th Meeting, 30 December 1949, PSF-NSC, Box 220.

basis." It recommended that the administration support voluntary regional associations of non-Communist states; cultivate
conditions in Asia conducive to economic recovery, the multilateral revival of trade, and eventual political stability; and in
general, encourage non-Communist forces to take the initiative. The United States had a legitimate interest in maintaining a defensive perimeter in the Pacific, declared the report,
but should disengage support of non-Communist elements in
China. Japan would be "reevaluated by the NSC after a decision regarding a peace treaty had been arranged." South Korea
should continue to receive United States political, economic,
technical, and military support. In regard to conflicts between
imperial and nationalist forces, particularly "the problem of
French Indo-China," Washington should assist the demands of
the nationalists while lessening the overt effects of such conflicts on European colonial powers. NSC 48/2 advised the administration to continue the policy set previously for Taiwan,
and immediately provide the nation the remaining $75 million
in funds from Section 303 of the Mutual Defense Assistance
Act. Truman approved the policy report, but indicated in a
margin note that he might be reluctant to follow up with funding to Taiwan. He added: "A program will be all right, but
whether we implement it depends on the circumstances."[80]

NSC 48/2 established the first long-range policy study of
American containment objectives for Asia. It compiled into one
policy statement the many policies on Japan, South Korea, and
Indochina the council had earlier coordinated and approved.
The defensive perimeter of Asia was reaffirmed, Japan's economic rehabilitation and an American military presence in Japan was assured until the arrangement of a peace treaty. South
Korea was guaranteed the continuation of American political
and economic help as well as non-combatant military technical
and advisory assistance. The United States was to support non-
Communist elements in French Indochina that might modify
French colonialism. In affirming the extension of previously assigned Mutual Defense Assistance funds to Taiwan, NSC 48/2
made a partial concession to the concerns of the Joint Chiefs

---

80. NSC 48/2, "The Position of the United States with Respect to Asia," 30
December 1949, *United States–Vietnam Relations*, 265–272; Etzold and Gaddis,
Containment, 269–276; *FRUS: 1949*, VII, 1215–1220; PSF-NSC, Box 207.

and the Department of Defense. Yet it kept intact the Department of State's opposition to a military commitment to Taiwan. Truman's approval of NSC 48/2 until the onset of the Korean War ensured the Department of State's position regarding China and Taiwan.

American policy toward Asia as Stalin recognized it initiated a Cold War rapprochment between Japan, Northeast Asia, and Southeast Asia. He also interpreted American policy toward Japan as a forward strategy, intended to revive Japan's presence on the Asian mainland and throughout the archipelagos. Japan had been a major geopolitical Asian rival of Russia since the Russo-Japanese War of 1904 and 1905, and the Soviet Union had been excluded from the military occupation of Japan. These two factors motivated Stalin by late 1949 to accept Mao's overtures for a new Sino-Soviet alliance and co-prosperity for Asia. If the USSR could not thwart Japan's Cold War reentry into Asia's power sphere, Stalin reasoned, collaboration between the Soviet Union and the People's Republic of China could unify the periphery of Asia against the United States and Japan.[81]

* * *

By late 1949 Truman and the NSC had affirmed that despite the success of the Chinese Communists on the mainland, containment policy toward Asia would remain limited in the scope and degree of economic, political, and military assistance. But as Mao's forces routed Jiang's Nationalists in China, two other events redirected the attention of the NSC from Asia back to the nation's vital containment interests—Western Europe and the Soviet Union. A serious dollar gap in Western Europe had revealed to Truman and the NSC by the summer and fall of 1949 that the Marshall Plan's ERP was not proving fully successful. And, the Soviet Union's detonation of an atomic bomb in late August ended the American monopoly of nuclear weapons, and gave allies reason to question the ability of the United States to defend them from a Soviet attack.

In mid-September the CIA warned the council that the ERP had become "a palliative, not a cure" for Western Europe.[82] Un-

81. Zubok and Pleshakov, *Inside the Kremlin's Cold War*, 56–60.
82. CIA-9–49, "Review of the World," PSF-NSC, Box 206.

der Secretary of State James Webb explained to the NSC that by concentrating on efforts to increase industrial production in Western Europe, the ERP was failing to attend to "distribution mechanisms." As demands for American imports grew faster than Western Europe's means of paying for them, a dollar gap widened through late 1949, particularly in Great Britain. By September the dollar gap crisis became so severe that the United Kingdom devaluated the British pound. Webb told the NSC that the British monetary crisis developed "as the world seller's market turned to a buyer's market" and the United Kingdom began drawing on its sterling credits.[83]

Truman and the NSC were acutely aware that the markets of Western capitalist countries were contracting, and they began to worry that the possible collapse of Western capitalism posed a serious threat to American hegemony. The dollar gap crisis was symptomatic of a problem that had become apparent when a domestic recession slowed the postwar economic growth of the United States earlier in 1949. The Cold War, moreover, had restricted Western European trade with Eastern European countries under Soviet control, peripherial markets in Asia that might have filled the void were not materializing, and Japan's industrial revival fell victim to a growing trade deficit and the declining value of the Japanese yen.[84]

The dollar gap crisis and contraction of Western markets gave Truman and the NSC good reason to reevaluate America's economic containment strategy. Soviet atomic capabilities as of August 29, 1949, also mandated a thorough reassessment of America's military containment strategies.

On September 3, an American B-29 reconnaissance plane over the northern Pacific collected an unusual rainwater sample. The AEC conducted several tests on the sample and deter-

83. Minutes of 45th Meeting, 16 September 1949, PSF-NSC, Box 22; Leffler, *A Preponderance of Power*, 303, 314–317. For a careful analysis of the dollar gap and sterling crisis see Michael J. Hogan, *The Marshall Plan: America, Britain, and the Reconstruction of Western Europe, 1947–1952* (Cambridge: Cambridge University Press, 1987), 238–292; Scott Newton, "The 1949 Sterling Crisis and British Policy Toward European Integration," *Review of International Studies* 11 (July 1985): 169–192.

84. Robert A. Pollard, *Economic Security and the Origins of the Cold War, 1945–1950* (New York: Columbia University Press, 1985), 161–165, 182–186; McCormick, *America's Half-Century*, 90–94; Leffler, *The Specter of Communism*, 89–91.

mined it contained elements of radioactive material. Souers immediately informed Truman that the Soviet Union had tested an atomic device. Unsure whether a nuclear accident had occurred or whether the USSR had detonated an atomic weapon, Truman dispatched planes from the Air Force Long Range Detection Staff for additional samples. The AEC called in its advisory committee of top nuclear physicists, and after several days of testing confirmed that the USSR had indeed exploded its first atomic bomb.[85]

Disbelief and shock swept Washington. Truman had been among many Americans who had believed that Moscow did not have the capability to produce an atomic bomb for at least four or five more years. Nearly a year earlier the CIA had reported to him that "the most probable date" the Soviet Union could perfect an atomic weapon "would be mid-1953."[86] But others, including some of the leading scientists, estimated that the Soviets would have an atomic bomb much earlier. Among them, Vannevar Bush told Forrestal in late 1945 that the Russians "might equal our 1945 position by 1950." And in a 1946 collection of essays on atomic energy entitled *One World or None*, physicists Hans Bethe and Fred Seitz predicted Soviet atomic capability as early as 1951.[87]

As the atomic cloud drifted across North America, over the Atlantic, and toward Western Europe, the AEC agreed that a public announcement of the discovery was necessary. Lilienthal cut short a vacation and arrived in Washington on September 20. He contacted Souers, who arranged an appointment with Truman for late that afternoon. Lilienthal pleaded with Truman for an immediate announcement. The president refused, telling Lilienthal that he feared an announcement so

85. Holloway, *Stalin and the Bomb*, 96–220; Richard G. Hewlett and Francis Duncan, *Atomic Shield, 1947–1952:* Volume II, *A History of the United States Atomic Energy Commission* (University Park: The Pennsylvania State University Press, 1969), 362–366; Raymond P. Brandt, "Inside Story of Announcement of Reds' Atom Bomb Revealed," *Washington Evening Star*, 28 September 1949.

86. CIA cited in Ranelagh, *The Agency*, 171.

87. Bush cited in Herbert F. York, *The Advisors: Oppenheimer, Teller, and the Superbomb* (Stanford: Stanford University Press, 1976), 35; Hans Bethe and Frederick Seitz, "How Close is the Danger," in Dexter Masters and Katharine Way, eds., *One World or None* (New York: McGraw-Hill, 1946), 42–46.

soon might provoke "chaos in Europe and hysteria in this country." The president explained that his reluctance was based on the recent British devaluation of their currency, as well as an economic slowdown and series of coal and steel strikes here at home. Showing Lilienthal to the door, Truman mentioned that he had not been convinced that the USSR really had the bomb. A discouraged Lilienthal left the meeting, only to be told by Souers that Bradley and Johnson and the JCS had urged Truman to make an announcement at once, albeit with no success. The next morning Souers informed the AEC that he thought the president would act by the end of the week.[88]

Only after Truman received a signed statement from each member of the AEC Advisory Committee of scientists swearing to believing that the USSR had detonated an atomic bomb did he begin to prepare to tell the public.[89] On the morning of September 23, he informed his cabinet and issued a short statement to the press. Carefully crafted, the public statement referred to the Soviet bomb only as "an atomic explosion," and called for future "effective enforceable international control of atomic energy."[90] In the words of one observer at the time, Truman made sure "the world received the sensational news without sensational reaction."[91]

Beyond the atomic bomb lay in the scientific imagination an even more powerful nuclear weapon, the hydrogen bomb. Known as the super bomb, it operated on a thermonuclear chain reaction, or fusion of light elements, triggered by an atomic weapon, and provided nearly one hundred times more explosive yield than the atomic bomb in America's stockpile. In 1945 and 1946 Edward Teller of the Los Alamos research labs had first explored theoretically the idea of fusion and a super bomb. By October 1949 a hydrogen bomb lobby had formed,

---

88. Hewlett and Duncan, *Atomic Shield*, 365–367; Truman cited in David E. Lilienthal, *The Journals of David E. Lilienthal:* Volume II, *The Atomic Energy Years* (New York: Harper & Row, 1964), 569–572.

89. York, *The Advisors*, 34; Lewis L. Strauss, *Men and Decisions* (New York: Doubleday, 1962), 205.

90. Brandt, *Washington Evening Star*, 28 September 1949; Strauss, *Men and Decisions*, 205; Hewlett and Duncan, *Atomic Shield*, 367–368; PPP: HST, 485.

91. Brandt, *Washington Evening Star*, 28 September 1949.

with Teller at its head, and it included strong support from AEC Commissioner Lewis Strauss, the Department of Defense, and the NSC.[92] In late July, Truman requested that a special NSC committee provide him with a complete review of the nation's atomic energy program. Truman had earlier approved a joint recommendation of the AEC and the JCS for a substantial three-year acceleration in the production of atomic materials and weapons. He directed Souers to form a committee made up of the secretaries of state and defense and the chair of the AEC. Called the Z Committee by members, its purpose was to provide an assessment of the stockpiling program and its relation to the fiscal year 1951 national security program.[93] The detonation of the Soviet weapon thus moved the administration to review its defense capabilities and decide quickly on the development of the hydrogen bomb.

One month after Truman learned that the USSR had exploded its atomic bomb, the Z Committee reported "that the proposed acceleration of the atomic energy program is necessary in the interests of national security." International controls on atomic energy, the report observed, had failed to develop; the growth of American defense commitments in Europe and elsewhere globally had expanded; American atomic testing programs in 1948 had achieved success and new breakthroughs; and the USSR now had atomic capability. The report concluded that it was imperative for the administration to act before the USSR developed a "significant" atomic stockpile of its own. A week after receiving the committee's report, Truman approved the expansion program.[94]

Strauss and Souers had become two of the earliest proponents of the hydrogen bomb. Strauss argued that the United States needed to regain its nuclear monopoly, which was achievable only with a "quantum jump" that the hydrogen

92. York, *The Advisors*, 21–24, 45; Holloway, *Stalin and the Bomb*, 300.

93. Harry Truman to Sidney Souers, 26 July 1949, NSC-Subject File, PSF-NSC, Box 198; *FRUS: 1949*, I, 501–503; Hewlett and Duncan, *Atomic Shield*, 182–183.

94. Report to the President by the Special Committee of the National Security Council on the Proposed Acceleration of the Atomic Energy Program, 10 October 1949, *FRUS: 1949*, I, 559–564; Leffler, *A Preponderance of Power*, 327. For a fuller analysis of the actions and assessments of the committee see David Alan Rosenberg, "American Atomic Strategy and the Hydrogen Bomb Decision," *Journal of American History* 66 (June 1979): 62–87.

bomb promised.[95] With the exception of AEC Commissioner Gordon E. Dean, Strauss found little support for the development of a thermonuclear weapon. Strauss then turned to Souers for advice. Like Strauss, Souers believed that the bomb was vital for national security. Souers told Strauss that he did not think Truman was aware of the possibility of a thermonuclear weapon. After approaching the president on the subject, Souers later informed Strauss that while Truman knew nothing about the hydrogen bomb, he "showed an immediate interest." Souers wanted Strauss "to force the issue up to the White House and do it quickly."[96]

In early November the AEC voted against the program, and Lilienthal forwarded the AEC report to Truman. The report listed several "general conclusions" the AEC believed should be considered before the United States proceeded with a hydrogen bomb. Although the report did not mention moral issues, its tone indicated that a majority of the members of the AEC had moral doubts.[97] Bradley informed Johnson that the JCS believed that a hydrogen bomb program should proceed immediately. The JCS harbored concerns that the Soviet Union could quickly perfect a hydrogen bomb. "Possession of a thermonuclear weapon by the U.S.S.R.," Bradley summed the thinking of the JCS, "without such possession by the United States . . . would be intolerable."[98]

Faced with the two conflicting proposals, Truman reappointed the Z Committee for the specific purpose of studying the proposal for a hydrogen bomb. Assisting it was a working group headed by Souers, composed of representatives from the Departments of State and Defense and the AEC.[99] The commit-

---

95. Memorandum, Lewis Strauss to AEC Commissioners, 5 October 1949, in Strauss, *Men and Decisions*, 216–217.

96. Souers cited in Roger M. Anders, ed., *Forging the Atomic Shield: Excerpts from the Office Diary of Gordon E. Dean* (Chapel Hill: University of North Carolina Press, 1987), 35; York, *The Advisors*, 60; Hewlett and Duncan, *Atomic Shield*, 373–374. For the debate within the AEC over the hydrogen bomb program see Anders, Ibid., 57–64; York, Ibid., 46–65.

97. David Lilienthal to Harry Truman, 9 November 1949, *FRUS: 1949*, I, 576–585; Holloway, *Stalin and the Bomb*, 301.

98. Memorandum, Omar Bradley to Louis Johnson, 23 November 1949, *FRUS: 1949*, I, 595–596.

99. Harry Truman to Sidney Souers, 19 November 1949, Ibid., 587–588; Anders, *Forging the Atomic Shield*, 62; York, *The Advisors*, 65–66; Truman, *Years of Trial and Hope*, 309.

tee convened in December, but the recalcitrance of Johnson and Lilienthal prevented a resolution.[100] Thereafter, several indecisive weeks passed during which Strauss, Johnson, the JCS, and the AEC lobbied Truman.[101] At the same time, Acheson, who had held reservations about the program, joined the hydrogen bomb lobby. Many officials in the Department of State, however, disagreed with Acheson's new-found position. Kennan, for one, had opposed escalating reliance on military rearmament as a strategy of the Cold War. In late fall he asked to be relieved as director of the PPS and began to turn much of his work over to his successor, Paul H. Nitze.[102]

In late December the president informed the Z Committee he wanted a decision at once. By the time the committee and its working group held a second meeting in early 1950, the hydrogen bomb forces had massed against Lilienthal and the AEC. Lilienthal pleaded forcefully his objections to the proposed program, saying repeatedly that he had a "visceral feeling this is wrong." Acheson and Johnson outvoted him. Following the vote in favor of a thermonuclear program, the committee issued a draft report based on recommendations proposed earlier by Nitze, who had served as a working group member while he was deputy director of the PPS. It suggested that Truman direct the AEC to "proceed with an accelerated program to test the possibility of a thermonuclear reaction"; and that State and Defense reexamine America's peacetime and wartime objectives and "their effect on strategic planning."[103]

---

100. Lilienthal, *The Journals of David E. Lilienthal*, Volume II, 613–614; Acheson, *Present at the Creation*, 348; Hewlett and Duncan, *Atomic Shield*, 398.
101. Strauss, *Men and Decisions*, 219; Hewlett and Duncan, *Atomic Shield*, 395–396; Lilienthal, *The Journals of David E. Lilienthal*, Volume II, 615; York, *The Advisors*, 66–67; Memorandum, Omar Bradley to Louis Johnson, 13 January 1950, *FRUS: 1950*, I, 503–511.
102. York, *The Advisors*, 66–67; Kennan, *Memoirs*, Volume I, 471; Miscamble, *George F. Kennan and the Making of American Foreign Policy*, 281–295; Leffler, *A Preponderance of Power*, 328–331.
103. York, *The Advisors*, 68; Hewlett and Duncan, *Atomic Shield*, 406–407; Acheson, *Present at the Creation*, 348–349; Lilienthal, *The Journals of David E. Lilienthal*, Volume II, 623–632; James R. Shepley and Clay Blair, Jr., *The Hydrogen Bomb: The Men, The Menace, The Mechanism* (Westport, CT: Greenwood Press, 1954), 87. For the context of Nitze's recommendations see Memorandum, Paul Nitze to Dean Acheson, 19 December 1949, *FRUS: 1949*, I, 610. Lilienthal's influence may have been weak because he had submitted his resignation from the AEC several months before the hydrogen bomb debate.

Souers delivered to Truman the committee's vote and report. "I don't think you have a choice, " he told the president. "It's either we make it or wait until the Russians drop one on us without warning."[104] In the early afternoon the committee met briefly with Truman, and each member—Acheson, Johnson, and Lilienthal—presented his conclusions orally. The president listened quietly, then told them he would approve their recommendations, saying that he believed the United States "should never use these weapons but the Russian's behavior left no choice but to make them."[105] A few hours later he issued a public statement that directed the AEC "to continue its work on all forms of atomic weapons."[106]

From 1945 to 1947, United States armed forces had declined from twelve million to one-and-a-half million men, and the Department of Defense came to rely more on atomic capabilities to make up for the loss in conventional manpower. Between 1947 and 1949 the Departments of Defense and State agreed that American power was limited and that programs of economic containment coupled with limited military assistance and covert actions would be sufficient to thwart Soviet expansion. Fears of growing inflation, however, led Truman's economic advisers to hold military spending to no more than $15 billion a year. This budget restraint was reinforced by the general assumption that the Soviet threat was intended to provoke the United States into excessive expenditures.[107] Those concerns would modify with Truman's directive to proceed with a hydrogen bomb program. With it he also added an order that the Departments of State and Defense proceed with a reevaluation of national security policy to be presented to the NSC as soon as possible.

Throughout much of 1949 the United States containment

---

104. Souers cited in Shepley and Blair, *The Hydrogen Bomb*, 88.

105. Ibid.; Hewlett and Duncan, *Atomic Shield*, 408; York, *The Advisors*, 69–70; Truman, *Years of Trial and Hope*, 309. The official written report by the NSC Special Committee would not be presented until March 1950, apparently because committee members preferred to give their oral reports to Truman beforehand.

106. Ibid.; PPP-HST, 1950.

107. Warner R. Schilling, "The Politics of National Defense: Fiscal 1950," in Warner R. Schilling, Paul Y. Hammond, and Glenn H. Snyder, *Strategy, Politics, and Defense Budgets* (New York: Columbia University Press, 1962), 100–106.

policies concentrated on vital American interests in Europe and peripheral interests in the Eastern Mediterranean and Asia. In absence of major differences between State, Defense, and the Joint Chiefs, the NSC's coordination processes worked well. Although early in the year Acheson and Kennan were having professional disagreements, the PPS influenced the council's coordinated policies for Yugoslavia, Eastern Europe, and China. Personal differences strained the working relationship between Acheson and Johnson that in turn made it difficult for the NSC to forge a consensus on policies for China, Taiwan, and much of Asia. The three crises of later 1949—the dollar gap in Western Europe, the Communist victory in China, and Moscow's acquisition of atomic capability—initiated NSC reassessments of the administration's containment objectives. The reorganization of the NSC also facilitated the coordination process that produced the first long-range policy study for Asia and aided Truman in his decision to proceed with a hydrogen bomb program for the United States.

Chapter Five

The NSC and
the Korean War

*The weak fear the strong; the strong fear the resolute; the
resolute fear the desperate.*

(Chinese aphorism)

The Truman administration had rhetorically presented a tough
containment policy, but by early 1950 a genuine siege mentality was gripping the country. Facilitating it were the fall of
China to Mao's Communists, the USSR's testing of its first
atomic weapon, the espionage cases of Alger Hiss in January
and Klaus Fuchs in February, the emergence of McCarthyism,
and a more general sense within much of the public that foreign forces were undermining the nation's values and institutions. Thus, months before war broke out in Korea, the NSC
began to militarize and expand the administration's containment objectives. Adding to domestic pressures was the economic crisis in Western Europe that signaled the possible
collapse of Western capitalism under the strains of a contracting world market, coupled with the concern that the Soviet
Union was launching an offensive—a perception reinforced
when North Korean forces attacked South Korean positions
south of the 38th parallel on June 25, 1950. Thereafter, what
had previously been a limited response by the NSC to the ex-

126

pansion of the Soviet Union became a global militancy against communism in differing forms.[1]

Two days after Truman authorized that work proceed on the hydrogen bomb, the British arrested nuclear physicist Fuchs for passing atomic secrets to the Soviet Union. A German emigré, he had worked on the Manhattan District Project during World War II and participated in the early fission conferences at Los Alamos in 1946.[2] In January 1950, while working in Great Britain, Fuchs confessed that he had been a Soviet agent since 1942. The AEC met three days after his confession and determined that he might have learned enough to pass on to the USSR information about the hydrogen bomb. Although the Z Committee dealing with atomic proliferation was informed of Fuchs's arrest when it convened in late January, no discussion of the matter occurred at the meeting.[3] Truman did not know of Fuchs's arrest until February 1, when Federal Bureau of Investigation Director J. Edgar Hoover phoned Souers and advised him that he "might want to inform the president."[4]

The news of Fuchs's confession and arrest confirmed in the minds of many in the military services that Soviet spies had passed along enough information to help the USSR construct a hydrogen bomb. In late February the JCS and Johnson urged Truman to speed up hydrogen bomb production.[5] In response to this request, the president reassembled the Z Committee. On March 9, the committee submitted its report on the development of thermonuclear weapons. It noted that work on the

---

1. CIA-2–50, "Review of the World," PSF-NSC, Box 207. The best account of the Hiss case is Allen Weinstein, *The Hiss-Chambers Case* (New York: Knopf, 1978). On the Fuchs case see Robert Chadwell Williams, *Klaus Fuchs, Atom Spy* (Cambridge: Harvard University Press, 1987). Several insightful works have been produced on McCarthyism such as Richard M. Freeland, *The Truman Doctrine and the Origins of McCarthyism: Foreign Policy, Domestic Politics, and Internal Security, 1946–1948* (New York: Knopf, 1972); Athan Theoharis and Robert Griffith, eds., *The Specter: Original Essays on the Cold War and the Origins of McCarthyism* (New York: New Directions, 1974); Richard M. Fried, *Nightmare in Red: The McCarthy Era in Perspective* (New York: Oxford University Press, 1990).

2. Williams, *Klaus Fuchs*, 64–91.

3. Ibid., 116, 123; York, *The Advisors*, 69; Holloway, *Stalin and the Bomb*, 220–221, 301–302.

4. Hoover cited in Williams, *Klaus Fuchs*, 116.

5. York, *The Advisors*, 70; Louis Johnson to Harry Truman, 24 February 1950, *FRUS: 1950*, I, 541–542; Truman, *Years of Trial and Hope*, 309–310.

bomb was under way, but recommended that Truman stress that the program was regarded "a matter of the highest urgency." Truman did not hesitate, and approved the report the next day, ordering the implementation of its findings.[6]

The United States would detonate its first hydrogen bomb in late 1952, and the USSR would perfect its first thermonuclear weapon in the summer of 1953. Planners began to forecast A-Day—the last time that the United States could launch a nuclear attack against the Soviet Union without risking direct retaliation. In April 1950, the NSC marked A-Day for sometime in 1954.[7] When Truman issued his directive to proceed with the hydrogen bomb, he instructed the secretaries of state and defense to provide a reevaluation of national security policy in light of the fall of China, the Soviet atomic bomb, and the American hydrogen bomb program.[8] Souers had already recommended a similar assessment on January 5, and the NSC had concurred in the proposal. The preliminary report was assigned to an ad hoc State-Defense Policy Group headed by Nitze, whom Kennan in 1949 had added to the PPS staff. On December 31, Kennan left the PPS and Nitze replaced him as the director.[9]

The State-Defense Policy Group worked diligently to produce a quick but thorough reevaluation of national security policy. Much of the drafting process went smoothly. But resistance came from Secretary Johnson, who argued that a reevaluation of policy needed to be restricted to current defense programs and budgets, and not applied to long-term guide-

---

6. Report to the President by the Special Committee of the National Security Council on the Development of Thermonuclear Weapons, 9 March 1950; *FRUS: 1950*, I, 538–539; Hewlett and Duncan, *Atomic Shield*, 417; York, *The Advisors*, 70; Truman, *Years of Trial and Hope*, 310.

7. For the development of the U.S. hydrogen bomb and Operation Ivy in 1952 see Hewlett and Duncan, *Atomic Shield*, 529–531, 539–545, 590–593; York, *The Advisors*, 75–83. For the Soviet hydrogen device see Holloway, *Stalin and the Bomb*, 294–319 and York, *The Advisors*, 89–93. "A-Day" prediction by the NSC can be found in NSC 68, *FRUS: 1950*, I, 267–268.

8. Harry Truman to Dean Acheson, 31 January 1950, *FRUS: 1950*, I, 141–142; Truman, *Years of Trial and Hope*, 311.

9. Memorandum, Sidney Souers to the NSC, 20 December 1949, "Assessment and Appraisal of U.S. Objectives, Commitments and Risks in Relation to Military Power," Minutes of the 51st Meeting, 5 January 1950, PSF-NSC, Box 207; Leffler, *A Preponderance of Power*, 355–360; idem, *The Specter of Communism*, 93–94.

Principle author of NSC 68, Director of the Policy Planning Staff Paul H. Nitze, 1951–1953. *(Courtesy of Harry S. Truman Library)*

lines. Tensions between Acheson and Johnson had materialized early in the year when Johnson tried to interfere with access by the Department of State to the military service secretaries. Not only did this interrupt the efforts of the NSC to coordinate political and military policy, but Acheson interpreted it to be an effort by Johnson to undermine his effectiveness.[10] As they labored with the State-Defense Policy Group, the departmental turf battle and the clash of personalities between the two surfaced.

On March 22, Johnson and Acheson tangled at a meeting of the group, called so members could review a lengthy preliminary final draft of the policy review before it was forwarded to the NSC. Copies of the policy had been circulated one week earlier, but after the meeting opened Johnson complained that the policy review had arrived on his desk only early that morning. Johnson accused Acheson, Bradley, and others of not having read the draft. In response, Acheson asked Nitze to summarize the main points for the group. Acheson was to recall that Johnson listened quietly for a short time, then lunged out of his chair and shouted: "No one . . . was going to make ar-

---

10. Acheson, *Present at the Creation*, 373; Prados, *Keepers of the Keys*, 37–38.

rangements for him to meet with another Cabinet officer and a roomful of people and be told what he was going to report to the President." Acheson tried to calm down the secretary of defense, but Johnson stormed out of the meeting.[11] One hour after the meeting concluded, Truman phoned Acheson and requested a report of "the slightest sign of obstruction or foot-dragging" from Johnson. From that time on, Truman's two most important NSC advisers rarely spoke to one another.

The State-Defense Policy Group continued its work without Johnson, and the final draft of the policy review was completed later in the month. In early April 1950 the group submitted it to the NSC as "United States Objectives and Programs for National Security" (NSC 68), the most significant national security policy statement of the United States during the Cold War.[12]

Although lengthy and rambling, the central message of NSC 68 was clear, and its discourse more hostile toward the Soviet Union than that of any before. It portrayed the USSR as aspiring to world hegemony, did not rule out the possibility of a war between the United States and the Soviet Union, and advocated a broader, more expensive, and global American effort to counter the threat of international communism.[13] The United States, NSC 68 held, was a free society; the USSR, a "slave state." The free society uses military force only when attacked. The slave society uses military force to threaten others. The document portrayed Kremlin leaders as hostile and uncompromising, determined to acquire "the domination of the Eurasian land mass" and dedicated to the subversion of the non-Soviet world. "The United States, as the principal center of power in the non-Soviet world . . . is the principal enemy" of the USSR.[14]

NSC 68 declared further that "the intensifying struggle" be-

11. Ibid.

12. Acheson, *Present at the Creation*, 373–374; Prados, *Keepers of the Keys*, 38; Paul Y. Hammond, "NSC-68: Prologue to Rearmament," in Schilling, Hammond, and Snyder, *Strategy, Politics, and Defense Budgets* (New York: Columbia University Press, 1962), 296–297. For the drafting of NSC 68 see Samuel F. Wells, Jr., "Sounding the Tocsin: NSC 68 and the Soviet Threat," *International Security* 4 (Fall 1979): 124–131.

13. For the complete text of NSC 68, "United States Objectives and Programs for National Security," 14 April 1950, see *FRUS: 1950*, I, 235–292; Etzold and Gaddis, *Containment*, 385–442.

14. *FRUS: 1950*, I, 238–248.

tween the United States and the USSR required the nation to admit that it could "expect no lasting abatement" of the Cold War. "The issues that face us," NSC 68 warned, "are momentous," and involved the continuation or the destruction of civilization. "Our free society, confronted by a threat to its basic value, naturally will take such action," NSC 68 confirmed, "including the use of military forces, as may be required to protect those values."[15] Unlike earlier recommendations for containment that fixed American efforts on certain limited and vital strong points in Europe and Asia, NSC 68 stressed that "a defeat of free institutions anywhere is a defeat everywhere." Therefore, it concluded, the only effective response to international communism would be an accelerated build-up of America's atomic, thermonuclear, and conventional military strength. Noting that "within the next four or five years the Soviet Union will possess the military capability of delivering a surprise atomic attack" upon the United States, "the risk of war with the USSR," NSC 68 warned, made dangerously inadequate the "present programs and plans." It concluded: "Without superior aggregate military strength, in being and readily mobilizable . . . a policy of 'containment'—which is in effect a policy of calculated and gradual coercion—is no more than a policy of bluff."[16]

Although NSC 68 advocated the globalization of containment efforts and the accelerated increase of American military capabilities, it was intentionally vague about the specific expansion of national security programs and their costs. But in calling for stepping up military expenditures, foreign military and economic aid programs, and measures for intelligence and covert operations, internal security and civil defense, NSC 68 was contemplating a departure in national security planning. It challenged the fiscally conservative assumptions from 1947 through 1949 that larger increases in postwar military expenditures would lead to inflation, higher taxes, and financial ruin. The authors of NSC 68 were influenced by the ideas of Leon Keyserling, the chairman of the Council of Economic Advisors. In early 1950, Keyserling had urged upon the administration a Keynesian economics, suggesting that government deficit

15. Ibid., 238, 244.
16. Ibid., 240, 253, 265–267, 282.

spending, coupled with an expanding economy and increased federal revenues, would provide more federal expenditures available for Truman's domestic Fair Deal program.[17] NSC 68 advanced a similar Keynesian argument. It pointed out that the nation's experience in World War II proved that the United States could afford both guns and butter. In what would be a message for Truman, the document insisted that "budgetary considerations will need to be subordinated to the stark fact that our very independence as a nation may be at stake." Acheson would remember the NSC statement was used as an instrument to "bludgeon the mass mind of 'top government' that not only could the President make a decision but that decision could be carried out."[18] But Truman, a fiscal conservative and earlier in life an unsuccessful small businessman, was concerned about the budgetary implications. He inquired about the probable cost of the programs. He also requested that the economic cooperation administrator, the director of the BOB, and the chairman of the council of economic advisers participate as an ad hoc committee in the council's consideration of NSC 68.[19]

On April 20, the council agreed to establish an ad hoc committee to respond to Truman's directive. The committee consisted of representatives designated by each NSC member, as well as representatives from the secretary of the treasury and from the three economic agencies, these last to be of Truman's choosing. The committee was assigned the task of preparing an assessment on programs and costs by August 1, but the Korean War postponed its work.[20] The war loosened Truman's fiscal restraint and convinced him that the United States needed to increase its military and international security programs. On September 21, the ad hoc committee submitted its report of

---

17. Ibid., 286, 256–258; Gaddis, *Strategies of Containment*, 93–94; H. W. Brands, *The Devil We Knew: Americans and the Cold War* (New York: Oxford University Press, 1993), 39–40. For Keyserling's impact on Fair Deal expenditures, see Alonzo L. Hamby, "The Vital Center, the Fair Deal, and the Quest for a Liberal Political Economy," *American Historical Review* 77 (June 1972): 633–665.

18. *FRUS: 1950*, I, 285; Acheson, *Present at the Creation*, 488.

19. Harry Truman to James Lay, 12 April 1950, PSF-NSC, Box 207; *FRUS: 1950*, I, 234–235; Leffler, *The Specter of Communism*, 96.

20. Memorandum, James Lay to the NSC, 17 April 1950, PSF-NSC, Box 208; Summary of Discussion at the 55th Meeting, 21 April 1950, Ibid., Box 220.

tentative cost estimates for national security programs from 1951 to 1955. On October 2 Truman, presiding over a meeting that considered the suggestions, proposed that the NSC approve the policy formulated, "but work out the details as the programs are developed." He praised the NSC for its accomplishments, saying that in constituting an "over-all approach" by departments and agencies vital to national security, the project was an innovation. Truman then directed the Senior NSC Staff to prepare revised cost estimates of NSC 68 and its annex, and "keep the entire study under continuous review." As the president had wished, the council adopted the conclusions of the report as a policy statement for the following four or five years. Truman agreed that "the implementing programs" should be acted upon quickly. The next day, September 30, 1950, nearly three months after the Korean War began, he approved NSC 68.[21]

By early December, the revisions of the policy and its annexes had been completed by the Senior NSC Staff and circulated to government officials as NSC 68/3. They included a table of cost estimates covering the programs and a statement by Keyserling on the implications of the proposed programs and their impact upon the domestic economy. Although he acknowledged that implementation of NSC 68 would be a "large-scale dedication" for the national economy, Keyserling stressed that the programs and their costs were "far short of an all-out . . . mobilization for war purposes."[22] On December 14, the council, with Truman presiding, considered all the efforts and annexes made to NSC 68/3. Some council members were hesitant to approve the cost estimates until Keyserling reassured them the economy could perform as the NSC required. After minor changes, the council adopted the amended version as NSC 68/4, and Truman issued a policy directive stating that it was approved "as a working guide for the urgent purpose of making an immediate start." Truman indicated that the programs contained in the new statement were provisional and di-

---

21. NSC 68/2, "United States Objectives and Programs for National Security," 30 September 1950, Ibid., Box 209; Summary of Discussion at the 68th Meeting, 2 October 1950, Ibid., Box 220; Hammond, "NSC-68," 355.

22. NSC 68/3 and Annexes to NSC 68/3, NSC, "Policies of the Government, 1950," 45, PSF-NSC, Box 195; *FRUS: 1950*, I, 430.

rected the Departments of State and Defense to conduct a joint review of political and military strategy. The joint review would stress "increasing and speeding up the programs outlined" and would be due on December 31, 1950.[23]

Paul Hammond suggests that NSC 68 "emphasized a general objective," and left "executive leadership the flexibility and discretion it would need to achieve that objective." The militarization of American containment policy, contends Thomas J. McCormick, "was the only choice that dealt with all the exigencies and long-term concerns generated by the crisis of 1949–50." By the end of 1950, Truman had requested from Congress $28.4 billion more for defense programs, and an additional $4 billion supplement for foreign military assistance. The fiscal year 1951 budget for defense programs accelerated from the original proposal of $13.5 billion to $48.2 billion, an increase of two hundred and fifty-seven percent. The total budget for both defense and international assistance increased from $17.7 billion in fiscal year 1950 to $52.6 billion in fiscal 1953. Funding supported programs for nuclear weapons, air base construction, the dispatch of four more army divisions to Western Europe, increased covert operations, augmented greater economic and military foreign assistance programs, and greater military commitments in Asia, including the American buildup in the defense of Korea and Taiwan, and assistance to the French in Indochina.[24]

As Walter LaFeber correctly maintains, "NSC-68 was a policy in search of an opportunity." Without the Korean War it is unlikely Truman would have authorized for such programs but a minimal budgetary increase over the guarded ceiling of $13 to $15 billion for defense. The American military commitment to South Korea, in Acheson's judgment, "removed the recommendations of NSC 68 from the realm of theory and made them immediate budget issues." The North Korean invasion of South Korea "could hardly have come at a better time

---

23. Summary of Discussion at the 75th Meeting, 16 December 1950, PSF-NSC, Box 220; NSC 68/4, "United States Objectives and Programs for National Security," 14 December 1950, Ibid., Box 210; Presidential Directive, NSC, "Policies of the Government, 1950," 45, Ibid., Box 195; Hammond, "NSC-68," 357.

24. Hammond, "NSC-68," 361, 351–359; McCormick, *America's Half-Century*, 97.

to ensure implementation of NSC-68," contends John Lewis Gaddis, because "the Korean War appeared to validate several of NSC-68's most important conclusions.[25]

NSC 68 represented the maturing of the NSC as an instrument of policy coordination, and the moment when the executive branch became fully reliant on the council as the primary formulator of Cold War strategy. "Its history," maintains Ernest R. May, "certainly provides an example of how officialdom can force a president to follow policies that are against his inclinations." For the duration of the Cold War, NSC 68 remained the American national security policy statement. Written by Nitze, a protégé of Forrestal's, it articulated Forrestal's earlier warnings that the military capabilities of the United States were inadequate to meet the nation's Cold War international commitments. Nitze recognized that the Joint Chiefs' recommendations for an accelerated program of nuclear weapons and the massive buildup of conventional armed forces had been restricted by Truman's budget ceiling. He and Acheson realized that economic constraints since 1949 had prevented Western European allies from providing a credible defensive force. And both understood that the United States had to expand its economic and military strength sufficiently to deter Soviet expansion and continue the defense of the nation's hegemonic interests.[26]

NSC 68 was placed on the council's agenda at a critical juncture of the Cold War. Its military Keynesian pump-priming injected into the nation's economic and political development an increase in defense spending programs and the expansion of foreign assistance. Military Keynesianism contributed to the development of the military-industrial complex because government purchasing programs and research subsidies targeted industries related to defense along with high technology indus-

25. LaFeber, *America, Russia, and the Cold War*, 98; Acheson, *Present at the Creation*, 420–421; Gaddis, *Strategies of Containment*, 109; Hammond, "NSC-68," 363.

26. Paul H. Nitze with Ann M. Smith and Steven L. Rearden, *From Hiroshima to Glasnost: At the Center of Decision* (New York: Grove Weidenfeld, 1989), 82–100; Steven L. Rearden, "Frustrating the Kremlin Design: Acheson and NSC 68" in Douglas Brinkley, ed., *Dean Acheson and the Making of U.S. Foreign Policy* (London: Mcmillan, 1993), 159–175; Ernest R. May, "Introduction: NSC 68: The Theory and Politics of Strategy," in idem, *American Cold War Strategy: Interpreting NSC 68* (Boston: Bedford Books, 1993), 16.

tries necessary for waging the Cold War. For many years, NSC 68 programs and projected cost estimates underwent continual review, primarily so each phase of Cold War national security objectives could be planned accordingly.[27]

*   *   *

Indicative of a superior coordination of political and military by the NSC were revised policies formulated in early 1950 concerning the Middle East and the French predicament in Indochina. Preceding the Korean War, but reevaluated during the council's work on NSC 68, strategies shaped by the NSC merged Department of State interests and concerns of the JCS to broaden the administration's activities for military and economic containment.

By late 1949 the situation in the Middle East had stabilized. The first Arab-Israeli War had concluded with a signing of an armistice. An embargo placed by the administration during the conflict on weapons shipped to Israel, while Britain and France extended arms sales to the Arab states, made Israel become more dependent on Soviet bloc countries for its weapons. Concerned about Soviet influences in the Middle East, the NSC adopted a conciliatory policy of lifting the arms embargo on Israel and cultivating friendly relations with the Arab states of Egypt, Transjordan, Lebanon, and Syria.[28]

In early 1950, as American and British military investments and interests increased in Egypt, it became necessary for the NSC to reevaluate American relations with the Middle East. "United States Policy Toward Arms Shipment to the Near East" (NSC 65) emphasized that if the region was to be "militarily strengthened for defense against Communist aggression," then American, British and Egyptian as well as other Anglo-Arab military cooperation efforts must be maintained.[29] The council considered the report and agreed to add a paragraph to it insisting that any United States armament exports to the Middle

27. McCormick, *America's Half-Century*, 95.
28. NSC 47/2, "United States Policy Toward Israel and the Arab States," 17 October 1949, PSF-NSC, NSC Memorandum Approvals, Box 193; *FRUS: 1949*, VI, 1087–1089; Memorandum, Sidney Souers to Harry Truman, 20 October 1949, Ibid.
29. NSC 65, "United States Policy Toward Arms Shipment to the Near East," 28 March 1950; *FRUS: 1950*, V, 131–135.

East should be made with full knowledge of the "undesirability of increasing the instability and uneasiness in the Arab-Israeli area." When Truman read NSC 65 he was concerned that it might be construed as too pro-Arab, and he returned the policy recommendation for revision.[30]

In the spring of 1950 the Department of State submitted as its view of NSC 65 that the administration should "avoid being drawn into any arms race in the area." The department favored "sympathetic consideration" of any Israeli requests for defensive military aid designed to "discourage attack beyond its borders." Anticipating the possibility that arms shipments provided by the United States, Great Britain, and France might provoke hostilities, it urged "public statements" that in case of renewed conflict Great Britain and France would take "vigorous action both within and without" the United Nations.[31]

The JCS reviewed NSC 65 and informed Johnson that the reference to a public commitment of the three powers to maintain peace in the Middle East was "incompatible" with the nation's security interests. Johnson proposed that the NSC add a sentence to the final report: "Such action would not involve the use of U.S. military forces." With those revisions, council members approved the report as NSC 65/3, and Truman had it implemented.[32]

Soon after NSC 65/3 became policy, Acheson met with British and French representatives in London to work out a Tripartite Declaration of arms shipments to the Middle East. Signed on May 25, 1950, the declaration announced that while Israel and the Arab states were entitled to "a certain level of armed forces for the purposes of assuring their internal security and their legitimate self-defense," the sale of armaments to countries of the Middle East would require assurances that they would not be used in aggression. The declaration also specified that if hostilities between Arabs and Israelis resumed, the three powers would take action consistent with UN obligations to

30. Summary of Discussion at the 54th Meeting, 7 April 1950, PSF-NSC, Box 220; Memorandum, James Lay to the NSC, 17 April 1950, Ibid., Box 207.

31. NSC 65/2, "United States Policy Toward Arms Shipments to the Near East," 10 May 1950, Ibid., Box 207.

32. NSC 65/3, "United States Policy Toward Arms Shipments to the Near East," 17 May 1950, NSC, "Policies of the Government, 1950," 26–27, Ibid., Box 195; *FRUS: 1950*, V, 163–166.

protect the established Middle East frontiers and armistice lines.[33] The recommendations the council made in NSC 65/3, and their culmination with the Tripartite Declaration, assured increased American armament assistance to Israel together with an expanded and continued British and French role in the Middle East, and thereby together prevented Israel from turning to the USSR under threat or the Arab states from doing so in frustration. At the same time the NSC helped Truman revise policy toward Israel and the Arab states, it undertook a reexamination of Southeast Asia.

*   *   *

In early January the USSR and the People's Republic of China recognized Ho Chi Minh's Democratic Republic of Vietnam as the legitimate government. Acheson responded quickly that the Soviet and Chinese acts of recognition revealed "Ho in his true colors as the mortal enemy of native independence in Indochina."[34] The CIA warned that the Soviet Union's recognition of Ho, coupled with that of Communist China, would "stiffen the spirit" of Ho's followers. Soviet endorsement of Ho, moreover, would lead to the shipment of quantities of military supplies from the People's Republic of China. The CIA concluded that Soviet and Chinese military assistance to the Democratic Republic of Vietnam could force a French withdrawal from Indochina "in less than two years," if the French did not receive assistance from the United States and other Western nations.[35]

France followed by granting independent status to Vietnam and the kingdoms of Laos and Cambodia as Associated States of the French Union. By early February, the United States had extended recognition to Vietnam, Laos, and Cambodia, while the Soviet Union and the People's Republic of China concluded a defensive alliance that targeted Japan and any ally of Japan.

---

33. "Tripartite Declaration Regarding Security in the Near East," 25 May 1950, *Department of State Bulletin* (5 June 1950): 886; Acheson, *Present at the Creation*, 396; Leffler, *A Preponderance of Power*, 352.

34. "Kremlin Recognizes Community Movement in Indonesia," Statement by Secretary Acheson, *Department of State Bulletin* (13 February 1950): 244.

35. CIA-2–50, "Review of the World," 15 February 1950, PSF-NSC, Box 207.

Soon thereafter, the Soviet Union increased its military supply assistance to North Korea.[36] Three weeks later the Department of State submitted a report on Indochina for the consideration of the NSC. The council studied the conditions and issued "The Position of the United States with Respect to Indochina" (NSC 64), the first version of what would become the domino theory. "Indochina is a key area of Southeast Asia and is under immediate threat," it declared. The policy report maintained that if Indochina was overtaken by communism, other countries of Southeast Asia, particularly neighboring Thailand and Burma, would likely succumb. NSC 64 recommended that the Departments of State and Defense prepare "as a matter of priority" a program to protect the security interests of the United States in Indochina.[37]

The Joint Chiefs and Johnson supported the development of the Department of State's objectives outlined in NSC 64. The loss of Southeast Asia, the JCS warned, would threaten the security of Japan, India, and Australia, the "three major non-Communist base areas" of the United States. Indochina's fall to Communist control, the Joint Chiefs warned, "would undoubtedly lead to the fall of the other mainland sections of Southeast Asia." The JCS recommended the implementation of military aid programs for Indochina, Indonesia, Thailand, the Philippines, and Burma, but urged that assistance be integrated with the administration's other economic and political programs.[38]

After receiving the views of the JCS, the entire council formally adopted NSC 64. Truman approved the new policy in late April, and directed the Departments of State and Defense to develop a program protecting the nation's security interests in Indochina.[39] On May 2, Truman released $10 million from MDAP funds and transferred it to the Department of Defense for French military assistance in Indochina. One week later, Acheson and French Foreign Minister Robert Schuman agreed

---

36. Acheson, *Present at the Creation*, 672; Memorandum, Dean Acheson to Harry Truman, 2 February 1950, *United States–Vietnam Relations*, 276–277.

37. NSC 64, "The Position of the United States with Respect to Indochina," 27 February 1950, *United States–Vietnam Relations*, 282–285; *FRUS: 1950*, VI, 744–747.

38. Memorandum, Omar Bradley to Louis Johnson, 10 April 1950, *United States–Vietnam Relations*, 308–313.

39. NSC, "Policies of the Government, 1950," 11, PSF-NSC, Box 195.

to a Franco-American pledge of cooperation in Indochina. After the outbreak of the Korean War the following month, Truman announced further assistance for France in Indochina. By the end of 1950 the administration had committed $133 million in American military assistance. NSC 64, then, had taken the country from hesitancy regarding Indochina to commitment, the first of many steps that would lead to direct American involvement in Southeast Asia.[40]

* * *

Just before dawn on Sunday, June 25, 1950, by Korean time, over one hundred thousand North Korean soldiers crossed the 38th parallel. As they moved down a corridor towards Seoul, the South Korean military recalled its forces, one-third of which were on weekend leave. Muccio cabled the Department of State. His message arriving in Washington at 9:26 p.m. on June 24, concluded: "It would appear from the nature of the attack and the manner in which it was launched that it constitutes an all-out offensive against the Republic of Korea."[41]

Spending a quiet Saturday night with his family in Independence, Missouri, Truman was unaware of the developments that would lead to what he would later recall as his "most important decision as President."[42] Assistant Secretary of State for Far Eastern Affairs Dean Rusk received Muccio's dispatch and immediately telephoned Acheson, who had been vacationing at his Maryland farm. At 11:20 p.m. Acheson phoned Truman in Independence. The president told Acheson that he would return to Washington at once, but Acheson persuaded him to wait until the Department of State could appraise the situation. Acheson recommended that the United States request an emergency meeting of the UN Security Council to declare that North Korea had committed an act of aggression and call for a cease-

---

40. Department of State Outgoing Telegram, 3 May 1950, *United States–Vietnam Relations*, 321; Acheson, *Present at the Creation*, 673; "U.S. Air and Sea Forces Ordered into Supporting Action," Statement by President Truman, *Department of State Bulletin* (3 July 1950): 5; Herring, *America's Longest War*, 13–23.

41. Muccio cited in Truman, *Years of Trial and Hope*, 333–334.

42. Merle Miller, *Plain Speaking: An Oral Biography of Harry S. Truman* (New York: Berkeley, 1974), 284; Truman, *Years of Trial and Hope*, 331–332.

fire. Truman agreed.[43] At 2:45 p.m. Sunday, Acheson called Truman a second time. He told the president that the UN Security Council would meet early that evening to consider the Department of State's resolution. He also informed Truman that the attack had been confirmed and that the South Korean front was disintegrating. Truman told Acheson that he would fly to Washington at once, and asked him to provide a list of criteria for his review.[44]

As Truman flew back to Washington he began to analyze the importance of the events in Korea. The time, he was to remember of that flight, had given him a chance to think about other historical acts of aggression—Manchuria, Ethiopia, and Austria. "Communism was acting in Korea just as Hitler, Mussolini, and the Japanese had acted ten, fifteen, and twenty years earlier," Truman concluded. From that analogy, the president arrived at a premise that would influence his decisionmaking in the following critical days: "If the Communists were permitted to force their way into the Republic of Korea without opposition from the free world . . . it would mean a third world war, just as similar incidents had brought on the second world war."[45]

Neither Truman nor the NSC was prepared for the North Korean attack on South Korea. During 1949 and 1950 the council, the JCS, and the Department of State had been preoccupied with the possibility of a Soviet war of aggression in Europe. Although NSC 68 had emphasized that Moscow's nuclear capabilities had converted future Cold War hostilities to "piecemeal aggression," and some Soviet analysts in the Department of State were expecting limited military action along the periphery of the USSR, Korea was not a concern.[46] "For some months, after tensions had mounted after the Berlin blockade," records Acheson's memoirs *Present at the Creation*, "we had exercises on danger spots for renewed Soviet probing of our de-

---

43. Thomas J. Schoenbaum, *Waging Peace and War: Dean Rusk in the Truman, Kennedy and Johnson Years* (New York: Simon and Schuster, 1988), 211; Truman, *Years of Trial and Hope*, 332.

44. Truman, *Years of Trial and Hope*, 332.

45. Ibid., 333.

46. Kennan, *Memoirs*, Volume II, 484–485.

termination. Korea was on the list but not among the favorites."[47]

Since the time that American troop evacuation began in early 1949, intelligence reports had increasingly warned of a North Korean troop build-up along the 38th parallel, but no single estimate indicated that a North Korean offensive would be imminent. The NSC received numerous intelligence reports suggesting the possibility of a North Korean attack, but many on the NSC doubted the validity of any North Korean hostilities.[48] For what was thought to be its failure to predict the invasion of South Korea the CIA received congressional criticism and press reports blamed the ineptness of intelligence. But the director of the CIA, Admiral Hillenkoetter, claimed that the agency had provided ample warnings and suggested that either the reports had not received correct evaluation, or else they had been passed over at the administration's departmental levels.[49] According to the intelligence historian Phillip Knightley, the reports were "ignored in Washington," because they "conflicted with the CIA's prevailing view on the East-West confrontation."[50] If Truman and the NSC had treated the reports seriously, a major reassessment would have been required as well of Sino and Soviet intentions.

Throughout early 1950 the administration's policy regarding East Asia continued to rely on the concept of a defensive perimeter. Acheson's famous National Press Club Speech of January 12, 1950, detailing the limits of American responsibility and interests in Asia and outlining the strategic military conclusions that the JCS and Department of Defense had reached months earlier, declared that the American defense perimeter ran from the Aleutians to the Philippines, including Japan and the Ryukyus but not Taiwan or Korea. Wars on the Asian mainland, Acheson stressed, should be fought only by Asians. Military protection alone, Acheson argued, could not ensure Asian stability. Asian nations could withstand Communist "subversion and penetration" only if they developed stable

---

47. Acheson, *Present at the Creation*, 405.

48. Truman, *Years of Trial and Hope*, 331; Jones, *The CIA and American Democracy*, 64–65; Schnabel and Watson, *History of the JCS*, III, 49–52.

49. Schnabel and Watson, *History of the JCS*, III, 50; Memorandum, Roscoe Hillenkoetter, 3 August 1950, PSF-IF, Box 250.

50. Knightley, *The Second Oldest Profession*, 267.

economies and democratic institutions. Outside its defense perimeter, the United States would offer its economic, technical, and political support, but should a military attack occur on the mainland, "the initial reliance" and burden of resistance would fall on the native people themselves.[51] By the end of the year the concept of a defensive perimeter had been repudiated, and the policies of containment coordinated by the National Security Council embraced all the principles of NSC 68.

*   *   *

Two days after the North Korean invasion Truman informed congressional leaders that the United States would take firm action in Korea. By that time, he had already met with his top national security advisers. Unlike the Berlin blockade, however, the invasion did not prompt him immediately to call a special meeting of the NSC. Preferring to wait for UN resolutions, congressional response, and what he called a "survey of the most recent developments reported from Korea," Truman did not convene the NSC until three days after the North Korean attack.[52] When the NSC met on June 28 and June 29, he requested that it recommend the deployment of American ground troops to South Korea. That decision would broaden the nation's commitment, and the president did not wish to make it without the council's consideration.

In the evening hours of June 25, Truman met briefly with thirteen national security advisers at the Blair House, his temporary residence across the street from the White House. At the meeting he ordered MacArthur to provide military supplies to the ROK and dispatched the Seventh Fleet north to be put under MacArthur's command.[53] Hours before the meeting the UN Security Council had voted unanimously, with the USSR delegate absent, for a North Korean withdrawal behind the 38th parallel, an immediate cease-fire, and assistance from UN member states "in the execution of the resolution."[54] At the

---

51. "Crisis in Asia—An Examination of U.S. Policy," Speech by Dean G. Acheson, *Department of State Bulletin* (23 January 1950): 111–118.

52. Truman, *Years of Trial and Hope*, 340.

53. Ibid., 333–336.

54. *FRUS: 1950*, VII, 1556–1557. The Soviet delegate, Jacob Malik, did not attend the UN Security Council meeting because the USSR was boycotting the exclusion of the People's Republic of China from admission.

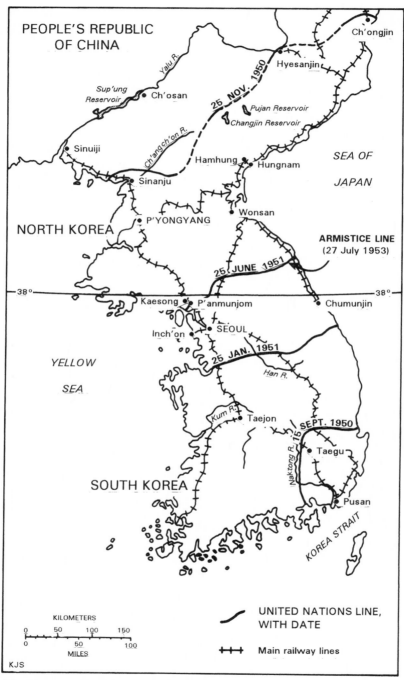

PEOPLE'S REPUBLIC
OF CHINA

Yalu R.

Sup'ung Reservoir

● Ch'osan

Ch'ongjin ●

Hyesanjin ●

25 NOV. 1950

Pujan Reservoir

Changjin Reservoir

Ch'angch'on R.

● Sinuiji

Hamhung ● Hungnam

SEA OF

JAPAN

● Sinanju

NORTH KOREA

● P'YONGYANG

● Wonsan

ARMISTICE LINE
(27 July 1953)

38°

25 JUNE 1951

38°

● Kaesong

P'anmunjom ●

● Chumunjin

YELLOW

SEA

Inch'on ●

● SEOUL

25 JAN. 1951

Han R.

Kum R.

● Taejon

15 SEPT. 1950

Naktong R.

● Taegu

SOUTH KOREA

● Pusan

KOREA STRAIT

KILOMETERS
0   50   100   150
0   50   100
MILES

UNITED NATIONS LINE,
WITH DATE

+++ Main railway lines

KJS

Map 5.   Korean War (1950–1953)

144

Blair House, Truman and others questioned for the first time the role of the USSR in North Korea's invasion. Though there was no evidence of direct involvement, Truman and his advisers assumed that the USSR had instigated the attack to deflect United States attention from Western Europe and Japan. General Bradley commented that the Soviet Union was "obviously testing us" in Korea, and Truman told the Blair House conference participants that he thought "the line would have to be drawn." As in Berlin, the "Reds" he concluded, "were probing for weaknesses in our armour," and Truman decided, "we had to meet their thrust without getting embroiled in a world-wide war."[55]

The general conclusion that Truman and his national security advisers made the evening of June 25 was that the Soviet Union had instigated the North Korean invasion of South Korea. In fact, the idea for the invasion came from North Korea's leader, Kim Il Sung. Kim had met with Stalin in April and assured him that North Korea could overrun the South within three days, leaving the United States very little time to intervene. Stalin granted his approval of the invasion and promised Soviet military supplies, but only on condition that no Soviet military forces directly participate. Stalin further mandated that Kim obtain Mao's approval for the offensive. Kim therefore dutifully visited Mao and received his approval. New studies of recently released Soviet documents reveal that Stalin reasoned he could take credit for a successful invasion and unification of Korea conducted by Kim. Or if the North Korean leader's plans failed, Stalin thought that he could encourage Mao to intervene in the conflict, thereby making the People's Republic of China dependent on the Soviet Union and checking Mao's nationalistic revolution and influence in Asia.[56]

---

55. Truman, *Years of Trial and Hope*, 335, 337.
56. Stueck, *The Korean War*, 34–39; LaFeber, *America, Russia, and the Cold War*, 100–102; Khrushchev, *Khrushchev Remembers*, 144–146; Leffler, *A Preponderance of Power*, 367; idem, *The Specter of Communism*, 97–98; Goncharov, Lewis, and Litai, *Uncertain Partners*, 130–154; Chen Jian, "The Sino-Soviet Alliance and China's Entry into the Korean War," Working Paper #1, Cold War International History Project, Woodrow Wilson International Center for Scholars; Weathersby, "Soviet Aims in Korea and the Origins of the Korean War, 1945–1950," Working Paper #8, Ibid.; idem, "New Findings on the Korean War," *Bulletin CWIHP* 1 (Fall 1993): 1, 14–18; idem, "Korea, 1949–50," *Bulletin CWIHP* 5 (Spring 1995): 1–9.

By June 26 the situation in South Korea had further deteriorated. As North Korean troops closed in on Seoul, and
Rhee's government prepared to evacuate the South Korean
capital, Truman called another emergency meeting at the Blair
House. He read a report from MacArthur predicting that a
"complete collapse [of South Korea] is imminent." Then, on
Acheson's recommendation, Truman dispatched the Seventh
Fleet to defend the Taiwan Strait, ordered MacArthur to commit air and naval forces to support the South Korean army, authorized increases in American assistance to the French in
Indochina, and approved aid to the Philippine government in
its efforts to suppress a strengthening Communist insurgency
movement.[57] Truman specified that all military operations be
restricted to south of the 38th parallel, and he did not commit
American ground troops. Bradley told the president that de-
ploying ground forces in South Korea would require complete
mobilization, and the JCS were reluctant to commit ground
troops on lesser terms. Truman agreed that the question of mobilization would require study beforehand by the Joint Chiefs,
and he added: "I don't want to go to war."[58] He also approved
the resolution the Department of State had drafted for proposal
before the UN Security Council. It requested all UN member
states to "provide assistance to the Republic of South Korea as
may be necessary to repel the armed attack and restore international peace and security in the area."[59]

The next day the UN Security Council adopted the resolution that Truman had approved hours earlier. The president
then informed the American public in a brief statement that he
had "ordered United States air and sea forces to give the Korean Government troops cover and support." Assuming that as
commander-in-chief he did not need formal approval from
Congress for air and naval deployment, before releasing his
statement he had merely briefed congressional leaders and
received their agreement.[60] The only other decisions that re-

57. MacArthur cited in Truman, *Years of Trial and Hope*, 337.
58. Ibid.; Truman cited in Schnabel and Watson, *History of the JCS*, III, 91.
59. Philip Jessup, Memorandum of Conversation, 26 June 1950, *FRUS: 1950*, VII, 178–183.
60. Truman, *Years of Trial and Hope*, 338–339; Richard E. Neustadt, *Presidential Power* (New York: John Wiley and Sons, 1980), 91; George M. Elsey Oral History Interview; Dean Rusk Oral History Interview.

mained for Truman were whether American ground troops should be committed to South Korea, and whether the United States should cross the 38th parallel, and they would rest upon the NSC's recommendations.

On June 28 the Senate voted by roll call to grant Truman the authority to activate armed forces reserves and extend the selective service. Yet, the focus of attention that day was a meeting of the NSC. Besides Truman, Vice President Alben Barkley, Acheson, Johnson, and Stuart Symington, the newly appointed chair of the National Security Resources Board, the statutory members of the NSC, twenty-two additional participants attended the meeting; including executive department and intelligence advisers, the entire JCS, and the military service secretaries. The only subject the NSC and Truman addressed was the Korean crisis and its global implications.[61]

Truman opened the meeting by reading a statement of the latest developments in Korea. He directed the NSC to undertake a complete review of all policies affecting the "entire perimeter of the USSR," and prepare for his consideration courses of action in the event that Soviet forces entered Korean hostilities. Truman agreed with Acheson that the Department of Defense needed to begin preparations for an NSC review of military capabilities and options. Secretary of the Army Frank Pace told the group that military intelligence had initiated a search for "clear evidence of Soviet participation" in the Korean War. Truman replied that he wanted "special attention" given to other sensitive areas, especially Soviet activities in the vicinity of Yugoslavia, Northern Europe, and Northern Iran. Special Assistant to the President Averell Harriman reported on the European reaction to the crisis in Korea, remarking that "Europeans were gravely concerned" that the administration would not meet the challenge. Truman's actions provided Europeans "great relief," said Harriman. The president then informed the council that some congressional leaders had questioned whether other UN nations were willing to help. Indicative of UN member assistance, he told the NSC, was a British offer of naval aid. The council agreed with Truman that the British offer should be accepted and Senate leaders informed.[62]

61. Truman, *Years of Trial and Hope*, 340–341; Minutes of the 58th Meeting, 28 June 1950, PSF-NSC, Box 208.

62. Summary of Discussion at the 58th Meeting, 29 June 1950, PSF-NSC, Box 220. For other less detailed and more personal recollections of the meeting

At the conclusion of the meeting military officials raised the question of whether American forces might cross the 38th parallel. Secretary of the Air Force Thomas K. Finletter announced that after two days of operation the air force was finding it difficult to deal with North Koreans over the South. The problem was that American forces had been prohibited from moving north of the 38th parallel. Until American air power could destroy North Korean bases and pursue Communist aircraft, Finletter concluded, "we could not effectively stop" the offensive. Truman acknowledged Finletter's concerns, but believed that the decision to cross the 38th parallel should be considered at a later time. Acheson replied that he "hoped the line would not be crossed by 'accident.'" Johnson reassured the NSC on the matter. Assessing American actions and responsibilities up to that point, Acheson observed that the administration might find "it imperative to accept full-out war." Truman then concluded that he believed that the United States "should not back out of Korea unless a military situation elsewhere demanded such action."[63]

Pressing the case for further involvement, the Joint Chiefs prepared a draft directive for MacArthur that authorized the extension of air and naval forces north of the 38th parallel. They recommended "as a matter of urgency" the commitment of token ground forces for communication and transportation services. The JCS argued that if the Soviet Union intervened openly in Korea or seized an opportunity to move aggressively in Western Europe, the United States should proceed with complete mobilization. Realizing that the deployment of ground troops would require Truman's authorization, Johnson called the president on June 29 and suggested another meeting of the NSC for its consideration. Truman agreed and called a meeting for later that afternoon.[64]

Johnson read before the council the JCS draft directive for MacArthur. Truman and Acheson supported the directive's orders for air and naval operations north of the 38th parallel, and for the commitment of limited ground forces. Truman objected

---

see Truman, *Years of Trial and Hope*, 340–341; Acheson, *Present at the Creation*, 411.
   63. Ibid.
   64. JCS cited in Schnabel and Watson, *History of the JCS*, III, 103–106.

to the last paragraph of the directive, however, telling the NSC that he "wished to give no implication that we were planning to go to war with Russia under present circumstances." Truman informed the council that while he wanted to do everything necessary to force North Korean troops back across the 38th parallel, air and naval operations into North Korea should aim only at munition stores. In conclusion, the president insisted that he wanted it understood that American operations were intended to "keep the peace" and "restore the border."[65]

The NSC discussed the People's Republic of China's denunciation of the administration's support of South Korea and the USSR's refusal of a request to mediate the crisis in Korea. Acheson read a statement from Moscow that condemned South Korea for starting the war and declared that the USSR would adhere to the "principle of the impermissibility of interference by foreign powers in the internal affairs of Korea." Acheson told the NSC that the two communications taken together "indicated that the Soviet Union would not intervene in Korea, but might utilize the Chinese Communists." He then asked for the public release of the American appeal to the USSR, and the council agreed. Acheson also reported that India, Australia, New Zealand, Canada, and the Netherlands had offered assistance. Truman responded that he wanted all offers accepted so that the response in Korea "may be truly representative of the United Nations." Truman concluded the meeting by announcing that he wanted UN armed force contingents placed under MacArthur's command, and that the general be directed "to make a full and complete report on the situation in the Far East each day."[66]

Later that evening Acheson and Johnson approved a new directive to MacArthur. It authorized him to use American air and naval forces to provide the "fullest possible support" for South Korean troops, and employ limited United States Army ground troops for "essential support service." It also directed MacArthur to defend Taiwan against a Communist Chinese attack as well as prevent the Chinese Nationalists from using Taiwan "as a base of operations against the Chinese Mainland."

---

65. Summary of Discussion at the 59th Meeting, 30 June 1950, PSF-NSC, Box 220. Also see Truman, *Years of Trial and Hope*, 341–342.
66. Ibid.

MacArthur was ordered to take only defensive measures and in the event of Soviet intervention in Korea, to report to Washington and "take no action to aggravate the situation."[67] Truman's orders to MacArthur reached Tokyo on the morning of June 30. The general had just returned from a personal visit to the front line in Korea, witnessed the North Korean capture and burning of Seoul, and ordered air strikes above the 38th parallel. From his battlefront observations MacArthur determined that combat troops would be necessary to halt the North Korean advance toward Pusan. After he arrived in Tokyo and received additional reports that North Korean forces had broken ROK defenses at the Han River and were moving to capture the whole peninsula, MacArthur sent an urgent request to Washington. The cable asked for one regimental combat team to strengthen American units and an additional two divisions to mount an early counteroffensive.[68]

MacArthur's dispatch arrived in Washington in the middle of the early morning hours of June 30. Pace telephoned Truman and relayed MacArthur's message. Truman immediately authorized the deployment of a regimental combat team, but not the two divisions for a counteroffensive. Later that morning he met with several national security advisers and informed them of MacArthur's request. The group did not object to the general's proposal to engage combat troops in a counteroffensive, and Truman decided shortly thereafter to allow MacArthur full authority to use American troops under his command in Japan for combat in Korea. In addition, Truman directed a naval blockade of North Korea.[69] "Friday's decisions," in Acheson's recollections, "were the culminating ones of a momentous week. We were then fully committed to Korea."[70] In 1948 and 1949, the NSC, the Department of State, and the JCS had determined that the Korean peninsula was only a peripheral interest to the United States. But in the days between June 25 and June 30, 1950, it became instead a central concern. "What Korea showed," points out one scholar of the

---

67. JCS cited in Schnabel and Watson, *History of the JCS,* III, 108–109.
68. Ibid., 110–113.
69. Ibid., 116, 127–129; Truman, *Years of Trial and Hope,* 343; Acheson, *Present at the Creation,* 412.
70. Acheson, *Present at the Creation,* 413.

Cold War, "was that even regions not deemed vital could become vital if threatened by a hostile military force."[71] For Truman and the NSC, Korea's loss to Communist control symbolized the first domino in the Far East.[72]

*   *   *

By the summer and fall of 1950, the United States had headed down the long road of Cold War globalism, the defensive perimeter had expanded to include Korea and Taiwan, and Americans were fighting on the Asian mainland in the interests of national security and worldwide containment. Within months the administration adopted the national security premises of NSC 68, enacted larger military budgets for the United States, and applied a new strategy to liberate all of Korea from Communist control.

The United States became committed to Korea before the NSC could provide Truman any short-term assessments and long-range policy objectives. Nor had the NSC been afforded enough time to formulate recommendations regarding the future of the Korean 38th parallel or the possibility of Korean unification. Because Korea was strategically located near the USSR, the first concern for the NSC was determining American policy toward the Soviet Union. In early July the NSC staff studied all policies affecting the entire perimeter of the USSR.

In a draft policy statement concerning Korea titled "The Position and Actions of the United States with Respect to Possible Further Soviet Moves in the Light of the Korean Situation" (NSC 73/4), the council in early July determined that there had been "no conclusive indication" that Moscow intended "to launch a global war." Yet the danger of the USSR initiating such a conflict, either by deliberation or by miscalculation, NSC 73/4 warned, "may have been increased by the Korean war." The report noted that "no conclusive evidence" existed that indicated the USSR would commit Soviet troops, either "alone or with satellite forces, in isolated or piecemeal attacks"

---

71. Gaddis, *The Long Peace*, 168.
72. For the symbol of Korea see Charles M. Dobbs, *The Unwanted Symbol: American Foreign Policy, the Cold War, and Korea, 1945–1950* (Kent: Kent State University Press, 1981).

along its periphery. NSC 73/4 concluded that the USSR would probably use Communist Chinese troops in Korea as well as against Taiwan, and encourage aggression from its satellites against Western Europe, Yugoslavia, Greece and Turkey, Hong Kong and Macao, and Southeast Asia.[73]

At the same meeting, Symington read and the NSC discussed a statement titled "Suggested Action by the NSC for Consideration of the President in the Light of the Korean Situation." Noting that the invasion of South Korea "came as a surprise and shock, not only to the people of the United States and the world, but also to the people around this table," Symington warned that, "there are further shocks which must be absorbed," and urged that the NSC propose a long-range strategic defense plan. He recommended that the council's staff consider his request in connection with its work on NSC 73/4. The members approved the request and circulated the statement to all departments and agencies concerned with the task of mobilization.[74] Symington's appeal did not bring the NSC to devise a coordinated policy. But portions of his report influenced Part II of NSC 73/4, in which the council proposed that the United States rapidly increase the build-up of its military strength, implement measures outlined in NSC 68, prepare "for fighting a global war should war prove unavoidable," and in the event of overt military action, "take appropriate air and naval action outside Korea against Communist China."[75]

At the same time the NSC considered the drafts of NSC 73/4, the UN Security Council confirmed the leading role of the United States in Korea. On July 7, it adopted a resolution establishing a unified command over all combined UN forces engaged in Korea, headed by a commander designated by the President of the United States. Truman had already named MacArthur as his choice for the position, and he approved

---

73. NSC 73/4, "The Position and Actions of the United States with Respect to Possible Further Soviet Moves in the Light of the Korean Situation," 25 August 1950, NSC, "Policies of the Government, 1950," 68–69, PSF-NSC, Box 195.

74. Memorandum, Stuart Symington to the NSC, 6 July 1950, Ibid., Box 208; Minutes of the 60th Meeting, 6 July 1950, Ibid.

75. NSC 73/4, "The Position and Actions of the United States with Respect to Possible Further Soviet Moves in the Light of the Korean Situation," 25 August 1950, NSC, "Policies of the Government, 1950," 70–74, Ibid., Box 195.

the UN Security Council's resolution that day.[76] Soon after MacArthur assumed his new position, North Korean troops forced UN ground units to retreat down the Korean peninsula. By early July they were confined to the Pusan perimeter. The North Korean advance made MacArthur revise his estimates upward, and he requested more American and UN reinforcements for a counteroffensive and an amphibious operation that would land behind North Korean lines at Inchon.[77] In response to MacArthur's proposed operations, Truman asked that the NSC provide him a recommendation that specified United States policy in the event that North Korean forces were driven back across the 38th parallel by UN units.[78]

As the NSC began work on Truman's directive, the prospects of Soviet intervention in the war seemed less ominous. Throughout July the USSR did not move toward military involvement in Korea. Believing that Moscow had been surprised by the rapid reactions of the UN and the intervention of military forces in Korea, the CIA concluded: "Nothing in the Korean situation as yet indicates that the USSR would deliberately decide to deploy Soviet forces in direct military action precipitating global war."[79] Instead of a general war, the CIA stressed, the United States could expect the USSR "to localize the Korean conflict" by providing arms and material assistance to North Korea.[80] Throughout the fall of 1950 the USSR maintained its distance from the conflict, and this encouraged MacArthur along with the NSC to pursue a more aggressive policy. Indicative of the NSC's lack of concern about immediate Soviet military intervention in Korea was the council's half-hearted adoption, and Truman's approval, of NSC 73/4 as a "working guide." The council, however, did not abandon its earlier warning that the United States must remain alerted to

76. Schnabel and Watson, *History of the JCS*, III, 134–135; John W. Spanier, *The Truman-MacArthur Controversy and the Korean War* (New York: W.W. Norton, 1965), 65–68.
77. Schnabel and Watson, *History of the JCS*, III, 178–202.
78. Memorandum, Harry Truman to James Lay, 17 July 1950, *FRUS: 1950*, VII, 410; Memorandum, James Lay to the NSC, 17 July 1950, PSF-NSC, Box 208.
79. CIA, Intelligence Memorandum No. 302, 8 July 1950, PHT-NSC, Box 1, HSTL, Independence, Missouri.
80. CIA, Intelligence Memorandum No. 300, 28 June 1950, Ibid.

Moscow's "overt use of organized Chinese Communist forces in Korea."[81]

The new suspicion of the People's Republic of China revealed that the NSC had become less willing to act in accordance with its earlier policies. At the same time, the Joint Chiefs reintroduced their interest in guaranteeing the administration's support of Taiwan. In late July the NSC adopted a JCS proposal that would strengthen Taiwan against invasion. "Immediate United States Courses of Action with Respect to Formosa" (NSC 37/10) recommended that "irrespective of the situation in Korea," the administration prepare to defend Taiwan from Communist forces. It also suggested reviewing its policy of denying military material and supplies to Jiang's government.[82] With the approval of NSC 37/10, the United States officially recognized the strategic importance of Taiwan. The Korean War had forced an end to the efforts of Acheson and Truman in 1949 to disengage the United States from the island. In August, Truman approved a military mission to advise Jiang's troops as well as $14 million in military assistance. As of October Acheson reluctantly agreed to work with the UN for the neutralization of Taiwan.[83]

To provide for an adequate defense of Taiwan the JCS followed up NSC 37/10 with a request that Johnson secure NSC approval for periodic photo reconnaissance flights south of the 32nd parallel. Intelligence reports, the Joint Chiefs observed, revealed "sufficient build-up of troops and water lift" by the People's Republic of China along its coastline, and without photographic reconnaissance an amphibious assault against Taiwan would be difficult to defeat.[84] The Department of State commented on the request, adding that MacArthur should "ex-

81. Minutes of the 66th Meeting, 24 August 1950, PSF-NSC, Box 209; NSC 73/4, "The Positions and Actions of the United States with Respect to Possible Further Soviet Moves in the Light of the Korean Situation," 25 August 1950, NSC, "Policies of the Government, 1950," 73, Ibid., Box 195.

82. Memorandum, Omar Bradley to Louis Johnson, 27 July 1950, Ibid., Box 208; NSC 37/10, "Immediate United States Courses of Action with Respect to Formosa," 3 August 1950, Ibid.; *FRUS: 1950*, VI, 413–414.

83. Memorandum, Harry Truman to Dean Acheson, 25 August 1950, *FRUS: 1950*, VI, 414n; Minutes of Discussion of the Taiwan Issue, 15 November 1950, Ibid., 556–572; Leffler, *A Preponderance of Power*, 375–376.

84. Memorandum, A. C. Davis to Louis Johnson, 28 July 1950, PSF-NSC, Box 208.

ercise caution to avoid creating hostilities" with the People's Republic of China, take care not to widen the Korean conflict, conduct reconnaissance "to the maximum extent possible outside Chinese territorial waters," and avoid giving the Chinese Communists "any impression" that American aircraft were "making a serious attempt to penetrate the mainland."[85] After the JCS accepted the Department of State's additions, the NSC approved the reconnaissance request in early August, and instructed the Departments of State and Defense together to devise its implementation. Within a week aerial reconnaissance missions began.[86]

Throughout July and August the administration did not publicly specify American military objectives beyond the language of the UN resolutions. But, with mid-term elections pending in November, Truman's critics, including Senator Joseph McCarthy and congressional members of the bipartisan China bloc, clamored for a military offensive against North Korea.[87] MacArthur also issued several optimistic statements touting his plans for a military conquest of North Korea and the eventual military occupation and political unification of all of Korea. When Generals J. Lawton Collins and Hoyt S. Vandenberg visited MacArthur at his headquarters in mid-July, MacArthur informed them of his perceived mission: total defeat of the North Korean forces. And, he added, after the defeat, "it might be necessary to occupy" as well as "compose and unite" Korea.[88]

In August the first clash took place between Truman and MacArthur. It occurred over the troublesome issue of Taiwan. MacArthur traveled to the island to strengthen his ties with Jiang, personal and military. Although the Joint Chiefs had ordered MacArthur to assess the defense requirements of Taiwan,

85. Department of State, Comment on the Recommendations of the Joint Chiefs of Staff on Photo Reconnaissance of Certain Portions of the China Coast, Ibid.

86. Minutes of the 63rd Meeting, 3 August 1950, Ibid.

87. For congressional reaction during July and August, see Ronald J. Caridi, *The Korean War and American Politics: The Republican Party as a Case Study* (Philadelphia: University of Pennsylvania Press, 1969). For McCarthy's criticisms a fine account is Thomas C. Reeves, *The Life and Times of Joe McCarthy: A Biography* (New York: Stein & Day, 1982), 327–333.

88. MacArthur cited in J. Lawton Collins, *War in Peacetime: The History and Lessons of Korea* (Boston: Houghton Mifflin, 1969), 82–83.

his unexpected visit irritated Truman. Newspaper headlines, moreover, suggested to Truman that MacArthur's trip may have been politically motivated. MacArthur praised Jiang during the visit, assured him of "effective military coordination between the [Nationalist] Chinese and American forces," and released a photograph of himself kissing Madame Jiang's hand.[89] Although aware that Republican members of the China bloc in Congress had courted MacArthur and that the general had recently revised upward his own military estimates of the importance of Taiwan, Truman responded quietly and cautiously. Orders were sent to MacArthur that explicitly emphasized limiting American policy toward Taiwan. Then Harriman met with MacArthur in Tokyo to explain to him why any alliance with Jiang was a disadvantage, and to make it clear that administration support for Taiwan at the time could endanger UN unity in Korea.[90]

Harriman informed Truman soon after that MacArthur had accepted the president's position and promised to obey his orders. But Harriman was not convinced, and he told Truman: "I explained in great detail why Chiang [Jiang] was a liability . . . and the great danger of a split in the unity of the United Nations. . . . He has a strange idea that we should back anybody who will fight Communism." One week after Harriman's visit with MacArthur, the general confirmed Harriman's doubts. In mid-August MacArthur issued a public statement that the American government had arranged his trip to Taiwan. He also further criticized the administration for refusing to accept the military usefulness of Jiang's forces in the Korean War, and blamed it for promoting "a policy of defeatism and appeasement." Fifteen days later, in a speech that he had prepared to deliver before a convention of Veterans of Foreign Wars, MacArthur attacked. Released three days before the convention was set to open MacArthur again took issue with Truman's policies. On August 28, the speech repeated his call for assistance to Jiang.[91]

---

89. Stueck, *The Korean War*, 66–68; Dean Acheson, *The Korean War* (New York: W.W. Norton, 1971), 43; Rudy Abramson, *Spanning the Century: The Life of W. Averell Harriman, 1891–1986* (New York: William Morrow, 1992), 447.

90. Acheson, *The Korean War*, 43–44; Abramson, *Spanning the Century*, 450–453.

91. Harriman cited in Abramson, *Spanning the Century*, 453; MacArthur cited in Acheson, *The Korean War*, 44; Stueck, *The Korean War*, 68.

When Truman read MacArthur's speech he gave serious thought to relieving the general from his command. By that time, though, the size of UN forces had increased significantly in Korea, and MacArthur's operational plans for the invasion of Inchon were in the making. Instead, Truman decided to order MacArthur to withdraw the speech. Meeting on August 26, with the JCS and Johnson, the president told the secretary of defense to transmit his order to MacArthur. This led to another conflict between Johnson and Acheson. Immediately after the meeting Johnson phoned the secretary of state and questioned Truman's logic. He told Acheson he believed the order should be rephrased so as to imply that the decision to withdraw the speech was "only one man's opinion and not the official policy of the Government." Acheson, appalled that Johnson would take such a position, retorted that he believed that "the issue seemed to be who was President of the United States." Truman reissued his order to Johnson, but the secretary of defense remained hesitant to follow through. Finally, Truman instructed Harriman to cable the order to MacArthur.[92] The president found Johnson's actions inexcusable, and he decided to demand the secretary's resignation. Johnson resigned on September 11, and ten days later General Marshall officially took over as secretary of defense. Soon thereafter, Lovett returned to assist Marshall as deputy secretary of defense, and a year later he succeeded Marshall. With these changes in place, the NSC's efforts at coordinating political and military objectives greatly improved, and the Department of State's policy of placing European over Asian concerns and issues returned. Truman's problems with MacArthur, however, did not disappear.[93]

With troop buildups continuing in Korea and MacArthur's operational plans clearer, Truman and the NSC began to consider seriously the possibility that North Korean troops would be driven across the 38th parallel and all of Korea liberated from communism and severed from the influence of the USSR and the People's Republic of China. In early September, one

92. Acheson, *The Korean War*, 45; Abramson, *Spanning the Century*, 454–455; Prados, *Keepers of the Keys*, 44.

93. Acheson, *The Korean War*, 45–46; Abramson, *Spanning the Century*, 455–457; Prados, *Keepers of the Keys*, 44. For an insightful study of the Marshall and Acheson relationship see Forrest C. Pogue, "Marshall and Acheson: The State Department Years, 1945–49," in Douglas Brinkley, ed., *Dean Acheson and the Making of U.S. Foreign Policy* (London: Macmillan, 1993), 211–232.

week before MacArthur's bold Inchon landing, the NSC staff offered suggestions concerning the possibilities in Korea. In "United States Courses of Action with Respect to Korea" (NSC 81), the NSC report indicated for the first time that the administration had made plans to cross the 38th parallel and roll back communism from the Korean peninsula. NSC 81 specified that:

> The United Nations forces have a legal basis for conducting operations north of the 38th parallel to compel the withdrawal of the North Korean forces behind this line or to defeat these forces. It would be expected that the UN Commander would receive authorization to conduct military operations . . . in pursuance of a roll-back in Korea north of the 38th parallel, for the purpose of destroying the North Korean forces, provided that at the time of such operations there had been no entry into North Korea by major Soviet or Chinese Communist forces.[94]

In addition, NSC 81 recommended that no UN operations extend "close to" the Manchurian and Soviet borders of North Korea. And it specified that in the event Soviet or Chinese Communist forces occupied North Korea, the UN commander "should reoccupy Korea up to the 38th parallel."[95]

At a council meeting in early September, Bradley read comments by the JCS on NSC 81. The Joint Chiefs agreed in principle with the policy but expressed doubt that the front should be stabilized along the 38th parallel. Acheson told Bradley that the members of the JCS were wrong to conclude that NSC 81 suggested that. He went on to request that before UN forces launched an invasion north of the parallel, MacArthur should come to Washington for a "final decision." Bradley and Johnson concurred in Acheson's proposal. The council then adopted NSC 81 subject to redrafting by the Departments of State and Defense.[96] The discussion led to an amended version labeled NSC 81/1. The new draft required advanced presidential ap-

---

94. NSC 81, "United States Courses of Action with Respect to Korea," 1 September 1950, *FRUS: 1950*, VII, 685–693.

95. Ibid.

96. Memorandum, Omar Bradley to Louis Johnson, 7 September 1950, PSF-NSC, Box 209; Summary of Discussion at the 67th Meeting, 8 September 1950, Ibid., Box 220.

proval before military operations could take place north of the 38th parallel. The prohibition of actions "close" to the Soviet and Manchurian borders was revised to forbid operations extending "across" borders. And political objectives for postwar military occupation of Korea were revised to include the adoption by the UN of three phases: military occupation until internal security of Korea had been established; free national elections held under UN auspices; and withdrawal of all non-Korean UN forces and the extension of assistance to the country's unification.[97]

Truman approved NSC 81/1 on September 11, four days later MacArthur staged his successful Inchon landing, and the nature of the war changed significantly. Within two weeks, MacArthur's forces had isolated North Korea's supply lines and liberated most of South Korea. Hopeful for a quick victory, the administration evoked the policy recommendations of NSC 81/1 report and thereby cleared the way for moving the war north of the 38th parallel. On September 27 Secretary of Defense Marshall asked that Truman approve a directive to MacArthur implementing the "military aspects" of NSC 81/1. He informed Truman that the president's authorization would permit MacArthur "to conduct the necessary military operations . . . to destroy North Korean forces." Without hesitation Truman authorized the directive.[98] Seoul was liberated the next day. On September 30, President Rhee reestablished the ROK government, and the first of South Korean troops crossed the 38th parallel. On October 7, troops moved north of the parallel, and the UN General Assembly voted to adopt the three proposals that the NSC had suggested for occupation and postwar unification.[99]

Truman hoped for a quick victory when he approved NSC 81/1 as policy and signed the directive authorizing MacArthur

97. NSC 81/1, "United States Courses of Action with Respect to Korea," 9 September 1950, *FRUS: 1950*, VII, 712–721; Dean Rusk Oral History Interview.

98. George C. Marshall to Harry Truman, 27 September 1950, PSF-KWF, Box 243, HSTL, Independence, Missouri; Leffler, *A Preponderance of Power*, 377; idem, *The Specter of Communism*, 105; Joseph C. Goulden, *Korea: The Untold Story of the War* (New York: McGraw-Hill, 1982), 210–237.

99. Goulden, *Korea*, 230, 239–243; Stueck, *The Korean War*, 85–87, 91–96; Spanier, *The Truman-MacArthur Controversy*, 88.

to launch a UN military campaign north of the 38th parallel. His historic decision to widen the war was influenced as well by two important domestic political opportunities. Truman understood that a new offensive for the liberation of Korea and a rollback of communism in Asia would stifle attacks from Senator McCarthy charging that the administration's earlier appeasements of Communist China were to blame for America's failures in Asia. In turn he also reasoned that the offensive would derail Republican critics who had pressed for an "Asia first" policy for nearly two years. The president further realized that a widening of the war would necessitate congressional approvals of the massive defense budgets recommended by NSC 68. The revised strategem that flowed from the provisions of NSC 81/1 granted Truman, as historian Walter LaFeber points out, "the opportunity to put the United States, finally, on full military footing to fight the larger Cold War."[100]

As MacArthur's forces drove north toward the Yalu River the NSC and Truman dismissed all previous concerns about crossing the 38th parallel, even though two NSC reports had considered and noted officially the possibility of Chinese military intervention in Korea. In late September Mao ordered his Foreign Minister Zhou Enlai to issue warnings through India that if UN ground forces crossed the 38th parallel the People's Republic of China would intervene to protect its borders. The administration discounted the communiques as bellicose propaganda bluffs and as part of a Sino-Soviet war of words to frighten troop withdrawal from Korea. The JCS and Truman directed MacArthur to continue military action "in the event of the open or covert employment anywhere in Korea of major Chinese Communist units." MacArthur did not believe that the Chinese would intervene in the war. When Truman met with MacArthur at Wake Island on October 15, the general assured him that "the victory was won in Korea," and emphatically noted that "the Chinese Commies would not attack."[101] Two days after Wake Island, as MacArthur's forces closed in on

---

100. LaFeber, *America, Russia, and the Cold War,* 117; Christensen, *Useful Adversaries,* 117; idem, "A Lost Chance for What?" 268–278.

101. Stueck, *The Korean War,* 94, 97; Draft Message, JCS to Commander in Chief UN Command (with Truman's signature of approval), 8 October 1950, PSF-KWF, Box 243; Wake Island Summary, Ibid.

Truman and General Douglas MacArthur, Wake Island Meeting, October 1950. *(From the album, The President's Trip to Wake Island; Courtesy of Harry S. Truman Library)*

Pyongyang, Truman publicly notified China that the United States had "no aggressive designs in Korea or in any other place in the Far East or elsewhere."[102] The Chinese were not convinced, and in less than a week the confidence of the administration as well as its credibility would be shattered.

Recently released Soviet and Chinese documents reveal that by early October the People's Republic of China was preparing to enter the Korean War. Mao's decision to send in Chinese volunteers may have been influenced as early as June, when Truman and the NSC dispatched the Seventh Fleet to defend Taiwan, interpreted by Mao as a hostile American effort to intervene in China's civil war. Although the People's Republic of China attempted to issue warnings in an effort to prevent the expansion of the conflict, historian Thomas J. Christensen correctly notes that "poor communication channels" between Beijing and Washington aggravated the efforts of Mao and Zhou. By early October the USSR was pressuring Communist

---

102. Truman cited in Spanier, *The Truman-MacArthur Controversy*, 120.

China to assume a military offensive if UN forces crossed the 38th parallel. Mao hesitated but caved in to Stalin's urgent reminders that as Moscow's ally in Asia it was Beijing's responsibility to resume Kim Il Sung's revolution. Stalin made it clear to Mao that he would directly engage the USSR in the Korean War at the time that American efforts threatened to jeopardize the future of world socialism. Russian historians Zubok and Pleshakov maintain that Stalin was directly challenging the legitimacy of the People's Republic of China. Mao had the duty, Stalin told him, "to fend off a regional imperialist offensive" led by the United States, while the USSR would wait and "save itself for an ultimate battle with the forces of imperialism."[103]

On October 16 the first Chinese armed volunteers crossed the Yalu River and fanned south. MacArthur's troops continued to drive north during mid-October. They encountered the first Chinese units forty miles south of the Yalu. American policy, however, did not change, and on October 31 the NSC and Truman approved a directive to MacArthur that ordered the occupation of North Korea.[104] The next day Chinese planes appeared along the Yalu, and Chinese troops began pouring over the river's bridges from Manchuria. In early November, MacArthur cabled Washington, declaring that "the only way to stop this reinforcement of the enemy is the destruction of the bridges by air attack."[105] The JCS directed him to proceed with bombing the northern borders, but restricted it to the "Korean end of the Yalu bridges." The NSC concurred with the JCS and authorized: "General MacArthur's directive should not be changed at present. Meantime, General MacArthur is free to do what he militarily can under his present directive without bombing Manchuria."[106] With United States bombing raids came a lull in the fighting. His confidence renewed, MacArthur began preparations for a new offensive that he claimed would

---

103. Christensen, *Useful Adversaries*, 174–175; Goncharov, Lewis, and Litai, *Uncertain Partners*, 168–202; Zubok and Pleshakov, *Inside the Kremlin's Cold War*, 67–68; LaFeber, *America, Russia, and the Cold War*, 114–115; Stueck, *The Korean War*, 52, 105–106.

104. Directive for the Occupation of North Korea, 31 October 1950, PSF-NSC, Box 210.

105. MacArthur cited in Schnabel and Watson, *History of the JCS*, III, 293.

106. Summary of Discussion at the 71st Meeting, 10 November 1950, PSF-NSC, Box 220.

bring about a final victory. Then, on November 26, as Mac-
Arthur began his final offensive and his forces closed in on
the border along the Yalu, two hundred thousand Chinese
troops counterattacked.[107] Thereafter, "an entirely new war," as
MacArthur defined it, began.[108] As his troops retreated south
toward the 38th parallel in disarray, MacArthur cabled that
he urgently needed more reinforcements; otherwise, he would
have to begin an evacuation of UN forces. As soon as Truman
received MacArthur's request, he called an emergency meeting
of the NSC on November 28. As in the instance of the Berlin
blockade nearly two and a half years earlier, the NSC provided
Truman the crisis forum he needed to reach a very difficult decision.[109]

   With the JCS, the three service secretaries, and their advisers present at the meeting, Bradley read MacArthur's cable. He
then told the council and the others that "the Chinese Communist offensive might be limited." Because the present JCS
directive "authorizes General MacArthur to take up defensive
positions," Bradley noted, no new directive would be needed at
least for the following day or two. After Bradley summed up
the situation in Korea, Marshall read a memorandum from the
military service secretaries. He told the NSC that the most important point raised in the memorandum was that the United
States "should not become engaged individually or as a member of the UN in a general war in China with the Chinese Communists." Bradley replied that the Joint Chiefs were against an
overt war with China, preferred waging a limited war, and
therefore advised that no additional troops be made available
to MacArthur. Vice President Barkley commented that the service secretaries' memorandum indicated a grave shortage of
manpower. He questioned whether without more reinforcements the UN troops could "hold the line." Marshall agreed
with Barkley that "it was a gloomy picture," and added that he
thought "the choice was between having our hands tied in a

---

   107. Stueck, *The Korean War*, 119; Schnabel and Watson, *History of the
JCS*, III, 321–335.
   108. MacArthur quote cited in Schnabel and Watson, *History of the JCS*,
III, 336.
   109. Ibid., 336–342; Minutes of the 73rd Meeting, 28 November 1950,
PSF-NSC, Box 210; Summary of Discussion at the 73rd Meeting, 28 November
1950, Ibid., Box 220.

war with China, or how we can withdraw with honor." Near the end of the meeting Acheson told the NSC that he believed "this development brings us much closer to the danger of a general war." Acheson emphasized that "we should not lose what we have." Then he advanced the argument that the administration needed to attempt to disengage from the Korean War in order for the United States to meet its commitment elsewhere. Acheson questioned whether MacArthur understood the directive and he told the NSC that it should be emphasized to MacArthur that American and UN policy was neither to occupy Korea nor to defeat the Chinese Communist troops there. Instead, he concluded: "The main objective we should try to achieve now is to terminate this Korean situation." After listening intently to the deliberations, Truman ended the meeting by telling the NSC that he believed "the most important thing now is to hold the line."[110]

The consensus that day had been unanimous. Earlier objectives that concentrated on the liberation, or rollback of all Communists from Korea, and the eventual postwar political unification of Korea were discarded. Truman and the NSC determined that by engaging in a general war with China or extending the war into China, the United States increased the risk of confrontation with the USSR in Western Europe. They therefore chose to limit the war. During the course of the NSC meeting the quest for the liberation of Korea had been eliminated, and containment again become the primary goal of American Cold War policy.

The consensus between State, Defense, and the Joint Chiefs that advanced the militarization of United States containment policy had begun officially with NSC 68. Coinciding were policies coordinated by the NSC that recommended greater military assistance to Israel and the Arab states as well as military aid for France's effort in Indochina. In Korea months later, the Cold War turned hot. And in the minds of many on the NSC it affirmed the basic premises of NSC 68. Although the July assessment of NSC 73/4 determined that the USSR posed no direct military threat of entering the Korean War, it warned that the United States could be faced with overt intervention of Chinese Communist military forces. Following the approval of

---

110. Ibid.; Stueck, *The Korean War*, 132–134.

NSC 73/4 as a working guide, a JCS proposal was adopted that recognized the wartime strategic importance of Taiwan. It signaled an end to the Department of State's efforts to maintain a neutral disengagement from Jiang, and provided the Department of Defense and the JCS with military justification for dispatching naval patrols into the Taiwan Strait and implementing aerial reconnaissance missions over China's southern coastline. NSC 81/1 of September called for the liberation, or rollback, of all Communist forces and influences from Korea, a point consistent with the recommendation of NSC 68 for "checking and rolling back" the Soviet Union's drive for hegemony. The rollback strategy met disaster when Chinese Communist forces entered the war in late November. In addition, Chinese intervention in Korea ended the efforts of the Department of State to accommodate non-Soviet forms of communism as well as instigate a split between the Soviet Union and the People's Republic of China. For the NSC, it reinforced the perception that the United States had to implement an activist, globalist, and militarized containment policy. By late 1950 any distinctions between vital and peripheral interests once articulated by the NSC had blurred. Thereafter, the national security of the United States and the security of the non-Communist world fused into a singular containment objective.

Chapter Six

Implementing Global Strategies

The wonder of it is how much was done.
(Dean G. Acheson, 1969)

The Korean War continued through the last two years of Truman's presidency and for six more months into 1953. Exempted from the Twenty-second Amendment of 1951 that denied a president more than two elected terms, Truman was, however, becoming physically weary and tiring of the responsibilities. As his rating in public opinion polls sunk to a low twenty-three percent in late 1951, Truman decided not to run for another full term. On March 29, 1952, he announced that he would not seek reelection. At the time he left office, the war brought the NSC to initiate significant changes in Truman's containment strategies regarding Western Europe, Japan, Indochina, and the Middle East. The council formulated several policies that helped the administration provide additional military assistance to Italy, Greece, Yugoslavia, and Spain. It further clarified and expanded CIA clandestine and covert operations during wartime, and authorized a coordinated program for foreign information and psychological warfare. United States security interests during the Korean War also gave the NSC cause for revised policies that strengthened the administration's economic and military support for Japan, the French effort in Indochina, and British influence in the Middle East.

166

In late November 1950, the Joint Chiefs sent a new directive to MacArthur to hold a line somewhere in Korea without substantial reinforcements, and inflict maximum damage on the enemy's positions. The JCS asked for MacArthur's comments on the directive and the situation in Korea. MacArthur's reply was a call for a widening of the war against China. He argued that if the United States or the UN understood "the State of War which has been forced upon us by the Chinese authorities," they would recognize the need for a naval blockade of China's coast, air and naval raids into Manchuria against industries contributing to the military, and the use of reinforcements from Jiang's forces both in Korea and on China's mainland.[1] MacArthur received no immediate reply from Washington regarding his proposal. Reports from the battlefield meanwhile worsened. In early January 1951, the Chinese launched a second offensive, driving MacArthur's forces south of the 38th parallel. General Matthew B. Ridgway, who had taken charge of the Eighth Army, retreated to Seoul, but was forced to evacuate the capital on January 4. Five days after the evacuation of Seoul the JCS informed MacArthur that any retaliatory actions against China must wait and that he must continue to defend Korea. MacArthur sent an immediate request for clarification to the Joint Chiefs, asking whether the administration's policy contemplated maintaining an indefinite military position in Korea or evacuating as soon as possible.[2]

When Truman received MacArthur's query he called a special meeting of the NSC.[3] Marshall read MacArthur's cable to the council and told the members that his first concern was "the state of morale in Korea." He proposed that Generals Collins and Vandenberg go to Korea to investigate. Truman and the NSC then approved a message that the JCS had proposed for MacArthur, emphasizing that the general hold the line as long as possible. Acheson said he believed that the administration needed to "let General MacArthur know more why

---

1. Collins, *War in Peacetime*, 246–248; Schnabel and Watson, *History of the JCS*, III, 397–400; Douglas MacArthur to the JCS, 30 December, *FRUS: 1950*, VII, 1630–1633; Goulden, *Korea*, 429–431.

2. Stueck, *The Korean War*, 127–130; Schnabel and Watson, *History of the JCS*, III, 406–411; Truman, *Years of Trial and Hope*, 433–434; Goulden, *Korea*, 433; *FRUS: 1951*, VII, pt. 1, 41–43, 55–56.

3. Truman, *Years of Trial and Hope*, 434.

The National Security Council, January 1951. From left to right: James S. Lay, Jr.; W. Stuart Symington; W. Averell Harriman; Walter Bedell Smith; Omar N. Bradley; George C. Marshall; Dean G. Acheson; Harry S. Truman; John W. Snyder. *(Courtesy of Bettmann Newsphotos, Inc./United Press International)*

it is desirable for us to stay in Korea." Marshall insisted that the message needed to clarify the importance of containing North Korean forces at the 38th parallel. Truman retorted that MacArthur "was liable to mix the political and military aspects anyway," but concluded that "we try to keep them clear." The NSC agreed that the Department of State should prepare a second message for MacArthur dealing with the politics of containment involved in Korea.[4] The next day Truman used State's draft to inform MacArthur of his goals in Korea. His personal message apparently relieved MacArthur, especially the president's statement that in the event of a withdrawal from Korea, the United States would "not accept the result politically or militarily until the aggression has been rectified." When Collins and Vandenberg arrived in Tokyo in mid-January, MacArthur informed them that he finally understood that he must remain in Korea indefinitely.[5] Despite the NSC's efforts, within two months MacArthur directly challenged Truman's policies to wage a limited war.

4. Summary of Discussion at the 79th Meeting, 13 January 1951, PSF-NSC, Box 200.
5. Truman, *Years of Trial and Hope*, 434–436; Acheson, *Present at the Creation*, 516; Collins, *War in Peacetime*, 254–255; Goulden, *Korea*, 445.

In mid-winter 1951 Ridgway's forces moved slowly back north toward the 38th parallel and recaptured Seoul. By the end of March his troops had reestablished a defensive position along the 38th parallel, removing any doubts about their ability to hold a line in Korea. As news of Ridgway's successes reached Washington, the Department of State began preparations for a UN cease-fire initiative.[6] In early March, MacArthur belittled Ridgway's limited war efforts with a barrage of public statements that would eventually give Truman reason to order his dismissal. By mid-March, still seeking total victory and the liberation of Korea, MacArthur began to exaggerate the military success of his campaigns. On March 24, he publicly demanded that the Chinese surrender before they met defeat on the battlefield. That unauthorized statement seriously damaged the Department of State's efforts to open UN armistice negotiations. The same week MacArthur demanded the Chinese surrender, he sent a letter to Congressman Joseph Martin, minority leader of the House of Representatives, criticizing the administration's policy of limited war in Korea as well as its refusal to use Jiang's troops for an offensive against China.[7]

MacArthur's proposals were in fact similar to two earlier recommendations during the darker days of the war that the NSC had considered but not adopted. In mid-January, the NSC staff issued a report that the JCS submitted to the council. The JCS called for a naval blockade of China, tactical air warfare against that nation, and increased anti-Communist guerrilla activities, using Nationalist troops from Taiwan, against and within China. Because the NSC found the report lacking a statement of American policy objectives, it referred it back to the NSC staff for further evaluation.[8] One week after the NSC considered the report, it received a different plan from Symington titled "Recommended Policies and Actions in Light of the

6. Truman, *Years of Trial and Hope*, 438–440; Goulden, *Korea*, 447–459.

7. Goulden, *Korea*, 478–485; Acheson, *Present at the Creation*, 528–530; Truman, *Years of Trial and Hope*, 440–442. For a complete account of events leading up to MacArthur's dismissal see Schnabel and Watson, *History of the JCS*, III, 505–562; Spanier, *The Truman-MacArthur Controversy*, 187–256.

8. NSC 101, "Courses of Action Relative to Communist China and Korea," 12 January 1951, PSF-NSC, Box 211; *FRUS: 1951*, VII, pt. 1, 79–81; Summary of Discussion at the 80th Meeting, 18 January 1951, PSF-NSC, Box 220.

Grave World Situation" (NSC 100) that called for an evacuation from Korea, followed by a nuclear attack against China by air and sea, and if necessary a nuclear campaign against the USSR.[9]

The primary concern of the NSC was should the administration use nuclear weapons to end the Korean War. Acheson observed that "if the United States followed certain courses recommended . . . it would probably bring on a third world war." Acheson pointed out, however, that NSC 100 contained "another idea . . . that we should at the present time make political use of the atomic bomb in our dealings with the Soviet Union." Symington agreed: "The bomb doesn't have to be a political threat, but it could well be a political ace." Truman had tested on his own the political merits and detriments of publicly suggesting that the atomic bomb had always been considered a weapon for use in Korea. At a press conference on November 30, 1950, he remarked that American efforts to wage a war against the People's Republic of China would include nuclear weapons. His comments provoked alarm in Western Europe and British Prime Minister Clement Attlee flew to Washington to urge American restraint.[10]

General Walter Bedell Smith, the new director of the CIA, then read an advance copy of an intelligence estimate before the council. It suggested that preventing the rearmament of Germany would be the more probable reason for the USSR's going to war. The estimate Smith insisted, demonstrated that a "grave danger of global war" existed if the administration pursued a policy to rearm Germany. Symington calculated that it might be more advantageous for the administration to scale back on conventional troops and "send other means of defending Western Europe." Bradley thought that because NSC 100 concerned United States "global policy" it should be referred to

9. NSC 100, "Recommended Policies and Actions in Light of the Grave World Situation," 11 January 1951, *Records of the National Security Council,* Parts 1–4: 1947–1953. Microfilm. (Washington, D.C.: University Publications of America, 1984).

10. Summary of Discussion at the 81st Meeting, 25 January 1951, PSF-NSC, Box 200; PPP:HST, 1950, 726–727; Ferrell, *Harry S. Truman,* 328–329; Hamby, *Man of the People,* 552–553; LaFeber, *America, Russia, and the Cold War,* 117–119; Stueck, *The Korean War,* 131.

the Departments of State and Defense. Truman, Acheson, Marshall, and other NSC members concurred that no action be taken on NSC 100 at that time until further study had been conducted.[11]

Although Truman and the council did not approve NSC 100, its existence made clear that the administration retained its option of using a nuclear threat if the circumstances warranted. Truman left the meeting with that in mind. Meanwhile, MacArthur may have learned through his Washington contacts of the pending NSC policies and determined that his own proposals for a wider war had finally achieved an impact on the war objectives of Truman and the NSC. On April 5, Congressman Martin read MacArthur's letter before the House of Representatives. When Truman heard the contents of the letter he decided to fire MacArthur. In exasperation on April 6, Truman wrote in his diary: "MacArthur shoots another political bomb. . . . This looks like the last straw. Rank insubordination . . . I've come to the conclusion that our Big General in the Far East must be recalled."[12]

The same day that Truman made his personal decision to recall MacArthur, he held a series of meetings with his national security advisers to discuss the matter. Truman's meeting with Bradley centered not on MacArthur but on Soviet military maneuvers in Manchuria and along the Pacific coast of Asia. Bradley told Truman that the USSR had increased its number of submarines stationed at Soviet bases in southern Sakhalin Island and at its Vladivostok base, and the USSR was engaged in troop maneuvers along the Yalu River. To deter direct Soviet intervention in the Korean War, Bradley urged, Truman should give serious consideration to a request by the Joint Chiefs for air strikes in Manchuria, and that he dispatch nuclear weapons to American bases in Okinawa and Guam. Truman did not call an emergency meeting of the NSC, but met privately with the new chair of the AEC, Gordon E. Dean. The president told Dean that he had a request from the JCS to release "nine

---

11. Summary of Discussion at the 81st meeting, 25 January 1951, PSF-NSC, Box 200.

12. Acheson, *Present at the Creation*, 520; Goulden, *Korea*, 484–486; Truman diary, 6 April 1951, in Ferrell, *Off the Record*, 210–211.

nuclears" to the custody of the air force. According to Dean, the president "hoped very much that there would be no necessity for using them; that before there was any decision to use them the matter would be fully explored by the special committee of the National Security Council." After Truman signed the transfer order for the bombs, Dean contacted newly appointed Executive Secretary James Lay to make sure that the NSC would be consulted on any plan to use the weapons.[13]

Truman's decision to transfer nuclear weapons to the Pacific was the second major policy he implemented without consulting the NSC. It remained top secret until after MacArthur's removal, and contributed to the final recommendation on April 8 by the Joint Chiefs that MacArthur be dismissed from his command. The general's political posturing and rank insubordination had undermined his credibility with Truman and the JCS, and neither would risk the chance of placing nuclear weapons in his control. Two days later, on April 10, Truman fired MacArthur and named Ridgway as UN Supreme Commander.[14]

The change in command led the Department of State to renew its efforts to open armistice negotiations with the People's Republic of China. In the spring of 1951 ground troops in Korea stalled along the 38th parallel, the war had become unpopular in the United States and among its allies, and the war effort was straining domestic politics and the economy. UN negotiations began in July at Kaesong, and after a brief disruption resumed in late October at Panmunjom, only to continue for nearly two more years.[15] As the situation improved in Korea

---

13. Michael Schaller, *Douglas MacArthur: The Far Eastern General* (New York: Oxford University Press, 1989), 235–236; Roger Dingman, "Atomic Diplomacy during the Korean War," *International Security* 13 (Winter 1988–89): 72–74; Anders, *Forging the Atomic Shield*, 137–143; Laura Belmonte, "Anglo-American Relations and the Dismissal of MacArthur," *Diplomatic History* 19 (Fall 1995): 662–663; Stueck, *The Korean War*, 67, 181.

14. For the steps that Truman took to dismiss MacArthur see Truman, *Years of Trial and Hope*, 442–450; Acheson, *Present at the Creation*, 521–522; Goulden, *Korea*, 548–586; Leffler, *A Preponderance of Power*, 406; idem, *The Specter of Communism*, 110–111; Stueck, *The Korean War*, 178–182. See also Belmonte, "Anglo-American Relations and the Dismissal of MacArthur" for an insightful analysis of British efforts to remove MacArthur.

15. Acheson, *Present at the Creation*, 529–538; Truman, *Years of Trial and Hope*, 455–462; Goulden, *Korea*, 548–586.

by early spring, the NSC staff began the revision of several containment policies, starting with Asia. The existing policy on Asia, NSC 48/2, had been accepted before the beginning of the Korean War. The dramatic changes of the war necessitated a revision. Renumbered NSC 48/5, the new version recommended several objectives in respect to Asia, the "ultimate objectives" of which would be the political, not military, unification of Korea through "appropriate UN machinery." The political unification of Korea, declared the document, would require the termination of all hostilities "under appropriate armistice arrangements," establishment of the ROK "over all Korea south of a northern boundary," withdrawal of non-Korean forces "by appropriate stages," and "the building of sufficient ROK military power to deter or repel a renewed North Korean aggression." After the achievement of these goals, a unification of the two Koreas might go forward.[16] NSC 48/5 also called for several current objectives in Asia while the political unification of Korea was being sought. Regarding Korea and the war there, it advised that the United States continue to oppose and penalize the aggressor; avoid extending hostilities "into a general war" with the Soviet Union or the People's Republic of China; continue the provision of military, economic, and political assistance for the defense of Taiwan; and expand American activities designed to "detach China as an effective ally of the U.S.S.R." NSC 48/5 suggested that the United States continue to assist nations in South and Southeast Asia "develop the will and ability to resist communism from within and without," conclude a peace treaty with Japan as well as the negotiation of a bilateral security agreement with Japan, and proceed with the provision of "timely and suitable military assistance" to the French effort in Indochina. Of all the objectives contained in NSC 48/5, the most significant was for the United States to limit the scope of fighting and end the conflict in Korea.[17]

Following the approval of NSC 48/5, Truman and the council received updated briefings on the course of the war and the

---

16. NSC 48/5, "United States Objectives, Policies and Courses of Action in Asia," 17 May 1951, *United States–Vietnam Relations*, 425–445; *FRUS: 1951*, VII, pt. 1, 35–37, 51–54, 439–442.

17. NSC 48/5 superseded policy statements in NSC 48/2 and the NSC 13 Series, the NSC 34 Series, the NSC 37 Series, and the NSC 81 Series constituted completed action on the NSC 101 Series.

situation in the Far East. By the summer of 1951 it was clear that Ridgway's counterattack was putting Chinese forces in trouble. In late June the NSC and the president were informed by director of central intelligence Smith that a special estimate revealed potential Soviet involvement in the war. Smith told Truman and the council that the CIA had evidence that "the Kremlin could not be certain that UN forces would not defeat the Chinese, unless the Russians intervened." Smith also warned that if UN forces approached Soviet borders the USSR could be provoked into entering the war.[18]

Acheson and Truman agreed that the success of UN forces in the field had placed the administration in a dilemma. "The better we do in Korea," Acheson observed, "the closer we get to World War III." Truman expressed concern that if a cease-fire was arranged, "popular clamor" for a quick withdrawal would leave "Korea wide open" for the USSR. "On balance," Acheson concluded, "an uneasy settlement in Korea would be less dangerous" than continuing the war effort. No further discussion followed, yet it became clear that Truman and the NSC were anxious for a conclusion to war, and aware that as the war continued, Soviet intervention loomed as a greater possibility. But the armistice negotiations were slow and tedious, and the United States found itself fighting largely alone, with UN allies seeking a way out. Soon thereafter, the JCS directed Ridgway to attack enemy forces and inflict maximum losses so the United States might "create conditions favorable to a settlement."[19]

By late 1951, as Ridgway's forces continued to hammer away at North Korean and Chinese units, the armistice talks had bogged down over demarcation and inspection arrangements. The Joint Chiefs became concerned about the prolonged negotiations and submitted a draft report to the NSC for consideration. It called for a review of United States military policy in Korea in the event that armistice negotiations failed. Instead of presenting the JCS report to the council, the Senior NSC Staff used it in connection with a similar study. In

---

18. Summary of Discussion at the 95th Meeting, 28 June 1951, PSF-NSC, Box 220.

19. Ibid.; Schnabel and Watson, *History of the JCS*, III, 492–495.

early December 1951, the staff finally completed a statement that Truman approved.[20]

"United States Objectives and Courses of Action in Korea" (NSC 118/2), the new policy statement, noted the limited war objectives recommended earlier, but added suggestions by the JCS concentrating on actions to be taken if an armistice in Korea could not be concluded. If no armistice materialized, NSC 118/2 recommended, the United States should intensify military operations in Korea. In addition, restrictions were to be removed "against advances or attacks in Korea," including restraints on unilateral air force strikes against Chinese air bases, if the president approved, and American bombing of "Yalu River dams and power installations" on the Korean side of the river. NSC 118/2 also proposed "a vigorous campaign of covert operations," designed to aid anti-Communist guerrillas in Korea and Communist China and disrupt enemy communications. It concluded that in case the adversary "deliberately" delayed armistice negotiations in order to increase purposefully offensive capabilities, the United States should "increase pressures on the aggressor by stages," including economic and political pressures "through U.N. and diplomatic channels," and execute military actions proposed in the event of an armistice failure.[21]

During the first four months of 1951 Truman and the NSC had been preoccupied with MacArthur's challenges and Soviet military maneuvers along North Korea's borders. Following MacArthur's removal, the council clarified the limited war objectives in Korea that the State and Defense Departments and the JCS had articulated. Progress toward ending the war began to materialize in UN negotiations that were under way by summer. Negotiations dragged on through 1952 and by spring were locked on the issue of prisoner-of-war exchange. With the ground war in Korea stalemated and no armistice imminent, the administration resorted to suggestions in NSC 118/2. In an attempt to force a settlement, the United States began satura-

---

20. Goulden, *Korea*, 567–585; Acheson, *Present at the Creation*, 537–538; NSC 118, "United States Courses of Action in Korea," 9 November 1951, PSF-NSC, Box 216; NSC 118/1, "United States Objectives and Courses of Action in Korea," 7 December 1951, *FRUS: 1951*, VII, pt. 1, 1259–1263.

21. NSC 118/2, "United States Objectives and Courses of Action in Korea," 20 December 1951, *FRUS: 1951*, VII, pt. 1, 1382–1399.

tion bombings of North Korean cities and Yalu River power installations. The strategy of saturation bombing, however, produced no formal armistice before Truman left office.[22] The Korean War continued for six more months into 1953. By the time an armistice was concluded on July 27, 1953, the war had initiated significant changes or modifications of containment policies and strategies regarding Western Europe, the intelligence community, Japan, Southeast Asia, and the Middle East.

*   *   *

Even as UN troops retreated south of the 38th parallel in 1951, the war's problems did not dislodge the NSC's interests from what had been its first Cold War priority—the defense of Western Europe. The North Atlantic Treaty of 1949 had merely initiated a collective security alliance that included the United States, the United Kingdom, France, Italy, the Netherlands, Canada, Denmark, Norway, Belgium, Luxembourg, Portugal, and Iceland. Despite United States military supply assistance to Western Europe under MDAP in 1949 and 1950, the administration made no military ground or air force commitments to Western Europe. When the Korean War began, the ability of European NATO members to defend themselves from Soviet aggression remained uncertain.[23]

With the beginning of the war, the NSC considered rearming the rest of Western Europe. In 1951 it completed several policy recommendations that it had initiated in mid-1950 that justified the rearmament of Italy, Germany, Greece, Turkey, and Spain on the basis of their importance to America's containment policies and their overall contribution to European defense.

In January 1951 the council adopted, and Truman approved, "The Position of the U.S. with Regard to the Communist Threat to Italy" (NSC 67/3) which recommended that the United States revise its peace treaty with Italy. The treaty had placed limitations on Italy's military buildup and restricted the

---

22. Acheson, *Present at the Creation*, 652–657; Goulden, *Korea*, 587–592, 618–623; Stueck, *The Korean War*, 220–298.
23. Acheson, *Present at the Creation*, 437; Leffler, *A Preponderance of Power*, 383–385.

possession of certain types of weapons. NSC 67/3 declared that it was "important to the security of the United States and other NATO countries that Italy meet in full its defense obligations as may be agreed in NATO." The Department of Defense supported the conclusions of the NSC report, and suggested that under the treaty the Italian army could not, "according to NATO standards, attain an effective strength and organization."[24] In November, British, French, and American negotiators acted to remove the treaty's limitations and the administration lifted all restrictions on military equipment to Italy under the MDAP.[25]

Unlike the arming of Italy, which had been accepted as a member of NATO in 1949, the rearmament of West Germany posed special problems for Washington's European allies. In the summer of 1950 the NSC considered reports from the Department of Defense and the JCS that recommended the arming of West Germany and establishing a German contribution to the the newly proposed Western European Defense Community. At that time, Truman and the Department of State believed the military's requests were premature.[26] But the war in Korea convinced Acheson that a forward strategy in Europe would be vital as well. Both were divided countries with an armed Communist government on one side. West Germany, Acheson concluded, might therefore become the next theater for deterring Soviet aggression.[27]

---

24. NSC 67/3, "The Position of the U.S. with Regard to the Communist Threat to Italy," 5 January 1951, PSF-NSC, Box 207; *FRUS: 1951,* IV, 543–545; "The Effects of Limitations Imposed by the Italian Peace Treaty on Italian Obligations Under N.A.T.O. Plans," 17 September 1951, *FRUS: 1951,* IV, 670–671.

25. Dean Acheson to Alberto Tarchiani, 21 December 1951, *Department of State Bulletin* (3 December 1951): 1050.

26. NSC 71, "United States Policy Toward Germany," 8 June 1950; NSC 71/1, "The Rearmament of Western Germany," 3 July 1950, PSF-NSC, Box 208; Memorandum, Dean Acheson to Harry Truman, 30 June 1950, Ibid.; Memorandum, Harry Truman to Dean Acheson, 16 June 1950, Ibid. The European Defense Community concept would be defeated by 1954 by France. However, at that time West German rearmament was underway.

27. Acheson, *Present at the Creation,* 437; Lawrence W. Martin, "The American Decision to Rearm Germany," in Harold Stein, ed., *American Civil-Military Decisions* (Birmingham: University of Alabama Press, 1963), 650. For a thorough assessment of Acheson's position see Lawrence S. Kaplan, "Dean Acheson and the Atlantic Community," in Douglas Brinkley, ed., *Dean Acheson and the Making of U.S. Foreign Policy* (London: Macmillan, 1993), 28–54.

Secretary of State Dean G. Acheson and President Truman discuss NATO policy, December 1950. *(Abbie Rowe; Courtesy of Harry S. Truman Library)*

At the same time that MacArthur's forces moved into North Korea the Departments of State and Defense sent a joint recommendation to the NSC that focused on Europe. "United States Position Regarding Strengthening the Defense of Europe and the Nature of Germany's Contribution Thereto" (NSC 82) advised that United States military forces be deployed to defend Europe and proposed a total combat-ready force in Western Europe of "about 4 infantry divisions and the equivalent of 1½ armoured divisions, 8 tactical air groups, and appropriate naval forces." It also urged that Americans hold all critical NATO positions, including that of the Supreme Commander of the European Defense Force. The more important point was that NATO "should proceed without delay with the formation of adequate West German units." The document emphasized that in the time that West German units could be trained and equipped "the appropriate framework for their integration into a European defense force" would be developed. NSC 82 did not go before the council for discussion. The NSC concurred, however, in its provisions, and in September 1950 Truman approved it. Nevertheless, he remained reluctant publicly to endorse West German rearmament and participation in NATO.

In announcing that the administration would send four combat divisions to Western Europe, he did not mention proposals for West Germany.[28]

Truman's endorsement of NSC 82 allowed Acheson to prepare for a new American policy toward Germany, and at the fifth North Atlantic Treaty Council session in New York he presented the substance of NSC 82. With little debate the delegates approved an integrated defense force for Western Europe, as well as an American Supreme Commander of NATO. A majority of delegates also agreed in principle that West Germany should participate in the defense of Europe. French opposition to German inclusion within a European army stalled until late in the year a final decision on West Germany's rearmament. In Brussels, at the next session of the North Atlantic Treaty Council, General Dwight D. Eisenhower was confirmed as the Supreme Commander of NATO, and the French agreed to accept German combat regimental teams, providing they would never exceed twenty percent of all NATO forces. The rearmament of West Germany and its future membership in NATO, however, remained unresolved. The process of formulating the European Defense Community under NATO continued through the end of Truman's presidency.[29]

In August 1951 the NSC and Truman concurred in another policy statement on West German rearmament that State and Defense had jointly presented. "Definition of United States Policy on Problems of the Defense of Europe and the German Contribution" (NSC 115) again called for West German participation in the European defense alliance, but recommended that NATO and the process of continental European integration must resolve the "individual fears" of the Europeans.[30] The North Atlantic Council ministers meeting in Lisbon in February 1952, agreed that the Allied occupation of West Germany

---

28. NSC 82, "United States Position Regarding Strengthening the Defense of Europe and the Nature of Germany's Contribution Thereto," 8 September 1950, NSC, "Policies of the Government, 1950," 5–9, Ibid., Box 195.

29. NSC Progress Report on NSC 82, 9 October 1950, Ibid., Box 209; Martin, "The American Decision to Rearm Germany," 657–659; Leffler, *A Preponderance of Power*, 408–415, 453–463; Acheson, *Present at the Creation*, 440, 457–459; General Lucius D. Clay Oral History Interview.

30. NSC 115, "Definition of United States Policy on Problems of the Defense of Europe and the German Contribution," 1 August 1951, approved by NSC Memoranda Action on 30 July 1951, **PSF-NSC**, Box 193.

would end and that twelve West German military divisions could enter a European Defense Community. The Lisbon session also approved an American resolution that called for doubling NATO forces to fifty divisions by the end of the year.[31] Thus, after several months of negotiations the policy statements recommended in NSC 82 and NSC 115 became reality. By the time Truman left office, NATO's conventional military forces had secured the defense of Western Europe as far as the Elbe River and West Germany would be making preparations for NATO membership by 1955. At the same time that the NSC proposed the rearmament of Italy and West Germany, it recommended adding Greece and Turkey to the NATO alliance. Both had received substantial military assistance, yet the NSC believed that both remained vulnerable to future Soviet military aggression. The more important consideration was that Greece and Turkey were strategic geographical positions for the NATO defense of Western Europe and for defending the oil-rich Arab states of the Middle East. In May of 1951 the NSC adopted and Truman approved two new policy reports, "The Position of the United States with Respect to Greece" (NSC 103/1) and "The Position of the United States with Respect to Turkey" (NSC 109). Acheson followed up with a request that the North Atlantic Council invite Greece and Turkey to join NATO. After changes were made in the NATO charter, delegates at the Lisbon session in February 1952 voted formally to admit Greece and Turkey. Thereafter, the NATO defense system extended from the Western hemisphere to the Caucasus Mountain borders of the USSR.[32]

The advent of the Korean War also caused Truman and the NSC concern about the vulnerability of Yugoslavia and Spain to Soviet attack. Although the NSC did not consider either country for NATO membership, it did recommend military assistance for both, as well as bilateral military cooperation with Spain.

The case of Yugoslavia had been important since 1949, when the NSC proposed economic assistance to Belgrade. In

31. LaFeber, *America, Russia, and the Cold War*, 128–129.
32. NSC 103/1, "The Position of the United States with Respect to Greece," 14 February 1951, PSF-NSC, Box 211; NSC 109, "The Position of the United States with Respect to Turkey," 11 May 1951, *FRUS: 1951*, V, 1148–1162.

early 1951 Yugoslav officials sought assurances from the administration that in the event Yugoslavia was attacked by the USSR or Soviet bloc countries, they would receive direct military aid from the United States. In a revised report on Yugoslavia, NSC 18/6, the NSC advised that in the event of a Soviet or Soviet-sponsored attack on Yugoslavia, direct military assistance, training, and technical support be provided the Belgrade government on "a status equal to that of N.A.T.O. countries," and "in cooperation" with them.[33] Truman agreed with NSC 18/6 and authorized that all new assistance to Yugoslavia be granted from MDAP. No other NSC policy change toward Yugoslavia occurred during Truman's presidency, but the help that the administration provided from 1949 through 1952 drew the former Soviet bloc nation closer to the Western alliance and secured the maintenance of an independent Yugoslavia for the future.[34]

Strategically located on the Iberian peninsula and the Atlantic seaboard, Spain as early as 1948 had drawn the attention of the NSC. At that time the council recommended that the administration normalize political and economic relations and the military services urged the acquisition of naval and air base rights in Spain. Truman, however, refused to consider either proposal. He not only personally disliked Spain's dictator, General Francisco Franco, but respected the practice among Washington's European allies of isolating Spain for its fascist ideology and military regime.[35] As the administration's attention shifted toward developing the European Defense Community and strengthening the NATO alliance, Spain again appeared on the agenda of the NSC. In 1950 the Department of Defense initiated a study on Spain that it ultimately submitted for NSC consideration. "United States Policy Toward Spain" (NSC 72/1) urged the United States and its allies to seek "mili-

33. CIA, NIE-29, "Probability of an Invasion of Yugoslavia in 1951," 6 March 1951, PSF-NSC, Box 211; NSC Progress Report on NSC 18/4 and NSC 18/2, 16 October 1950, Ibid., Box 209; NSC 18/6, "The Position of the United States with Respect to Yugoslavia," 7 March 1951, Ibid., Box 211.

34. NSC 18/6, "The Position of the United States with Respect to Yugoslavia," 7 March 1951, Ibid., Box 211; Leffler, *A Preponderance of Power*, 417–418.

35. NSC 3, "United States Policy Toward Spain," 17 December 1948, NSC, "Policies of the Government, 1947–1948," 28, PSF-NSC, Box 195; Theodore J. Lowi, "Bases in Spain," in Stein, *American Civil-Military Decisions*, 673–676.

tary accessibility and military cooperation with Spain" in order to ensure the fullest defense of Western Europe from Soviet attack. Believing that military cooperation with the Franco government might be a hindrance to NATO objectives, Truman returned the proposed policy to the NSC for further evaluation.[36]

A bloc supportive of Spain nonetheless formed in Congress in alliance with military service representatives. In conjunction, they pushed through a $62.5 million loan for Franco's government. In early 1951 the JCS proposed that the United States recommend NATO membership for Spain.[37] After several months of work, the NSC staff issued a report incorporating advice from the Department of State that Spain's membership in NATO be delayed in favor of a military and mutual security arrangement between Spain and the United States. In late June the NSC approved the revised policy as NSC 72/6, and after careful consideration Truman gave his assent. To implement NSC 72/6, Truman sent a military team to Madrid for negotiations over base rights. In November 1953 an official treaty was concluded, providing that in return for the use of Spanish bases and the construction of new American air and naval bases, the administration agreed to supply Spain nearly $250 million in military assistance.[38] The eventual acquisition of the rights to establish bases in Spain provided an important defensive position for Western Europe, and ensured that Franco's government would not become politically neutral in any future Cold War conflict or military confrontation.

Policies formulated by the NSC that provided for the rearmament of Italy and West Germany, additional MDAP assistance for Yugoslavia, and the admission of Greece and Turkey to NATO posed no difficulty for the council in 1952 since in light of the Korean War the State and Defense Departments

---

36. NSC 72, NSC 72/1, "United States Policy Toward Spain," 8 June, 3 July 1950, PSF-NSC, Box 208; Memorandum, Dean Acheson to Harry Truman, 30 June 1950, Ibid.

37. LaFeber, *America, Russia, and the Cold War*, 127; Lowi, "Bases in Spain," 677–682; NSC 72/3, "United States Policy Toward Spain," 29 January 1951, PSF-NSC, Box 211.

38. NSC 72/6, "United States Policy Toward Spain," 27 June 1951, PSF-NSC, Box 213; NSC Progress Report on NSC 72/6, 7 September 1951, Ibid., Box 214; *FRUS: 1951*, IV, pt. 1, 818–822, 834–835; LaFeber, *America, Russia, and the Cold War*, 127–128.

ICELAND

NORTH
SEA

NORWAY

SWEDEN

FINLAND

IRELAND   UNITED
           KINGDOM   DENMARK

ATLANTIC

OCEAN

BALTIC SEA

U.S.S.R.

NETH.

G.D.R.   POLAND

BELGIUM

F.R.G.

CZECH.

LUX.

FRANCE   SW.   AUST.

HUNG.

ROMANIA

BLACK SEA

PORTUGAL

SPAIN

ITALY

YUGOSLAVIA

BULGARIA

ALB.

GREECE

MEDITERRANEAN SEA

TURKEY

0   KILOMETERS   300

0   MILES   200

KJS

**KEY TO ABBREVIATED COUNTRY
NAMES**

	NATO MEMBERS
	SOVIET BLOC COUNTRIES
	OTHER COUNTRIES

ALB.	ALBANIA
AUST.	AUSTRIA
CZECH.	CZECHOSLOVAKIA
F.R.G.	FEDERAL REPUBLIC OF
	GERMANY
G.D.R.	GERMAN DEMOCRATIC
	REPUBLIC
HUNG.	HUNGARY
LUX.	LUXEMBOURG
NETH.	NETHERLANDS
SW.	SWITZERLAND

Map 6.   NATO Europe (1952)

183

were in agreement that the organization of a European Defense Community was critical. A policy for Spain's membership in NATO, however, required coordination by the council. The Defense Department and the JCS argued that a complete defense of Western Europe necessitated Spain's military participation in the European Defense Community. Truman's reluctance to accept the proposal delayed approval of the policy recommendation. When NSC 72/6 merged with the position of the Department of Defense and the Joint Chiefs the Department of State's suggestion that Spain's membership in NATO be delayed until official bilateral military arrangements were made, Truman changed his mind. The work of the council had been indispensible.

*   *   *

During the Korean War both the military services and the executive departments demanded greater intelligence information, psychological warfare, and covert paramilitary operations than the CIA provided. Coinciding with the Korean War was the replacement of Hillenkoetter with General Smith. During his tenure the CIA entered a phase of rapid growth with new planning, management, and implementation mechanisms as well as additional personnel added to clandestine intelligence and covert operations. To improve the CIA's intelligence estimates Smith created a separate Office of National Estimates, and appointed as its chief William Langer, a professor of diplomatic history at Harvard University and former World War II director of OSS Research and Analysis. Then to develop timely coordination of intelligence reports, he insisted that intelligence units in the Department of State and the military services participate in the drafting of the office's estimates.[39] Smith spent much effort as well in streamlining the coordination of CIA clandestine operations. In January 1951 he re-

---

39. Jones, *The CIA and American Democracy*, 67; Ray S. Cline, *Secrets, Spies, and Scholars: Blueprint of the Essential CIA* (Washington, D.C.: Acropolis Books, 1976), 111–112; Montague, *General Walter Bedell Smith as Director of Central Intelligence*, 129–140. Cline worked with Langer at that time. The CIA's National Intelligence Estimates (NIE) replaced the earlier monthly reports "Review of the World Situation," which were discontinued on 1 December 1950.

cruited Allen Dulles to serve as deputy director for plans at the CIA. Dulles managed the CIA's two units responsible for collecting clandestine intelligence, the OPC and the Office of Special Operations. In August 1951 Dulles became deputy director of central intelligence. The following year, the NSC approved the official merger of OPC and the Office of Special Operations into a new Directorate of Plans, headed by Frank Wisner.[40]

The major growth within the CIA during the Korean War occurred in the clandestine services. From 1950 to 1952 the OPC grew from about three hundred staff members to nearly ten times that number, and included an additional three thousand overseas contract personnel. At the same time its budget expanded from $4.7 million to $82 million, and its field stations increased from seven to forty-seven.[41] Covert operations, as opposed to espionage, were becoming the primary task of the CIA.[42] Both the Department of State and the JCS recommended the use of covert paramilitary operations to augment regular military operations in Korea and China.[43] The NSC, moreover, had described the USSR as waging a worldwide "struggle for men's minds" and called for a counteroffensive that would include covert as well as psychological, economic, and political warfare against Communist regimes.[44] In response to the growing paramilitary support in Korea, Truman and the NSC approved in October 1951 "an intensification of covert action" and granted greater responsibility to the DCI in carrying out covert operations.[45]

Psychological warfare, another strategy that owed much to the Korean War and the NSC, had been of interest to Truman as early as 1949, when he approved a coordinated program for

40. Ray S. Cline, *Secrets, Spies and Scholars*, 113–114; Prados, *Presidents' Secret Wars*, 82–85; Montague, *General Walter Bedell Smith as Director of Central Intelligence*, 4, 217–218, 220–227.
41. Cline, *Secrets, Spies and Scholars*, 115; Church Committee, 31.
42. Jones, *The CIA and American Democracy*, 68; Church Committee, 38.
43. Church Committee, 31. For details on the paramilitary operations conducted or developed by the CIA in Korea or China see Prados, *Presidents' Secret Wars*, 61–78, 88–89; Alfred H. Paddock, Jr., *U.S. Army Special Warfare— Its Origins: Psychological and Unconventional Warfare, 1941–1952* (Washington, D.C.: National Defense University Press, 1982); William M. Leary, *Perilous Missions: Civil Air Transport and CIA Covert Operations in Asia* (University, AL: The University of Alabama Press, 1984).
44. Church Committee, 32.
45. Ibid.; Prados, *Presidents' Secret Wars*, 84.

foreign information and psychological warfare within the Department of State.[46] In April 1950, in response to Soviet propaganda and jamming of Voice of America signals, Truman called for a "Campaign of Truth," directing information specialists to counter "Communist-inspired lies" about the United States.[47] A few months later, the Department of State submitted "A Plan for National Psychological Warfare" (NSC 74). The Senior NSC Staff also prepared a reference memorandum on the subject. In January 1951, the NSC considered the staff's memorandum, and Truman referred it, along with JCS comments, to Souers and the BOB for further study.[48] In response to Truman's request, Souers submitted a recommendation that called for the establishment of an interagency Psychological Strategy Board, made up of the undersecretary of state, the deputy secretary of defense, the DCI, and a representative of the JCS, and headed by a director appointed by the president. Reporting directly to the NSC, the Psychological Strategy Board would authorize and coordinate all national psychological operations, policies, and programs. Truman approved the recommendations of Souers and the BOB and, in a secret directive, authorized the creation of the board.[49]

The first director of the Psychological Strategy Board that Truman appointed was Gordon Gray, former secretary of the army. Gray served from July 1951 until February 1952, when he resigned to return to the presidency of the University of North Carolina. Later Gray would recall that he had assumed the position at a time when the United States "had to do more than we had done in the past to win and hold the confidence of our friends abroad and weaken the will of our enemies."[50] Al-

---

46. See earlier reference to NSC 43, "Planning for Wartime Conduct of Overt Psychological Warfare," 23 March 1949.

47. PPP-HST, 260–264.

48. NSC 74, "A Plan for National Psychological Warfare," 10 July 1950, Appendix C. Annotated List of NSC Reports, NSC, "Policies of the Government, 1950," 121, PSF-NSC, Box 195; Memorandum, James Lay to the NSC, "The National Psychological Effort," 14 September 1950, Ibid., Box 210; Minutes of the 77th Meeting, 4 January 1951, Ibid.; "Whispers," *U.S. News and World Report*, 9 March 1951, 6.

49. "Psychological Strategy Board," NSC, "Policies of the Government, 1950," 168–169, PSF-NSC, Box 195; Montague, *General Walter Bedell Smith as Director of Central Intelligence*, 204–205.

50. Gordon Gray to Harry Truman, and attached "The PSB Concept," 22 February 1952, HTP-WHCF, Box 165, HSTL, Independence, Missouri; Prados,

though the Psychological Strategy Board had difficulty compelling other agencies, particularly the CIA, to follow its policy decisions, it coordinated a number of psychological warfare plans that the NSC had authorized and the administration implemented. The first Psychological Strategy Board plan, approved in late 1951, established international programs under the Mutual Security Agency and the Department of State to resettle and provide for emigrés from Soviet bloc nations. Others executed in 1952 included a psychological operations program designed to promote UN Korean War cease-fire negotiations, an emergency plan in the event Korean armistice negotiations broke down, and establishment of national objectives to be executed upon presidential proclamation in the event of a general war.[51]

The Campaign of Truth that Truman and the NSC had developed as psychological warfare included an increase in the broadcasting efforts of the Voice of America, greater intelligence support for the Voice of America, and the expansion of the Department of State's international information and cultural exchange programs. Among other devices was the placing of American business ads in foreign magazines and newspapers and on foreign radio programs as well as selling calendars abroad that depicted scenes of life in the United States.[52] Along with the OPC's support for Radio Free Europe was the funding by the CIA and the OPC of radio broadcasting operations for a new program, Radio Liberty. Headed by American Committee for Freedom for the Peoples of the USSR, by 1951 Radio Liberty was beaming American information programs directly into the

---

Presidents' Secret Wars, 86–87; Gordon Gray Oral History Interview, Oral History Collection, HSTL, Independence, Missouri. Successors of Gray included Dr. Raymond B. Allen and Admiral Alan G. Kirk.

51. Appendix D to No. 6, "The National Psychological Program" of NSC 135, Summary of a Report from the CIA, 1 August 1952, PSF-NSC, Box 218; Report to the President, NSC Reporting Unit, Brief No. 6, "The National Psychological Effort," 2 September 1952, Ibid.; PHT-RPSB, Boxes 1, 2, 8, 14, 31, 32, 33, HSTL, Independence, Missouri.

52. NSC 66/1, "Intelligence Support for the Voice of America with Regard to Soviet Jamming," 19 January 1951, adopted by NSC Memoranda Action on 27 February 1951, approved by Truman on 28 February 1951, PSF-NSC, Box 193; Edward W. Barrett, "U.S. Informational Aims in the Cold War," *Department of State Bulletin* (19 June 1950): 992–995; John M. Begg, "The American Idea: Package It for Export," *Department of State Bulletin* (12 March 1951): 409–412.

Soviet Union. The most innovative psychological warfare strategy conceived during the last years of Truman's presidency involved a Free Europe Committee balloon launch that dropped millions of anti-Communist leaflets over Soviet bloc countries in August 1951.[53]

In addition to psychological warfare organization and implementation, Truman and the NSC expanded the collection of communications, or signals intelligence, under the Armed Forces Security Agency. Composed of the three military services signals intelligence units, the Armed Forces Security Agency monitored Soviet signals and radio messages routinely until late 1952. It was replaced by the National Security Agency in November 1952. The National Security Agency reported to the Department of Defense and became the sole agency responsible for the collection of intelligence concerning signals communications. Operating under the advisory body of the United States Communication Intelligence Board, which reported to the NSC and the CIA, the National Security Agency did not receive its official status until Truman in December 1952 issued an NSC intelligence directive for collection of signals communications. Within weeks after he approved the creation of the National Security Agency, Truman left office. American signals intelligence operations and systems remained thereafter as one of the closely guarded secrets of the Cold War.[54]

From late 1948 the Departments of State and Defense had differed on terms for Japan's peace treaty. But because the Korean War intensified the NSC's concerns for the security of Japan, the two departments resolved their differences. In the fall of 1950, they issued a joint memorandum to Truman suggesting that the United States proceed with the final phase of negotiations for a peace treaty. Truman approved the memorandum and sent it to the staff of the NSC, which also concurred.[55] Sim-

---

53. Mickelson, *America's Other Voice*, 56, 63–67; Prados, *Presidents' Secret Wars*, 35; Jones, *The CIA and American Democracy*, 60.

54. James Bamford, *The Puzzle Palace: A Report on America's Most Secret Agency* (Boston: Houghton Mifflin, 1982), 2–3; John Prados, *The Soviet Estimate: U.S. Intelligence Analysis and Russian Military Strength* (New York: Dial Press, 1982), 27.

55. NSC 60/1, "Japanese Peace Treaty," 8 September 1950, NSC, "Policies of the Government, 1950," 15–17, PSF-NSC, Box 195; Leffler, *A Preponderance of Power*, 391–393.

ply titled "Japanese Peace Treaty" (NSC 60/1), the policy outlined the terms Truman's leading negotiator, John Foster Dulles, had followed in his month-by-month deliberations with Japan and the Allied powers. It recommended major stipulations necessary for the formulation of a final treaty. The treaty would become effective only when American interests dictated and "in no event until after favorable resolution of the present United States military situation in Korea." It would provide that "foreign forces unacceptable to the United States not be permitted" in the Japanese islands south of Sakhalin and the Kurile Islands. The treaty was to assure that all Japanese resources "be denied to the USSR." It must guarantee continued "United States strategic trusteeship over the Mariana, Caroline, and Marshall Islands," as well as "United States exclusive strategic control" of Marcus Island, the Ryukyu Islands, and the southern Nanpo Shoto Islands. The treaty would not prohibit Japanese self-defense, would provide for initial garrisoning in Japan of "forces acceptable to the United States under a United States military command," would not prohibit American forces garrisoned in Japan from putting down "large-scale internal riots and disturbances" if requested by the Japanese government, and would guarantee the United States "the right to maintain armed forces in Japan, however, for so long, and to such extent as it deems necessary."[56]

After the NSC specified the major terms of the treaty and Dulles secured them in text and ratification, a convention of world delegates was called for its signing. In early September 1951, some fifty nations attended the San Francisco Conference. When the conference agreed to follow the strict rules that the United States had established prohibiting any alteration of the treaty, Soviet, Czechoslovak, and Polish delegates walked out. Despite Soviet protest, forty-nine nations signed the treaty on September 8, restoring Japan's sovereign status and opening the way for the end of occupation by April 1952.[57] The Japanese Peace Treaty was nonpunitive and free of stipulations, and it

56. Ibid.
57. "The Position of the United States Delegation at the San Francisco Peace Conference," 29 August 1951, Ibid.; Leffler, *A Preponderance of Power*, 432; Schaller, *The American Occupation of Japan*, 293–294; Acheson, *Present at the Creation*, 541–550.

looked to create a stable and economically prosperous non-Communist Japan.[58] Nevertheless, the NSC concluded that one additional matter needed clarification—the rearmament of Japan and its defensive alignment with the United States.

In February 1952, the Department of State sent Truman a draft report for interim policy guidelines on Japan. Truman agreed with the report's basic objective, that the security of Japan was too important to America's containment policies and hegemonic interests in the Pacific for hostile forces to gain control of any part of its territory. Truman sent the report to the NSC, which agreed and issued a statement of its own, "Interim Policy with Respect to Japan" (NSC 125).[59] The Senior NSC Staff used it in preparing a policy recommendation that it had under way on the security of Japan. In July 1952, the staff completed the work and issued NSC 125/2, which declared that the United States "would fight to prevent hostile forces from gaining control of any part" of Japan. It recommended that the administration develop Japan's military strength and "capability for self-defense" so that it could contribute to the security of the Pacific area, develop a prosperous economy and politically stable representative government, and "return to the international community." NSC 125/2 advised in addition that the United States "in the foreseeable future" retain armed forces in Japan and the Pacific to strengthen the security of Japan from any military threat by Soviet or Chinese Communist forces.[60]

By late 1952 economic assistance and military was augmenting Japan's National Police Force and Maritime Security Force. The security arrangement outlined in NSC 125/2 proceeded slowly, and the Japanese government resisted American

---

58. For the context of the Japanese Peace Treaty see United States Department of State, *American Foreign Policy: Basic Documents 1950–1955*, Volume II (Washington, D.C.: G.P.O., 1957), 425–440.

59. Memorandum, Acting Secretary of State and Secretary of Defense to Harry Truman, 15 February 1952, *FRUS: 1952–1954*, XIV, pt. 2, 1159–1165; NSC 125, "Interim Policy with Respect to Japan," Appendix B. Annotated List of NSC Reports, NSC, "Policies of the Government and the United States of America Relating to the National Security, Volume V, 1952," 141, PHT-NSC, Box 17.

60. NSC 125/1, NSC 125/2, "United States Objectives and Courses of Action with Respect to Japan," 18 July, 7 August 1952, *FRUS: 1952–1954*, XIV, pt. 2, 1300–1308; Summary of Discussion at the 121st Meeting, PSF-NSC, Box 220; Memorandum, James Lay to Harry Truman, 7 August 1952, Ibid., Box 218.

pressure for rearmament. As a result, for years after the end of Truman's presidency an American military force remained at installations. The markets of China and Southeast Asia that the NSC had envisioned for Japan, moreover, did not materialize during the Korean War years. But by 1951 and 1952, American military procurement programs were beginning to rely on Japanese technology. Thereafter, American military purchases contributed to the economic, technological, and military recovery of Japan, helped establish a new relationship between the two countries, and provided the initiative for an innovative Cold War economic miracle for decades to come.[61]

From the beginning of the Korean War, the administration was convinced that America's containment policies for Asia were linked to the fate of Indochina. This had been the preliminary position of the NSC since 1949 and early 1950. It became firmer in the spring of 1950, when Truman and the NSC determined officially that Indochina was the "most strategically important area" of Southeast Asia. At that time the administration accepted the premise of NSC 64, an early rendering of what would become the domino theory.[62] In response to reports in April 1950 that the People's Republic of China had established military training programs in South China for Vietminh battalions and provided extensive military equipment to Vietminh forces, the administration authorized increased military assistance for the French effort and provided a Military Advisory Group to Saigon under the command of Brigadier General Francis G. Brink.[63]

As its extended military commitments in Korea and Western Europe increased during 1951 and 1952, the administration allowed France the primary responsibility of containing communism in Indochina. The NSC had recommended in 1950 that even in the event of overt Communist Chinese intervention in Indochina, the United States should avoid a military commitment and instead rely on accelerated economic, military, and technical aid to France. In May 1951 the council in NSC

61. Leffler, *A Preponderance of Power*, 465–469; Schaller, *The American Occupation of Japan*, 293–298.

62. NSC 64, "The Position of the United States with Respect to Indochina," 27 February 1950, *United States–Vietnam Relations*, 282–285; *FRUS: 1950*, VI, 744–747.

63. NSC Progress Report on NSC 64, 15 March 1951, PSF-NSC, Box 212.

48/5 reaffirmed this position.[64] And through the remainder of his presidency Truman stuck to that advice. But to keep the French fighting, plus encourage their badly needed support for West German rearmament and entrance into the European Defense Community, the administration accelerated its economic and military aid to France. For fiscal year 1951 the United States supplied France $21.8 million in economic and technical assistance, and $425.7 million in military aid, and for fiscal 1952 $24.6 million in economic and technical help and $520 million in military assistance.[65] Acheson would later define the dilemma thrust upon the administration: "withholding help to France would, at most, have removed the colonial power. It could not have made the resulting situation a beneficial one for Indochina or for Southeast Asia, or in the more important effort of furthering the stability and defense of Europe."[66]

In December 1951 the French sustaining heavy losses in Indochina, requested a military consultation between the United States, France, and Great Britain regarding concerted action in the event of Chinese military intervention. Military representatives met in Washington in early January 1952, but no assurances were given France as to what course would be taken if the People's Republic of China became militarily involved. After Acheson reviewed the tripartite military discussions, he informed French diplomats in Saigon that the JCS could not indicate the extent of military assistance that might follow a Chinese invasion. But he told them that General Bradley had indicated he would recommend to the president that the White House should issue a declaration to the People's Republic of China stating "retaliation would follow any aggression" in Indochina.[67]

---

64. NSC 64, "The Position of the United States with Respect to Indochina," 27 February 1950, NSC 48/5, "United States Objectives, Policies and Courses of Action in Asia," 17 May 1951, *United States–Vietnam Relations*, 282–285, 436.

65. NSC Progress Report on NSC 64, 15 March 1951, PSF-NSC, Box 212; Allan B. Cole, ed., *Conflict in Indochina and International Repercussions: A Documentary History, 1945–1955* (Ithaca, NY: Cornell University Press, 1956), 259–261.

66. Acheson, *Present at the Creation*, 673.

67. Ibid., 675; David Bruce to Dean Acheson, 22 December 1951, Dean Acheson to Saigon, 15 January 1952, *United States–Vietnam Relations*, 460–467.

Following the tripartite military discussions and the proposed American warning to China, the NSC began work on a reevaluation of policy toward Southeast Asia. In February 1952 the staff issued the first of a series of policy reports from the Department of State on the region. "United States Objectives and Courses of Action with Respect to Communist Aggression in Southeast Asia" (NSC 124) warned that the loss of Southeast Asia to the Communists would put economic and political pressures on Japan, open sources of strategic materials to the Soviet bloc, jeopardize communication lines and trade routes to South Asia, and render "precarious" the American position in the Pacific. NSC 124 suggested that if the People's Republic of China intervened in Indochina, "the U.S. should take appropriate military action as part of an UN action or in conjunction with others" to support France.[68] NSC 124 received critical comments from the CIA and the JCS. In late February the CIA estimated that a unilateral warning against Communist Chinese intervention in Southeast Asia would deter the People's Republic of China. But it also believed that any UN action would probably bring about a response similar to that in Korea. The Joint Chiefs expressed concern that any military operation in defense of Indochina would risk direct military retaliation on Communist China itself—a course of action that might result in a long and expensive war.[69]

In early March 1952, the council considered NSC 124 and comments of the JCS, and all council members agreed that the greater danger to Southeast Asia was subversion, not external aggression. The NSC, nevertheless, recommended that the military implications of going to war with the People's Republic of China be studied further and referred the report back to the staff for reconsideration. Meanwhile, the French determination to remain in Indochina appeared to be weakening.[70]

---

68. NSC 124, "United States Objectives and Courses of Action with Respect to Communist Aggression in Southeast Asia," 1 February 1952, PSF-NSC, Box 120; Annex to NSC 124, 13 February 1952, *United States–Vietnam Relations*, 468–476.

69. CIA, SE-22, "Consequences of Certain Possible U.S. Courses of Action with Respect to Indochina, Burma, or Thailand," 29 February 1952. Memorandum, Hoyt S. Vandenberg to the NSC, 4 March 1952, *United States–Vietnam Relations*, 477–493; Leffler, *A Preponderance of Power*, 469–470.

70. Summary of Discussion at the 113th Meeting, 6 March 1952, PSF-NSC, Box 220.

In late June the revised report returned to the council, which after making minor changes approved it. So did Truman, and he ordered it implemented as policy. NSC 124/2 reasserted the objectives toward Southeast Asia that the earlier report had outlined. The primary purpose of American policy would be "to prevent the countries of Southeast Asia from passing into the Communist orbit." The United States should "continue to assure the French that the United States regards the French effort in Indochina as one of great strategic importance in the general international interest rather than in the purely French interest." The administration should use a variety of political, economic, military, and social programs to ensure American influence in Indochina, provide increased assistance on a high-priority basis, oppose any French withdrawal from Indochina, and seek a UN warning and collective military action against any Communist Chinese intervention.[71]

In indicating a willingness on the part of Truman and the NSC to intervene militarily, if necessary, to stop the spread of Sino-Soviet influence in Southeast Asia, the report departed from other documents. Motivating the change was the fear that the loss of Indochina to communism, particularly the new aggressive Sino-Soviet brand of communism that revealed itself in Korea, would lead to the loss of all of Southeast Asia. The administration could have disengaged from Indochina. NSC 124/2 instead increased the nation's commitment there.

Concerns that Chinese Communist aggression in Asia could threaten the security of Japan and Indochina allowed the NSC to resolve State and Defense differences regarding a peace treaty with Japan and the rearmament of that country. Joint recommendations of the two departments provided for NSC 60 and NSC 125/2. Policy coordinated by the council also proved very capable in resolving differences between the Department of State's position and concerns of the Joint Chiefs about an American plan of containment for Southeast Asia. NSC 124/2 established a consensus that a Communist Chinese interven-

---

71. Summary of Discussion at the 120th Meeting, 26 June 1952, Ibid.; NSC 124/2, "United States Objectives and Courses of Action with Respect to Southeast Asia," 25 June 1952, Ibid., Box 217; Memorandum, James Lay to Harry Truman, 25 June 1952, Ibid. For other citations of NSC 124/2 see *United States–Vietnam Relations*, 520–534; *FRUS: 1952–1954*, XII, pt. 1, 123–134.

tion in Indochina could bring an American military response, though only as part of a multilateral or collective UN armed effort.

*   *   *

In the Middle East, like Indochina a region where events during 1951 and 1952 gave Truman and the NSC reason to re-evaluate America's containment policies, instability worsened as growing nationalism turned anti-Western. Although direct Soviet military action was not considered a possibility, the NSC became concerned that if open confrontations erupted against Western interests, Moscow's influence could expand. But as Middle Eastern nationalism became hostile to the British, the administration's policy of Anglo-American collaboration in the region was strained while American access to Persian Gulf oil was put at risk. When traditional diplomatic approaches failed to improve American-Arab relations, the Department of State began to rely on American oil companies to promote the ad-ministration's interests and influence with the oil-rich states. The involvement of the oil companies expanded after the Ko-rean War began when in December 1950 ARAMCO adopted with Saudi Arabia an agreement for equal distribution of prof-its. The Department of State supported the arrangement, and the Saudi government benefited as well from increased oil rev-enues.[72]

As the American relationship with Saudi Arabia developed in 1951, Nationalists in Egypt and Iran began to challenge Brit-ish influence. In March 1951, the NSC accepted and Truman approved NSC 47/5. It served as a revised policy for the Middle East, allocating to Great Britain the primary responsibility for the defense of Israel and the Arab states. But the NSC acknowl-edged that the United States had a vested interest in the Middle East and it recommended that discussions take place on the critical political and military questions. The talks would de-fine the character of Anglo-American collaborative efforts "in

---

72. For a more thorough analysis of the conflicts and the ARAMCO-Saudi arrangement see Painter, *Oil and the American Century*, 153–171; Irvine Ander-son, *ARAMCO, the United States and Saudi Arabia: A Study of the Dynamics of Foreign Oil Policy, 1933–1950* (Princeton: Princeton University Press, 1981); Aaron David Miller, *Search for Security: Saudi Arabian Oil and American For-eign Policy, 1939–1949* (Chapel Hill: The University of North Carolina Press, 1980).

strengthening the several Arab States and Israel."[73] As a result, in November 1951, the United States, Great Britain, France, and Turkey agreed to establish a collective security arrangement called the Middle East Command, seeking the cooperation "of all interested States" in the Middle East that were "willing and able to undertake the initial defense of their area." Participants in turn assisted the Middle East Command by providing the organization, military equipment, and technical training. Yet Truman and the NSC found it increasingly difficult to maintain American and Western interests in the region.[74]

In 1951, then, the United States was increasing its presence in the Middle East, but preferred to allow Great Britain the chief role in defense of the region. "United States Policy Toward the Arab States and Israel" (NSC 129/1) suggested that the major objectives of the United States in the Middle East for 1952 should include overcoming or preventing further instability in the Arab states and Israel that would threaten the West, preventing "the extension of Soviet influence" in the region, and strengthening that of the West ensuring that "the resources of the area are available to the United States and its allies." More important was the declaration that the United States "should be prepared to play a larger role in safeguarding Western interests in the area."[75]

Both NSC 47/5 and NSC 129/1 emphasized the concern of Truman and the NSC that the instability of the Middle East could allow Soviet expansion or influence in the region. That concern found an occasion when a major dispute broke out in 1951 between the Iranian government and the Anglo-Iranian

---

73. NSC 47/5, "United States Policy Toward the Arab States and Israel," 17 March 1951, NSC, "Policies of the Government of the United States of America Relating to the National Security, Volume IV, 1951," 29–31, PSF-NSC, Box 195, HSTL, Independence, Missouri.

74. Leffler, *A Preponderance of Power*, 425, 476–477; NSC Progress Report on NSC 47/2, NSC 47/5, and NSC 65/3, 23 April 1952, Ibid., Box 216; Acheson, *Present at the Creation*, 562–568. The Middle East Command was opposed by Egypt on 15 October 1951, and never materialized fully during the last year of the Truman administration.

75. NSC 129/1, "United States Objectives and Policies with Respect to the Arab States and Israel," 24 April 1952, NSC, "Policies of the Government, 1952," 28–33, PSF-NSC, Box 195; Memorandum, James Lay to Harry Truman, 24 April 1952, Ibid., Box 216; *FRUS: 1952–1954*, IX, 222–226.

Oil Company (AIOC) of Great Britain. Iranian Nationalists denounced British exploitation of their country's oil resources. The "very size and importance" of the AIOC, observes Barry Rubin, "came to symbolize foreign domination of Iranian affairs."[76] In April, after the AIOC refused to grant equitable profit-sharing as ARAMCO had done in Saudi Arabia, Iran, under the leadership of Prime Minister Mohammed Mossadeq, nationalized its oil industry. Later in the year, strikes forced the AIOC to close its operations, and Great Britain imposed a boycott on Iranian oil.[77]

From 1947 through 1950 the United States had pursued toward Iran a policy of neutrality and nonintervention. Now the NSC and the CIA worried that the British boycott of Iranian oil might bring on an economic collapse, which would give the growing pro-Soviet Tudeh Party in Iran an opportunity to take over the government. Another possibility that the CIA projected was that if the crisis became "prolonged by an unyielding attitude on the part of the British, or by some unpredictable development," then Moscow would undertake armed intervention. The NSC began work on a new policy. "The Position of the United States with Respect to Iran" (NSC 107/2) recommended that the administration strive to resolve the differences between the Iranians and the British.[78] At about the same time, Great Britain demanded full compensation from Iran for nationalizing the industry and the resulting loss of British oil profits, and Mossadeq refused. The administration quickly initiated negotiations with British and Iranian officials, and Truman sent Harriman to London and Tehran in an effort to

---

76. Barry Rubin, *Paved with Good Intentions: The American Experience and Iran* (New York: Oxford University Press, 1980), 43; Painter, *Oil and the American Century*, 173; Acheson, *Present at the Creation*, 503. For a thorough recent study of the American, British, Iranian oil conflict see Mary Ann Heiss, *Empire and Nationhood: The United States, Great Britain, and Iranian Oil, 1950–1954* (New York: Columbia University Press, 1997).
77. Rubin, *Paved with Good Intentions*, 51, 61, 63; Painter, *Oil and the American Century*, 173; Acheson, *Present at the Creation*, 503.
78. Under Secretary's Meeting, "The Position of the United States with Respect to Iran," 17 May 1949, RG 59-RSS, NA; CIA, Special Estimate-3, "The Current Crisis in Iran," 16 March 1951, PSF-NSC, Box 212; Minutes of the 87th Meeting, 21 March 1951, Ibid.; NSC 107/2, "The Position of the United States with Respect to Iran," 21 March 1951, NSC, "Policies of the Government, 1951," 17–23, PSF-NSC, Box 195.

defuse the crisis and break the impasse. Acheson and Harriman both concentrated on arranging an agreement whereby the British would recognize Iranian nationalization in return for financial recompense. Their efforts failed when Great Britain agreed to accept nationalization on the premise that AIOC management would retain control over Iran's oil production.[79]

Although sporadic, negotiations between Tehran and London continued through late 1951, the crisis worsened as the boycott depleted Iran's oil revenues. As economic collapse threatened and Tudeh Party opposition mounted against Mossadeq, Iran sought financial assistance from the United States. The administration agreed to provide limited technical and military aid but could promise no substantial loan until Iran settled its differences with Great Britain and the AIOC. In August 1951, Acheson informed the NSC that the British "were trying desperately to meet the Iranian demands," but he expressed regret that any agreement still hung on concessions that limited Iranian sovereignty and gave them "a monopoly on the sale of Iranian oil." Acheson warned the NSC that Mossadeq "would be compelled to resign if the talks did finally and irrevocably break down."[80] One month later the CIA reported that Iran would "probably remain internally unstable" through 1953, and concluded that a failure of Anglo-Iranian negotiations "may well lead to economic chaos and increase the danger of a Communist [Tudeh] coup."[81]

In 1952 the situation changed as a frustrated Mossadeq turned to the USSR for an oil purchase agreement, began to issue public pronouncements that called for Iranian neutrality in the Cold War, and acquired emergency dictatorial powers that gave him control of Iranian armed forces. Iran's apparent rapprochement with the USSR required an immediate reevalu-

79. Memorandum, Henry S. Villard to Paul Nitze, 9 November 1951, RG 59-PPS, NA; Leffler, *A Preponderance of Power*, 422–423; Rubin, *Paved with Good Intentions*, 65–68; Painter, *Oil and the American Century*, 174–179; Acheson, *Present at the Creation*, 506–509, 679–680.

80. Rubin, *Paved with Good Intentions*, 72; Summary of Discussion at the 100th Meeting, 23 August 1951, PSF-NSC, Box 220. Regretfully, several of the NSC meeting discussions on the subject of Iran during 1951 and 1952 are still severely censored.

81. CIA, Special Estimate-13, "Probable Developments in the World Situation Through Mid-1953," 24 September 1951, PSF-NSC, Box 215.

ation of American policy.[82] "The Present Situation in Iran" (NSC 136/2) proposed that the United States prepare "to take necessary measures to help Iran start up her oil industry and to secure markets for her oil," provide economic assistance to Iran, pending the restoration of the Iranian oil industry and markets, and through presidential authority sanction "voluntary agreements and programs under Section 708 (a) and (b) of the Defense Production Act of 1950" in which American companies would purchase and market Iranian oil. In late November 1952 the NSC and Truman approved the report.[83]

Truman made one last effort to solve the crisis. He approved a $100 million loan to Iran in return for future Iranian oil deliveries to the United States and requested American companies to increase their purchase of Iranian oil, either alone or from the AIOC. At the time, oil companies were facing an antitrust suit by the Department of Justice.[84] The Departments of State, Defense, Interior, and Commerce each argued before the NSC that prosecution of criminal proceedings against the oil companies would jeopardize American interests in Iran and the arrangements under way to stabilize Iran's economy and politics. In response, the NSC issued "National Security Problems Concerning Free World Petroleum Demands and Potential Supplies" (NSC 138/1), recommending that the Department of Justice drop all criminal charges against American oil companies and prepare a civil antitrust suit for a later date. Truman told the council that while he "had always been a strongly antitrust President" his conviction "that the national security was at stake," had persuaded him to approve the recommendations.[85] He authorized the cancellation of the criminal suit, and

82. Rubin, *Paved with Good Intentions*, 72–73.

83. NSC 136/2, "The Present Situation in Iran," 20 November 1952, NSC, "Policies of the Government of the United States of America Relating to the National Security, Volume V, 1952," 35–36, PSF-NSC, Box 195.

84. Leffler, *A Preponderance of Power*, 483–484; Rubin, *Paved with Good Intentions*, 75; Painter, *Oil and the American Century*, 186–188; Acheson, *Present at the Creation*, 683–684.

85. Summary of Discussion at the 127th Meeting, 17 December 1951, PSF-NSC, Box 219; Summary of Discussion at the 128th Meeting, 9 January 1953, Ibid.; NSC 138/1, "National Security Problems Concerning Free World Petroleum Demands and Potential Supplies," 8 January 1952; *FRUS: 1952–1954*, IX, 637–655.

American companies consented to an arrangement worked out by the Department of State that allowed them to purchase Iranian oil from the AIOC. In January 1953, the AIOC and American agreement was presented to Mossadeq as part of a Anglo-American proposal. But because the British demanded full compensation for past losses, Mossadeq rejected the final offer.[86]

In spite of the determination of Truman and the NSC to settle the Iranian crisis, time ran out. Like the Korean War, the question of rearming West Germany, and the problem of Indochina, the impasse in Iran continued into 1953, long after Truman's presidency ended on January 20.[87] Had the administration demanded greater concessions from the AIOC or understood Washington's subtle support of British demands forced Mossadeq to employ a traditional Iranian tactic, that of playing off one world power against another, the mediation efforts might have made a difference for American policy in the Middle East. Because Truman and the NSC believed that Soviet influence in the Middle East and Iran constituted a greater threat to American security interests than did the appearance of Anglo-American collaboration, policy that the NSC articulated in 1951 and 1952 instead contributed to the region's instability for decades to come.

Throughout 1952 the NSC worked well and operated as its creators had intended. As the council during the year shaped and revised the nation's containment policies, few differences emerged between State, Defense, and the Joint Chiefs. NSC 48/5 and NSC 118/2 clarified the country's war objectives in Korea. The tentative emergence of a European Defense Community and the expansion of NATO membership ensured the

---

86. Painter, *Oil and the American Century*, 188–189.

87. A joint CIA-British intelligence plan to overthrow the Mossadeq government was considered during the last weeks of the Truman presidency. However, DCI Smith and Deputy Director Dulles believed that neither Truman nor Acheson would approve the covert action. Nevertheless, the CIA continued its planning, and under the Eisenhower administration, in August 1953, orchestrated an Iranian-CIA sponsored coup which removed Mossadeq from office and thereafter established Shah Reza Pahlevi as the sole ruler of Iran through 1979. For details of the CIA-sponsored coup see Kermit Roosevelt, *Countercoup: The Struggle for the Control of Iran* (New York: McGraw-Hill, 1979).

rearmament of Western Europe. Covert intelligence capabilities of the CIA grew further in response to the requirements for a global strategy of psychological warfare. And the United States reaffirmed and strengthened its economic and military commitments to Japan, Southeast Asia, and the Middle East. Yet many more Cold War situations and policies toward other areas of the world remained unaddressed by Truman and the NSC, a task that the council had well prepared for during its tumultuous initial six years.

Conclusions

The early years of the Cold War brought about tremendous change and creativity in American foreign policy as the Truman administration struggled to deal with the disorder left by World War II and close the gap between the nation's new world responsibilities and the obsolete ad hoc structures of Roosevelt's presidency. Harry S. Truman presided from 1947 into 1953 over the growth, nurtured by the NSC, of what was to become known as the national security bureaucracy. The containment policies formulated for Truman by the NSC expressed the council's struggle to respond to a relentless succession of events and conditions: the political and military weaknesses and economic calamities in Western Europe; challenges from communism in Eastern Europe, China, Greece, Italy, Indochina, Korea, and the Middle East; the division of Germany; a military and economic power vacuum in Japan; unique options and possibilities of Titoism; and above all the perception of the Soviet Union as the primary threat to American hegemony, liberal democracy, and Western capitalism. The doctrine of containment itself did not, however, provide a long-term formula for the council's particular policies. With each year and each situation assessed by the council a Cold War containment policy developed.

From 1947 through 1949 the NSC determined that the major threat to American political and economic hegemony was the upset of the balance of power in Europe. The devastation of World War II and the dislocations that followed in the immediate postwar years were so disruptive in Europe by 1947 and 1948 that Communist political parties in Greece, France, and

202

Italy had gained adherents and were in positions to gain power. Their possible success would put Europe under the direct political influence of the Soviet Union. Fixing from 1947 through 1949 on Europe as the nation's region of vital interest, the NSC gave policy priority to continued assistance toward the reconstruction of Western Europe, covert political countermeasures to undermine European Communist parties, the revival of Germany's industrialization under the auspices of a separate West Germany, and following the Berlin blockade, American participation in the collective security alliance of NATO. Insisting on the importance of Europe, the NSC attempted to minimize American involvement in East Asia, the Middle East, and Southeast Asia. When the NSC examined regions it then considered peripheral interests, it formulated specific policies to contain the USSR as well as defend American hegemonic resources. Such were strategies for Scandinavia and the Eastern Mediterranean, and courses of action for reviving Japan's economy.

The crises of late 1949 provoked much insecurity and uncertainty for the United States, and greatly influenced Cold War containment policies the NSC formulated during the last years of Truman's presidency. The NSC anticipated as the USSR built a nuclear arsenal and expanded its global interests, while Western capitalistic markets continued to contract, and revolutionary nationalism gained momentum in the underdeveloped world, that the next three years would threaten the nation's hegemony as well as challenge its credibility.

The Korean War that erupted in June 1950 affirmed reassessments of American containment and national security policies the NSC had undertaken in late 1949 and early 1950, particularly as articulated in NSC 68. Although NSC 68 did not dictate that the United States intervene in Korea, it was critical in the militarization and eventual globalization of containment policies from 1950 through 1952. In September 1950, the NSC tested basic containment premises when it adopted for Korea a policy of liberation, or rollback. Liberation failed the test when UN forces encountered the massive Chinese Communist counteroffensive, and the NSC quickly resorted to a defensive containment strategy that called for a negotiated settlement along the 38th parallel. Throughout 1952 Truman and the council adopted an evermore activist containment

mentality that made no distinction between vital and peripheral interests, instead contemplating a global contest based on
positions of strength and designed to check the power of what
was thought to be a monolithic Soviet bloc. By 1952, policies
formulated by the NSC transformed NATO into a European
defensive alliance under the command of the United States
and increased military rearmament and assistance to NATO
members. Not only had it become evermore critical that stable
relations continue with Great Britain and France, but to contain Soviet influence and expansion in Southeast Asia and the
Middle East, Truman and the NSC implemented policies that
supported the French effort in Indochina and the British occupation in the Middle East. Those policies had long-term and
momentous costs, giving Asian and Arab nationalists reason to
perceive the United States as a surrogate colonial power in
both regions for decades after the Truman era of the Cold War
had ended.

Domestic politics had their own influence on the council's
decisions. From late 1947 through most of 1949 demobilization
and political fiscal conservatism limited defense spending and
American military power. The anti-Communist rhetoric that
Truman and his officials employed in the earliest years of the
Cold War was quite successful in obtaining public and congressional support for ERP, approval of the country's participation
in NATO, and endorsement of an economic recovery program
for Japan as well as extended military assistance programs for
Western Europe and Nationalist China. But when the Communists overtook China and the Soviet Union and acquired
nuclear capabilities, the anti-Communist militancy that the administration had evoked turned politically against it. In late
1949 and 1950 public opinion and right-wing attacks on the
administration's foreign policies encouraged Truman and the
NSC to formulate a more aggressive form of containment,
which became militarized and global during the years of
McCarthyism and the Korean War.

*   *   *

From 1947 through 1952 the NSC operated as an interdepartmental council. During that time its ability to coordinate
Truman's containment policies depended not only on the orga-

nization of representative departments but on the personal relationships of its leading officials.

Because the defense establishment—the Department of Defense, the Joint Chiefs, and the three military services— operated with considerable dispersal of authority, unified policy recommendations were rare. The JCS commonly sent its opinions and policy suggestions to the secretary of defense. Bureaucratic differences, even serious distrust, among the Departments of the Army, Navy, and Air Force hindered the effective composition of military statements of goals and requests. Most policy recommendations from the Department of Defense were based on strategic and budgetary concerns and the advice of the Joint Chiefs.

Within its earliest months, work of forming and coordinating NSC policies came to be dominated by the Department of State, particularly its PPS under the direction of George Kennan. Secretary George Marshall had established the PPS in early 1947 to develop long-term foreign policy objectives for the Department of State. Kennan and his successor Paul Nitze retained a small staff of policy specialists. The streamlined structure and operations of the PPS allowed Kennan and Nitze efficiently and effectively to produce NSC policy recommendations. As a result, the council became an ideal vehicle for the introduction of the policies and containment objectives of the two.

From 1947 through 1952 the success of the NSC largely resulted from the influence of its key participants. Most important were Forrestal, Lovett, Marshall, and Acheson, a unique small group composed of two Wall Street bankers, a general, and an attorney.

During the council's first two years the working relationship between Secretary of Defense James Forrestal, Secretary of State Marshall, and Undersecretary of State Robert Lovett was quite good. Each understood the value of objective policy evaluation and how it applied to coordinating the political with the military components of foreign and national security policy. Forrestal and Marshall met frequently to discuss objectives. When Marshall was engaged in foreign conferences Lovett and Forrestal, close friends and former neighbors as well as Wall Street colleagues, collaborated on shaping policy.

The deliberations of Forrestal, Marshall, and Lovett at NSC meetings were important to the integration of diplomatic and military objectives, and greatly assisted in the formation of a consensus at times when the council's recommendations or decisions were critical. For example, throughout 1948 Forrestal, Marshall, and Lovett facilitated the NSC's coordination of policies on technical and advisory military assistance for Greece, American membership in NATO and military assistance to it, the administration's decisions to deploy and extend the Berlin airlift, and a policy recommendation to proceed with a program to revive Japan's economy and begin negotiations for a peace treaty with Japan.

Forrestal worked hard to create for the NSC during its earliest years a congruent process for coordinating policy. Oftentimes he requested papers or recommendations from the NSC, or personally formulated a policy proposal and forwarded it to the council for bringing it into consonance with the wishes of the Department of State. In 1948, for example, he asked the NSC to establish a policy on atomic weapons custody and to reconcile differences within the NSC 20 series concerning military preparedness. He also requested the council give direction to policy or concerns related to the Department of Defense such as the decisions to evacuate American military forces from Tsingtao and to use troops as part of a UN peace-keeping mission in Palestine. But the goodwill and open communications that Forrestal labored to establish through the NSC were disrupted in early 1949 when he, Marshall, and Lovett resigned.

Throughout 1949 and 1950 personal tensions and bureaucratic differences between Secretary of Defense Johnson and Secretary of State Acheson strained NSC meetings and ad hoc committee deliberations as well as the efforts of the council to produce coordinated containment policies. Unlike Marshall, Acheson preferred to formulate policy for the Department of State and for advice he relied on specialists from its Executive Secretariat along with the help of the PPS. Like Forrestal, Johnson preferred hands-on control over proposals and communications. But he was less experienced in matters of foreign policy than Forrestal and often exhibited greater concern for defending his and the department's political interests than for building a consensus with Acheson and others on the NSC. Aggravating antagonism between Johnson and the Eurocentrist

Acheson was the insistence of the secretary of defense that NSC policy reassess containment strategy for Asia and request greater assistance to Jiang Jieshi. Johnson's agenda and recalcitrance gave Truman reason to relieve him of his duties in September 1950. Marshall succeeded him for nearly a year, then resigned in ill health to be replaced by Lovett.

The working relationship between State and Defense essential to the NSC policy process stabilized when Marshall returned and Lovett followed him as secretary of defense. In turn, Acheson became much less defensive and the ability of the council to coordinate political and military policy greatly improved. By that time the reorganization of the NSC had been completed. The amendments of 1949 had made the secretary of state a coequal of the secretary of defense on the council and the NSC officially became a part of Truman's Executive Office. Truman's directives of July 1950 creating a Senior NSC Staff responsible for reconciling departmental recommendations and requiring that the council meet weekly quickened the pace of its work. Thereafter, the NSC worked extremely well and the containment policies that resulted were far superior to those produced by the council in the years before reorganization. It provided Truman the decision-making forum he needed during the critical time of the Korean War and, from the proposals of the Department of State and those that the Department of Defense and the Joint Chiefs composed, recommendations that fulfilled the national security guidelines and the military and global requirements articulated in NSC 68 and NSC 48/5.

*   *   *

Truman delegated to the NSC the responsibility for formulating and bringing order to policy. He relied heavily on the council's recommendations that came to him, approved its policies, and ordered their implementation. Truman rarely acted as a policymaker. Only two instances stand out. Against the advice of leading council members in 1948 he decided to recognize the new state of Israel. And during the time when he had to cope with MacArthur's challenge to his authority he ordered the transfer of nuclear weapons to the Pacific without consulting the NSC. In retrospect, Truman established a successful record in foreign policy because he understood the necessity for Cold War containment strategies in which political and military objectives worked together. Truman realized, moreover, that the doctrine of containment could become feasible only if it was molded case by case into a policy that effectively applied to the uncertain international conditions and domestic demands of the Cold War. For that purpose he had created the NSC.

When Truman left office on January 20, 1953, relations between the United States and the Soviet Union had transformed the Cold War into a zero-sum contest driven by bipolar suspicion and distrust. Changes in the leadership of both powers during early 1953 did not lessen tensions: a nuclear arms race developed, war stalemated in Korea, and diplomatic impasses undermined negotiation. For over three decades after the end of Truman's presidency, Americans and Russians remained committed to the Cold War. During that time, the NSC continued to serve as Truman had intended. And the geopolitical premises of his and the council's containment policies provided the United States with its foundations for waging the Cold War and established the nation's national security strategy for much of the last half of the twentieth century. In retrospect the basic premises of those same policies contributed to the end of the Cold War.

After considerable costs, America's containment policies checked the advances of the USSR; however, the demise of the Cold War only took place when the internal forces of Soviet authoritarianism self-destructed. In the early 1990s, upon the collapse of the Soviet Union and its empire and with the survival of only a few Communist states, containment as an anti-Communist policy has become a historical artifact of the Cold War. Yet at the close of the century, containment remains a viable strategy applicable to expansionist and troublesome non-Communist states that threaten the nation's hegemony or its hegemonic resources.

With the end of the Cold War some argue that bureaucratic entities such as the NSC should be dismantled. But the Cold War imposed on nations and peoples its own structures, however bleak, and its ending has unleashed multiple disintegrative processes: a resurgence of ultranationalism, various nationalistic separatist movements and ethnic rivalries, refugee problems and resettlement, the redrawing of boundaries, the rapid expansion of international industrialization and communication technology into the developing world, and along with it a variety of new economic, environmental, political, and social forces that accompany a growing global marketplace all confront and confound American policymakers at century's end. Although the international tensions and disorders may not fully equate to those following World War II, conditions in our new postwar world are just as volatile and unpredictable. American foreign policy again must be formulated on a case by case basis, and the NSC that President Truman established for the coordination of containment might once more serve us well.

Appendix A

Statutory Members of President Truman's NSC

September 1947 – January 1953

1947–1948
Harry S. Truman, The President of the United States, Chairman
George C. Marshall, The Secretary of State
James V. Forrestal, The Secretary of Defense
Kenneth C. Royall, The Secretary of the Army
John L. Sullivan, The Secretary of the Navy
W. Stuart Symington, The Secretary of the Air Force
John R. Steelman, The Acting Chairman, National Security Resources
    Board
Arthur M. Hill, The Chairman, National Security Resources Board

1949
Harry S. Truman, The President of the United States, Chairman
Alben W. Barkley, Vice President of the United States
Dean G. Acheson, The Secretary of State
George C. Marshall, The Secretary of State
Louis A. Johnson, The Secretary of Defense
James V. Forrestal, The Secretary of Defense
Gordon Gray, The Secretary of the Army
Kenneth C. Royall, The Secretary of the Army
Francis P. Matthews, The Secretary of the Navy
John L. Sullivan, The Secretary of the Navy
W. Stuart Symington, The Secretary of the Air Force
John R. Steelman, The Acting Chairman, National Security Resources
    Board

1950
Harry S. Truman, The President of the United States, Chairman
Alben W. Barkley, Vice President of the United States
Dean G. Acheson, The Secretary of State
George C. Marshall, The Secretary of Defense
Louis A. Johnson, The Secretary of Defense
W. Stuart Symington, The Chairman, National Security Resources Board
John R. Steelman, The Acting Chairman, National Security Resources Board

1951
Harry S. Truman, The President of the United States, Chairman
Alben W. Barkley, Vice President of the United States
Dean G. Acheson, The Secretary of State
George C. Marshall, The Secretary of Defense
Robert A. Lovett, The Secretary of Defense
Jack O. Gorrie, The Chairman, National Security Resources Board
W. Stuart Symington, The Chairman, National Security Resources Board
W. Averell Harriman, The Director for Mutual Security

1952–Jan. 1953
Harry S. Truman, The President of the United States, Chairman
Alben W. Barkley, The Vice President of the United States
Dean G. Acheson, The Secretary of State
Robert A. Lovett, The Secretary of Defense
Jack O. Gorrie, The Chairman, National Security Resources Board

Appendix B

Organizational Charts of the NSC

(1947 and 1949)

1947

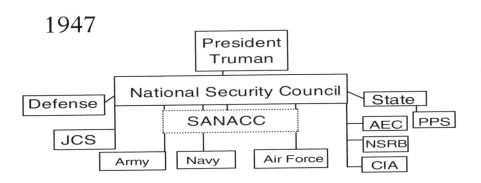

1949

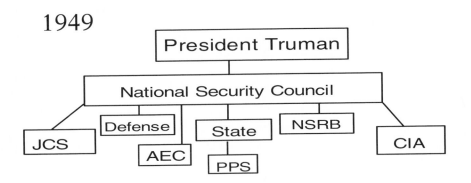

Bibliography

MANUSCRIPT COLLECTIONS
Harry S. Truman Library, Independence, Missouri.
Dean Acheson Papers
Clark M. Clifford Papers
George M. Elsey Papers
Richard E. Neustadt Papers
Sidney W. Souers Papers
Harry S. Truman Papers: National Security Council Files
Harry S. Truman Papers: President's Official Files
Harry S. Truman Papers: President's Secretary's Files
Harry S. Truman Papers: Records of the Korean War
Harry S. Truman Papers: Records of the Psychological Strategy Board
Harry S. Truman Papers: White House Confidential Files

National Archives, Washington, D.C.
Records of the Secretary of State: General Records of the Office of the Executive Secretariat, Record Group 59
Records of the Secretary of State: Records of the Policy Planning Staff, Record Group 59

Seeley G. Mudd Library, Princeton University Library, Princeton, New Jersey.
Allen W. Dulles Papers
Ferdinand Eberstadt Papers
James V. Forrestal Papers
George F. Kennan Papers

ORAL HISTORIES
Duke University Living History Program.
W. Averell Harriman
Dean Rusk

Harry S. Truman Library Oral History Collection.
Lucius D. Clay
Clark M. Clifford
George M. Elsey
Gordon Gray
Robert A. Lovett
Charles Saltzman
W. Stuart Symington

MICROFILM COLLECTIONS

Records of the National Security Council: First Supplement. Washington, D.C.: University Publications of America, 1981.
Records of the National Security Council: Second Supplement. Washington, D.C.: University Publications of America, 1984.

PUBLISHED DOCUMENTS AND UNITED STATES GOVERNMENT PUBLICATIONS

Bernstein, Barton J. and Allen J. Matusow, eds. *The Truman Administration: A Documentary History.* New York: Harper & Row, 1966.
Cole, Allan B., ed. *Conflict in Indochina and International Repercussions: A Documentary History, 1945–1955.* Ithaca, NY: Cornell University Press, 1956.
Commission on Organization of the Executive Branch of the Government. *Foreign Affairs: A Report to the Congress by the Commission on Organization of the Executive Branch of the Government, February 1949.* Washington, D.C.: G.P.O., 1949.
Commission on Organization of the Executive Branch of the Government. *The National Security Organization: A Report to the Congress by the Commission on Organization of the Executive Branch of the Government, February 1949.* Washington, D.C.: G.P.O., 1949.
Gaddis, John Lewis and Thomas H. Etzold, eds. *Containment: Documents on American Policy and Strategy, 1945–1950.* New York: Columbia University Press, 1978.
Jackson, Henry M., ed. *The National Security Council: Jackson Subcommittee Papers on Policy-Making at the Presidential Level.* New York: Praeger, 1965.
Leary, William M. *The Central Intelligence Agency: History and Documents.* University: The University of Alabama Press, 1984.
Nelson, Anna Kasten, ed. *The State Department Policy Planning Staff Papers, 1947–1949.* 3 volumes. New York: Garland Publishing, 1983.
Ryan, Allan A., Jr. *Klaus Barbie and the United States Government: The Report, with Documentary Appendix, to the Attorney General of the United States.* Frederick, MD: University Publications of America, 1984.
U.S. Congress. *The Atomic Energy Act of 1946, Public Law 585.* 79th Cong., 1st sess. Washington, D.C.: G.P.O., 1946.
_____. *The National Security Act of 1947, Public Law 253.* 80th Cong., 1st sess. Washington, D.C.: G.P.O., 1947.
_____. *The National Security Act of 1947, As Amended, Public Law 216.* 81st Cong., 1st sess. Washington, D.C.: G.P.O., 1949.
_____. Senate. Committee on Foreign Relations. *A Decade of American Foreign*

Policy: Basic Documents, 1941–1949. 81st Cong., 1st sess. Washington, D.C.: G.P.O., 1957.

_____. Committee on Armed Services and Foreign Relations. *Military Situation in the Far East.* 82d Cong., 1st sess. Washington, D.C.: G.P.O., 1951.

_____. Committee on Naval Affairs. *Unification of the War and Navy Departments and Postwar Organization for National Security.* 79th Cong., 1st sess. Washington, D.C.: G.P.O., 1945.

_____. Select Committee to Study Governmental Operations with Respect to Intelligence Activities. *Supplementary Detailed Staff Reports on Foreign and Military Intelligence* Book IV. 94th Cong., 2d sess. Washington, D.C.: G.P.O., 1976.

_____. Subcommittee on National Policy Machinery of the Committee on Government Operations. *Organizational History of the National Security Council.* 86th Cong., 2d sess. Washington, D.C.: G.P.O., 1960.

U.S. Department of the Army. Office of the Chief of Military History. *Military Advisors in Korea: KMAG in Peace and War.* By Robert K. Sawyer. Washington, D.C.: G.P.O., 1962.

U.S. Department of Defense. *United States–Vietnam Relations, 1945–1967* Book 8. Washington, D.C.: G.P.O., 1971.

U.S. Department of Justice. *Robert Jan Verbelen and the United States Government: A Report to the Assistant Attorney General, Criminal Division, U.S. Department of Justice, June 1988.* By Neal M. Sher. Washington, D.C.: U.S. Department of Justice, 1988.

U.S. Department of State. *American Foreign Policy 1950–1955: Basic Documents* Volume I. Washington, D.C.: G.P.O., 1957.

_____. *American Foreign Policy 1950–1955: Basic Documents* Volume II. Washington, D.C.: G.P.O., 1957.

_____. *Department of State Bulletin, 1949–1951.* Washington, D.C.: G.P.O.

_____. *Foreign Relations of the United States.* Washington, D.C.: G.P.O.

FRUS, 1947, V: The Near East and Africa (1971).

FRUS, 1947, VI: The Far East (1972).

FRUS, 1947, VII: The Far East: China (1972).

FRUS, 1948, II: Germany and Austria (1973).

FRUS, 1948, III: Western Europe (1974).

FRUS, 1948, IV: Eastern Europe; The Soviet Union (1974).

FRUs, 1948, VI: The Far East and Australia (1974).

FRUS, 1948, VII: The Far East: China (1973).

FRUS, 1948, VIII: The Far East: China (1973).

FRUS, 1949, I: National Security Affairs: Foreign Economic Policy (1976).

FRUS, 1949, IV: Western Europe (1975).

FRUS, 1949, V: Eastern Europe; The Soviet Union (1976).

FRUS, 1949, VI: The Near East; South Asia and Africa (1977).

FRUS, 1949, VII, pt. 1: The Far East and Australasia (1975).

FRUS, 1949, VII, pt. 2: The Far East and Australasia (1976).

FRUS, 1949, IX: The Far East: China (1974).

FRUS, 1950, I: National Security Affairs: Foreign Economic Policy (1977).

FRUS, 1950, III: Western Europe (1977).

FRUS, 1950, IV: Central and Eastern Europe; The Soviet Union (1980).

FRUS, 1950, V: The Near East; South Asia and Africa (1978).

FRUS, 1950, VI: East Asia and the Pacific (1976).

FRUS, 1950, VII: Korea (1976).

FRUS, 1951, IV, pt. 1: Europe: Political and Economic Developments (1985).

FRUS, 1951, IV, pt. 2: Europe: Political and Economic Developments (1985).

FRUS, 1951, V: *The Near East and Africa* (1982).
FRUS, 1951, VII, pt. 1: *Korea and China* (1983).
FRUS, 1952–1954, IX: *The Near and Middle East* (1984).
FRUS, 1952–1954, XII, pt. 1: *East Asia and The Pacific* (1984).
FRUS, 1952–1954, XIV, pt. 2: *China and Japan* (1985).
_____. *United States Relations with China: With Special Reference to the Period 1944–1949.* Washington, D.C.: G.P.O., 1949.
U.S. Joint Chiefs of Staff. Historical Division. *The History of the Joint Chiefs of Staff:* Volume I, *The Joint Chiefs of Staff and National Policy, 1945–1947.* By James F. Schnabel. Wilmington, DE: Michael Glazier, 1979.
_____. *The History of the Joint Chiefs of Staff:* Volume II, *The Joint Chiefs of Staff and National Policy, 1947–1949.* By Kenneth W. Condit. Wilmington, DE: Michael Glazier, 1979.
_____. *The History of the Joint Chiefs of Staff:* Volume III, *The Joint Chiefs of Staff and National Policy, The Korean War.* By James F. Schnabel and Robert J. Watson. Wilmington, DE: Michael Glazier, 1979.
U.S. National Military Establishment. *First Report of the Secretary of Defense.* Washington, D.C.: G.P.O., 1948.
U.S. President. *Public Papers of the Presidents of the United States.* Washington, D.C.: Office of the *Federal Register,* National Archives and Records Service, 1961–1966. *Harry S. Truman, 1945–1953.*
_____. *Survival in the Air Age: A Report by the President's Air Policy Commission.* Washington, D.C.: G.P.O., 1948.
Warner, Michael, ed. *CIA Cold War Records: The CIA Under Harry Truman.* Washington, D.C.: CIA History Staff Center for the Study of Intelligence, Central Intelligence Agency, 1994.

NEWSPAPERS AND PERIODICALS

Collier's
Eastern Underwriter
Harper's
The New York Times
The New York Times Magazine
The Reporter
Saturday Evening Post
St. Louis Post-Dispatch
U.S. News and World Report
Washington Star

ARTICLES

Alsop, Joseph and Stewart. "How Our Foreign Policy Is Made." *The Saturday Evening Post* 224, 4 (April 30, 1949): 30, 113–116.
Belmonte, Laura. "Anglo-American Relations and the Dismissal of MacArthur." *Diplomatic History* 19 (Fall 1995): 641–667.
Bethe, Hans and Frederick Seitz. "How Close is the Danger." In *One World or None,* eds. Dexter Masters and Katharine Way, 42–46. New York: McGraw-Hill, 1946.
Braden, Tom. "The Birth of the CIA." *American Heritage* 27 (February 1977): 11–13.
Brands, Henry W., Jr. "Redefining the Cold War: American Policy toward Yugoslavia, 1948–60." *Diplomatic History* 11 (Winter 1987): 41–53.

Chen Jian. "The Myth of America's 'Lost Chance' in China: A Chinese Perspective in Light of New Evidence." *Diplomatic History* 21 (Winter 1997): 77–86.

Christensen, Thomas J. "A Lost Chance for What? Rethinking the Origins of U.S.-PRC Confrontation." *Journal of American-East Asian Relations* 4 (1995): 249–278.

Clifford, Clark. "Recognizing Israel." *American Heritage* 28 (April 1977): 4–11.

Clifford, Garry. "Bureaucratic Politics." In Thomas G. Paterson et al., "A Round Table: Explaining the History of American Foreign Relations." *Journal of American History* 77, 1 (June 1990): 161–168.

Cohen, Warren I. "Acheson, His Advisers, and China, 1949–50." in *Uncertain Years: Chinese-American Relations, 1947–1950*, eds. Dorothy Borg and Waldo Heinrichs, 13–53. New York: Columbia University Press, 1980.

_____. "Conversations with Chinese Friends: Zhou Enlai's Associates Reflect on Chinese-American Relations in the 1940s and the Korean War." *Diplomatic History* 11 (Summer 1987): 283–289.

Combs, Jerald A. "The Compromise that Never Was: George Kennan, Paul Nitze, and the Issue of Conventional Deterrence in Europe, 1949–1952." *Diplomatic History* 15 (Summer 1991): 361–386.

Cummings, Bruce. "Kennan, Containment, Conciliation: The End of Cold War History." *Current History* 94 (November 1995): 359–363.

Current Biography, 1950 ed., s.v. "James S. Lay." New York: H.W. Wilson, 1950.

Dingman, Roger. "Atomic Diplomacy during the Korean War." *International Security* 13 (Winter 1988–89): 50–91.

Divine, Robert A. "The Cold War and the Election of 1948." *Journal of American History* 59 (June 1972): 90–110.

Eisenberg, Carolyn. "U.S. Policy in Post-War Germany: The Conservative Restoration." *Science and Society* 46 (Spring 1982): 24–38.

Etzold, Thomas H. "American Organization for National Security, 1945–1950." In *Containment: Documents on American Policy and Strategy, 1945–1950*, eds. John Lewis Gaddis and Thomas H. Etzold. New York: Columbia University Press, 1978.

Fischer, John. "Mr. Truman's Politburo." *Harper's Magazine* 202 (June 1951): 29–36.

Folly, Martin H. "Breaking the Vicious Circle: Britain, the United States, and the Genesis of the North Atlantic Treaty." *Diplomatic History* 12 (Winter 1988): 59–77.

Foot, Rosemary. "Making Known the Unknown War: Policy Analysis of the Korean Conflict in the Last Decade." *Diplomatic History* 15 (Summer 1991): 411–431.

Gaddis, John Lewis. "Containment: A Reassessment." *Foreign Affairs* 55 (July 1977): 873–887.

_____. "The Emerging Post-Revisionist Thesis on the Origins of the Cold War." *Diplomatic History* 7 (Summer 1983): 171–190.

_____. "Harry S. Truman and the Origins of Containment." In *Makers of American Diplomacy: From Benjamin Franklin to Henry Kissenger*, eds. Frank J. Merli and Theodore A. Wilson, 189–218. New York: Scribner's, 1974.

_____. "Korea in American Politics, Strategy, and Diplomacy, 1945–1950." In *The Origins of the Cold War in Asia*, eds. Yonosuke Nagai and Akira Iriye. New York: Columbia University Press, 1977.

_____. "Was the Truman Doctrine a Real Turning Point?" *Foreign Affairs* 52 (January 1974): 386–402.

Garver, John W. "Little Chance." *Diplomatic History* 21 (Winter 1997): 87–94.
Hall, David K. "The 'Custodian-Manager' of the Policymaking Process." In *Decisions of the Highest Order: Perspectives on the National Security Council*, eds. Karl F. Inderfurth and Loch K. Johnson, 146–154. Pacific Grove, CA: Brooks/Cole, 1988.
Hamby, Alonzo L. "Harry S. Truman: Insecurity and Responsibility." In *Leadership in the Modern Presidency*, ed. Fred T. Greenstein, 41–75. Cambridge: Harvard University Press, 1988.
_____. "The Vital Center, the Fair Deal, and the Quest for a Liberal Political Economy." *American Historical Review* 77 (June 1972): 653–678.
Hammond, Paul Y. "NSC-68: Prologue to Rearmament." In *Strategy, Politics and Defense Budgets*, eds. Warner Schilling, Paul Y. Hammond, and Glenn Snyder, 267–378. New York: Columbia University Press, 1962.
Henrikson, Alan K. "The Creation of the North Atlantic Alliance, 1948–1952." *Naval War College Review* 32 (May–June 1980): 4–39.
Herring, George C. "The Truman Administration and the Restoration of French Sovereignty in Indochina." *Diplomatic History* 1 (Spring 1977): 97–117.
Hess, Gary R. "The First American Commitment in Indochina: The Acceptance of the 'Bao Dai Solution,' 1950." *Diplomatic History* 2 (Fall 1978): 331–350.
Jones, Howard and Randall B. Woods. "The Origins of the Cold War: A Symposium." *Diplomatic History* 17 (1993): 251–276.
Kaplan, Lawrence S. "Dean Acheson and the Atlantic Community." In *Dean Acheson and the Making of U.S. Foreign Policy*, ed. Douglas Brinkley, 28–54. New York: St. Martin's, 1993.
Kennan, George F. "The Sources of Soviet Conduct." *Foreign Affairs* XXV (July 1947): 566–582.
LaFeber, Walter, "NATO and the Korean War: A Context." *Diplomatic History* 13 (Fall 1989): 461–478.
Lay, James S., Jr. "National Security Council's Role in the U.S. Security and Peace Program." *World Affairs* 115 (Summer 1952): 33–63.
Lees, Lorraine M. "The American Decision to Assist Tito, 1948–1949." *Diplomatic History* 2 (Fall 1978): 407–433.
Leffler, Melvyn P. "The American Conception of National Security and the Beginnings of the Cold War, 1945–48." *American Historical Review* 89 (April 1984): 346–381.
_____. "Inside Enemy Archives: The Cold War Reopened." *Foreign Affairs* 75 (July/August 1996): 120–135.
_____. "Negotiating from Strength: Acheson, the Russians and American Power." In *Dean Acheson and the Making of U.S. Foreign Policy*, ed. Douglas Brinkley, 176–210. London: Macmillan, 1993.
_____. "Strategy, Diplomacy, and the Cold War: The United States, Turkey, and NATO, 1945–1952." *Journal of American History* 71 (March 1985): 807–825.
_____. "The United States and the Strategic Dimensions of the Marshall Plan." *Diplomatic History* 12 (Summer 1988): 277–306.
Lichterman, Martin. "To the Yalu and Back." In *American Civil-Military Decisions*, ed. Harold Stein, 469–642. University: The University of Alabama Press, 1963.
Lowi, Theodore J. "Bases in Spain." In *American Civil-Military Decisions*, ed. Harold Stein, 667–702. University: The University of Alabama Press, 1963.

Lundestad, Geir. "Empire by Invitation? The United States and Western Europe, 1945–1952." *SHAFR Newsletter* 15 (September 1984): 1–12.

Martin, Lawrence W. "The American Decision to Rearm Germany." In *American Civil-Military Decisions*, ed. Harold Stein, 643–665. University: The University of Alabama Press, 1963.

May, Ernest R. "The American Commitment to Germany, 1949–1955." *Diplomatic History* 13 (Fall 1989): 431–460.

_____. "The Development of Political-Military Consultation in the United States." *Political Science Quarterly* 70 (June 1955): 161–180.

_____. "NSC 68: The Theory and Politics of Strategy." In *American and Cold War Strategy: Interpreting NSC 68*, ed. idem, 1–19. Boston: Bedford Books, 1993.

McCullough, David. "Harry S. Truman 1945–1953." In *Character Above All: Ten Presidents from FDR to George Bush*, ed. Robert H. Wilson, 39–59. New York: Simon and Schuster, 1995.

Miller, James E. "Taking Off the Gloves: The United States and the Italian Elections of 1948." *Diplomatic History* 7 (Winter 1983): 35–56.

Nelson, Anna Kasten. "National Security I: Inventing a Process (1945–1960)." In *The Illusion of the Presidency*, eds. Hugh Helco and Lester M. Salamon, 229–262. Boulder, CO: Westview Press, 1981.

_____. "President Truman and the Evolution of the National Security Council." *Journal of American History* 72 (September 1985): 360–378.

Newton, Scott. "The 1949 Sterling Crisis and British Policy Toward European Integration." *Review of International Studies* 11 (July 1985): 169–192.

Nitze, Paul H. "The Development of NSC 68." *International Security*, 4 (Spring 1980): 170–176.

Paterson, Thomas G. "The Search for Meaning: George F. Kennan and American Foreign Policy." In *Makers of American Diplomacy: From Benjamin Franklin to Henry Kissinger*, eds. Frank J. Merli and Theodore A. Wilson, 249–284. New York: Scribner's, 1974.

Platt, Alan A. and Robert Leonardi. "American Foreign Policy and the Postwar Italian Left." *Political Science Quarterly* 93 (Summer 1978/1979): 197–215.

Pogue, Forrest C. "Marshall and Acheson: The State Department Years, 1945–49." In *Dean Acheson and the Making of U.S. Foreign Policy*, ed. Douglas Brinkley, 211–232. London: Macmillan, 1993.

Rosenberg, David Alan. "American Atomic Strategy and the Hydrogen Bomb Decision." *Journal of American History* 66 (June 1979): 62–87.

_____. "The Origins of Overkill: Nuclear Weapons and American Strategy." In *The National Security: Its Theory and Practice, 1945–1960*, ed. Norman A. Graebner, 123–195. New York: Oxford University Press, 1986.

Sale, Sara L. "Admiral Sidney W. Souers and President Truman." *Missouri Historical Review* 86 (October 1991): 55–71.

Sander, Alfred. "Truman and the National Security Council, 1945–1947." *Journal of American History* 59 (September 1972): 369–388.

Schaller, Michael. "Consul General O. Edmund Clubb, John P. Davies, and the 'Inevitability' of Conflict Between the United States and China, 1949–50: A Comment and New Documentation." *Diplomatic History* 9 (Spring 1985): 149–160.

_____. "Securing the Great Crescent: Occupied Japan and the Origins of Containment in Southeast Asia." *Journal of American History* 69 (September 1982): 392–414.

Schilling, Warner R. "The Politics of National Defense: Fiscal 1950." In *Strat-

egy, Politics, and Defense Budgets, eds. Warner Schilling, Paul Y. Hammond, and Glenn Snyder, 1–266. New York: Columbia University Press, 1962.

Schlesinger, Arthur, Jr. "Origins of the Cold War." *Foreign Affairs* 46 (October 1967): 22–52.

Schonberger, Howard. "The Japan Lobby in American Diplomacy, 1947–1952." *Pacific Historical Review* 46 (August 1977): 327–359.

Sheng, Michael. "The Triumph of Internationalism: CCP-Moscow Relations Before 1949." *Diplomatic History* 21 (Winter 1997): 95–104.

Siracusa, Joseph M. "NSC 68: A Reappraisal." *Naval War College Review* 33 (1980): 4–14.

Smith, E. Timothy. "The Fear of Subversion: The United States and the Inclusion of Italy in the North Atlantic Treaty." *Diplomatic History* 7 (Spring 1983): 139–155.

Snyder, Glenn H. "The 'New Look' of 1953," In Warner R. Schilling, Paul Y. Hammond and Glenn H. Snyder. *Strategy, Politics, and Defense Budgets.* New York: Columbia University Press, 1962.

Souers, Sidney W. "Policy Formulation for National Security." *American Political Science Review* 43 (June 1949): 534–543.

Truman, Harry S. "Our Armed Forces Must Be Unified." *Collier's* (August 26, 1944): 63–64.

Tucker, Nancy Bernkopf. "China's Place in the Cold War: The Acheson Plan." In *Dean Acheson and the Making of U.S. Foreign Policy*, ed. Douglas Brinkley, 109–132. London: Macmillan, 1993.

Weathersby, Kathryn. "New Findings on the Korean War." *Bulletin of the Cold War International History Project* 3 (Fall 1993): 1, 14–18.

_____. "Korea, 1949–50: To Attack, or Not to Attack? Stalin, Kim Il Sung, and the Prelude to War." *Bulletin of the Cold War International History Project* 5 (Spring 1995): 1–9.

_____. "The Soviet Role in the Early Phase of the Korean War: New Documentary Evidence." *Journal of American-East Asian Relations* 2 (1993): 425–458.

Wells, Samuel F., Jr. "Sounding the Tocsin: NSC 68 and the Soviet Threat." *International Security* 4 (Fall 1979): 116–158.

Westad, Odd Arne. "Losses, Chances, and Myths: The United States and the Creation of the Sino-Soviet Alliance, 1945–1950." *Diplomatic History* 21 (Winter 1997): 105–115.

_____. "Rivals and Allies: Stalin, Mao, and the Chinese Civil War, January 1949." *Bulletin of the Cold War International History Project* 6–7 (Winter 1995–96): 219, 226–227.

Wyeth, George A., Jr. "The National Security Council." *Journal of International Affairs* (1954): 185–195.

BOOKS

Abramson, Rudy. *Spanning the Century: The Life of W. Averell Harriman, 1891–1986.* New York: William Morrow, 1992.

Acheson, Dean. *The Korean War.* New York: W.W. Norton, 1971.

_____. *Present at the Creation, My Years in the State Department.* New York: Penguin, 1969.

Allison, Graham T. *Essence of Decision: Explaining the Cuban Missile Crisis.* Boston: Little, Brown, 1971.

Ambrose, Stephen E. *Rise to Globalism: American Foreign Policy Since 1938.* 5th ed. New York: Penguin, 1988.

Anders, Roger M., ed. *Forging the Atomic Shield: Excerpts from the Office Diary of Gordon E. Dean*. Chapel Hill: University of North Carolina Press, 1987.

Anderson, Irvine. *ARAMCO, the United States and Saudi Arabia: A Study of the Dynamics of Foreign Oil Policy, 1933–1950*. Princeton: Princeton University Press, 1981.

Anderson, Patrick. *The Presidents' Men: White House Assistants of Franklin D. Roosevelt, Harry S. Truman, Dwight D. Eisenhower, John F. Kennedy and Lyndon B. Johnson*. New York: Doubleday, 1968.

Anderson, Terry H. *The United States, Great Britain, and the Cold War, 1944–1947*. Columbia: University of Missouri Press, 1981.

Bamford, James. *The Puzzle Palace: A Report on America's Most Secret Agency*. Boston: Houghton Mifflin, 1982.

Barnet, Richard J. *Roots of War: The Men and Institutions Behind U.S. Foreign Policy*. Baltimore: Penguin Books, 1972.

Bethell, Nicholas. *Betrayed*. New York: Times Books, 1984.

Bill, James. *The Eagle and the Lion: The Tragedy of American Iranian Relations*. New Haven: Yale University Press, 1988.

Blaufarb, Douglas S. *The Counterinsurgency Era: U.S. Doctrine and Performance 1950 to the Present*. New York: Free Press, 1977.

Blum, Robert M. *Drawing the Line: The Origin of American Containment Policy in East Asia*. New York: W.W. Norton, 1982.

Borden, William S. *The Pacific Alliance: United States Foreign Economic Policy and Japanese Trade Recovery, 1947–1955*. Madison: University of Wisconsin Press, 1984.

Borg, Dorothy and Waldo Heinrichs, eds. *Uncertain Years: Chinese-American Relations, 1947–1950*. New York: Columbia University Press, 1980.

Bradley, Omar N. and Clay Blair. *A General's Life*. New York: Simon and Schuster, 1983.

Brands, H. W. *The Devil We Knew: Americans and the Cold War*. New York: Oxford University Press, 1993.

_____. *Inside the Cold War: Loy Henderson and the Rise of the American Empire 1918–1961*. New York: Oxford University Press, 1991.

_____. *Into the Labyrinth: The United States and the Middle East 1945–1993*. America in Crisis Series. New York: McGraw-Hill, 1994.

Brinkley, Douglas, ed. *Dean Acheson and the Making of U.S. Foreign Policy*. London: Macmillan, 1993.

Bundy, McGeorge. *Danger and Survival: Choices About the Bomb in the First Fifty Years*. New York: Random House, 1988.

Burch, Philip H., Jr. *Elites in American History*. 3 volumes. New York: Holmes and Meier, 1981.

Burns, Richard Dean, ed. *Harry S. Truman: A Bibliography of His Times and Presidency*. Wilmington, DE: Scholarly Resources, 1984.

Callahan, David. *Dangerous Capabilities: Paul Nitze and the Cold War*. New York: Harper Collins, 1990.

Campbell, David. *Writing Security: United States Foreign Policy and the Politics of Identity*. Minneapolis: University of Minnesota Press, 1992.

Campbell, John C. *The United States in World Affairs, 1945–1947*. New York: Harper & Brothers, 1947.

_____. *The United States in World Affairs, 1947–1948*. New York: Harper & Brothers, 1948.

Caraley, Demetrios. *The Politics of Military Unification: A Study of Conflict and the Policy Process*. New York: Columbia University Press, 1966.

Caridi, Ronald J. *The Korean War and American Politics: The Republican Party as a Case Study*. Philadelphia: University of Pennsylvania Press, 1969.

Chang, Gordon H. *Friends and Enemies: The United States, China, and the Soviet Union, 1948–1971.* Stanford: Stanford University Press, 1990.

Chen Jian. *China's Road to the Korean War: The Making of the Sino-Soviet Confrontation.* The U.S. and Pacific Asia Series. New York: Columbia University Press, 1994.

Christensen, Thomas J. *Useful Adversaries: Grand Strategy, Domestic Mobilization, and Sino-American Conflict, 1947–1958.* Princeton Studies in International History and Politics Series. Princeton: Princeton University Press, 1996.

Clay, Lucius D. *Decision in Germany.* Garden City, NY: Doubleday, 1950.

Clifford, Clark with Richard Holbrooke. *Counsel to the President: A Memoir.* New York: Random House, 1991.

Cline, Ray S. *Secrets, Spies and Scholars: Blueprint of the Essential CIA.* Washington, D.C.: Acropolis Books, 1976.

Cohen, Michael J. *Truman and Israel.* Berkeley: University of California Press, 1990.

Cohen, Warren I. *America's Response to China: An Interpretive History of Sino-American Relations.* New York: John Wiley and Sons, 1971.

Colby, William and Peter Forbath. *Honorable Men: My Life in the CIA.* New York: imon and Schuster, 1978.

Collins, J. Lawton. *War in Peacetime: The History and Lessons of Korea.* Boston: Houghton Mifflin, 1969.

Cummings, Bruce. *The Origins of the Korean War:* Volume I, *Liberation and the Emergence of Separate Regines, 1945–1947.* Princeton: Princeton University Press, 1981.

_____. *The Origins of the Korean War:* Volume II, *The Roaring of the Cataract, 1947–1950.* Princeton: Princeton University Press, 1990.

Dallek, Robert. *The American Style of Foreign Policy: Cultural Politics and Foreign Affairs.* New York: Oxford University Press, 1983.

Daniels, Jonathan. *The Man of Independence.* Philadelphia: Lippincott, 1950.

Darling, Arthur B. *The Central Intelligence Agency: An Instrument of Government, To 1950.* University Park: The Pennsylvania State University Press, 1990.

Destler, I. M., Leslie H. Gelb and Anthony Lake. *Our Own Worst Enemy: The Unmaking of American Foreign Policy.* New York: Simon and Schuster, 1984.

Dobbs, Charles M. *The Unwanted Symbol: American Foreign Policy, the Cold War, and Korea, 1945–1950.* Kent: Kent State University Press, 1981.

Donaldson, Gary A. *America at War: Politics and Diplomacy in Korea, Vietnam, and the Gulf War.* Westport, CT: Praeger, 1996.

Donovan, Robert J. *Conflict and Crisis: The Presidency of Harry S. Truman, 1945–1948.* New York: W.W. Norton, 1977.

_____. *Tumultuous Years: The Presidency of Harry S. Truman, 1949–1953.* New York: W.W. Norton, 1982.

Dorwart, Jeffery M. *Eberstadt and Forrestal: A National Security Partnership, 1909–1949.* College Station: Texas A&M University Press, 1991.

Feis, Herbert. *The China Tangle.* Princeton: Princeton University Press, 1953.

_____. *From Trust to Terror: The Onset of the Cold War, 1945–1950.* New York: W.W. Norton, 1970.

Ferrell, Robert H. *Choosing Truman: The Democratic Convention of 1944.* Columbia: University of Missouri Press, 1994.

_____. *George C. Marshall.* Vol. 15 of *The American Secretaries of State and Their Diplomacy.* New York: Cooper Square Publishers, 1966.

_____, ed. *Dear Bess: The Letters from Harry to Bess Truman 1910–1950*. New York: W.W. Norton, 1983.

_____. *Harry S. Truman: A Life*. Columbia: University of Missouri Press, 1994.

_____. *Harry S. Truman and the Modern American Presidency*. Boston: Little, Brown, 1983.

_____, ed. *Off the Record: The Private Papers of Harry S. Truman*. New York: Harper & Row, 1980.

Foot, Rosemary. *A Substitute for Victory: The Politics of Peacemaking at the Korean Armistice Talks*. Ithaca: Cornell University Press, 1990.

_____. *The Wrong War: American Policy and the Dimensions of the Korean Conflict, 1950–1953*. Ithaca: Cornell University Press, 1985.

Freeland, Richard M. *The Truman Doctrine and the Origins of McCarthyism: Foreign Policy, Domestic Politics, and Internal Security, 1946–1948*. New York: Knopf, 1972.

Fried, Richard M. *Nightmare in Red: The McCarthy Era in Perspective*. New York: Oxford University Press, 1990.

Gaddis, John Lewis. *The Long Peace: Inquiries into the History of the Cold War*. New York: Oxford University Press, 1987.

_____. *Strategies of Containment: A Critical Appraisal of Postwar National Security Policy*. New York: Oxford University Press, 1982.

_____. *The United States and the Origins of the Cold War 1941–1947*. New York: Columbia University Press, 1972.

_____. *The United States and the End of the Cold War: Implications, Reconsiderations, Provocations*. New York: Oxford University Press, 1992.

Gallicchio, Marc S. *The Cold War Begins in Asia: American East Asian Policy and the Fall of Japanese Empire*. New York: Columbia University Press, 1988.

Gardner, Lloyd C. *Architects of Illusion: Men and Ideas in American Foreign Policy, 1941–1949*. Chicago: Quadrangle, 1970.

_____. *A Covenant with Power: America and World Order from Wilson to Reagan*. New York: Oxford University Press, 1984.

_____. *Approaching Vietnam: From World War II Through Dienbienphu 1941–1954*. New York: W.W. Norton, 1988.

_____., ed. *The Korean War*. New York: Quadrangle Books, 1972.

Goncharov, Sergei N., John W. Lewis, and Xue Litai. *Uncertain Partners: Stalin, Mao, and the Korean War*. Stanford: Stanford University Press, 1993.

Goode, James F. *The United States and Iran, 1946–1951: The Diplomacy of Neglect*. New York: St. Martins, 1989.

Goulden, Joseph C. *Korea: The Untold Story of the War*. New York: McGraw-Hill, 1982.

Graebner, Norman, ed. *The National Security: Its Theory and Practice, 1945–1960*. New York: Oxford University Press, 1986.

Grasso, June M. *Harry Truman's Two-China Policy, 1948–1950*. Armonic, New York: ME Sharpe, 1987.

Greenstein, Fred T., ed. *Leadership in the Modern Presidency*. Cambridge: Harvard University Press, 1988.

Hadley, Eleanor M. *Antitrust in Japan*. Princeton: Princeton University Press, 1970.

Hahn, Peter L. *The United States, Great Britain, and Egypt, 1945–1956: Strategy and Diplomacy in the Early Cold War*. Chapel Hill: The University of North Carolina Press, 1991.

Halle, Louis J. *The Cold War as History*. New York: Harper & Row, 1967.

226   BIBLIOGRAPHY

Hamby, Alonzo L. *Beyond the New Deal: Harry S. Truman and American Liberalism*. New York: Columbia University Press, 1973.
_____. *Man of the People: A Life of Harry S. Truman*. New York: Oxford University Press, 1995.
Harper, John Lamberton. *American Visions of Europe: Franklin D. Roosevelt, George F. Kennan, and Dean G. Acheson*. New York: Cambridge University Press, 1994.
Hartmann, Susan M. *Truman and the 80th Congress*. Columbia: University of Missouri Press, 1971.
Heiss, Mary Ann. *Empire and Nationhood: The United States, Great Britain, and Iranian Oil, 1950–1954*. New York: Columbia University Press, 1997.
Helco, Hugh and Lester M. Salamon, eds. *The Illusion of the Presidency*. Boulder: Westview Press, 1981.
Heller, Francis H., ed. *The Truman White House: The Administration of the Presidency 1945–1953*. Lawrence: The Regents Press of Kansas, 1980.
Herken, Gregg. *The Winning Weapon: The Atomic Bomb in the Cold War, 1945–1950*. New York: Vintage Books, 1982.
Herring, George C. *America's Longest War: The United States and Vietnam, 1950–1975*, 3rd ed. America in Crises Series. New York: McGraw-Hill, 1996.
Hess, Gary R. *The United States' Emergence as a Southeast Asian Power, 1940–1950*. New York: Columbia University Press, 1987.
Hewlett, Richard G. and Francis Duncan. *Atomic Shield, 1947–1952:* Volume II, *A History of the United States Atomic Energy Commission*. University Park: The Pennsylvania State University Press, 1969.
Hillman, William, ed. *Harry S. Truman in His Own Words*. New York: Bonanza Books, 1984.
Hixon, Walter L. *George F. Kennan: Cold War Iconoclast*. New York: Columbia University Press, 1989.
Hogan, Michael J., ed. *The End of the Cold War: Its Meaning and Implications*. New York: Cambridge University Press, 1992.
_____. *The Marshall Plan: America, Britain, and the Reconstruction of Western Europe, 1947–1952*. Cambridge: Cambridge University Press, 1987.
Holloway, David. *Stalin and the Bomb: The Soviet Union and Atomic Energy, 1939–1956*. New Haven: Yale University Press, 1994.
Hoopes, Townsend and Douglas Brinkley. *Driven Patriot: The Life and Times of James Forrestal*. New York: Alfred A. Knopf, 1992.
Inderfurth, Karl F. and Loch K. Johnson, eds. *Decisions of the Highest Order: Perspectives on the National Security Council*. Pacific Grove, CA: Brooks/Cole, 1988.
Ireland, Timothy P. *Creating the Entangling Alliance: The Origins of the North Atlantic Treaty Organization*. Westport: Greenwood Press, 1981.
Iriye, Akira. *The Cold War in Asia: A Historical Introduction*. Englewood Cliffs, NJ: Prentice-Hall, 1974.
Isaacson, Walter and Evan Thomas. *The Wise Men: Six Friends and the World They Made*. New York: Simon & Schuster, 1986.
James, D. Clayton. *The Years of MacArthur: Triumph and Disaster, 1945–1964*, Vol. 3. Boston: Houghton Mifflin, 198 5.
Jeffreys-Jones, Rhodri. *The CIA and American Democracy*. New Haven: Yale University Press, 1989.
Jones, Howard. *"A New Kind of War": America's Global Strategy and the Truman Doctrine in Greece*. New York: Oxford University Press, 1989.
Jones, Joseph M. *The Fifteen Weeks*. New York: Viking press, 1965.

Kaplan, Lawrence S. *NATO and the United States: The Enduring Alliance*. New York: Twayne, 1994.

_____. *The United States and NATO: The Formative Years*. Lexington: University Press of Kentucky, 1984.

Karnow, Stanley. *Vietnam: A History*. New York: Viking, 1983.

Kaufman, Burton I. *The Korean War: Challenges in Crisis, Credibility, and Command*. Philadelphia: Temple University Press, 1986.

Kennan, George F. *Memoirs*, Volume I. Boston: Little, Brown, 1967.

Khrushchev, Nikita Sergeyevich. *Khrushchev Remembers: The Glasnost Tapes*. Boston: Little, Brown, 1990.

Knightley, Phillip. *The Second Oldest Profession: Spies and Spying in the Twentieth Century*. New York: W.W. Norton, 1986.

Kofsky, Frank. *Harry S. Truman and the War Scare of 1948: A Successful Campaign to Deceive the Nation*. New York: St. Martin's Press, 1993.

Kohn, Harold Honju. *The National Security Constitution: Sharing Power After the Iran-Control Affair*. New Haven: Yale University Press, 1990.

Kolko, Gabriel. *Anatomy of a War*. New York: Pantheon, 1985.

Kolko, Joyce and Gabriel. *The Limits of Power: The World and United States Foreign Policy, 1945–1954*. New York: Harper & Row, 1972.

Krock, Arthur. *Memoirs: Sixty Years on the Firing* Line. New York: Funk & Wagnalls, 1968.

Kuniholm, Bruce R. *The Origins of the Cold War in the Near East: Great Power Conflict and Diplomacy in Iran, Turkey, and Greece*. Princeton: Princeton University Press, 1980.

LaFeber, Walter. *America, Russia, and the Cold War, 1945–1996*, 8th ed., America in Crisis Series. New York: McGraw-Hill, 1997.

Laquer, Walter. *A World of Secrets: The Uses and Limits of Intelligence*. New York: Basic Books, 1985.

Larson, Deborah Welch. *Origins of Containment: A Psychological Explanation*. Princeton: Princeton University Press, 1985.

Leary, William M. *Perilous Missions: Civil Air Transport and CIA Covert Operations in Asia*. University: The University of Alabama Press, 1984.

Leffler, Melvyn P. *A Preponderance of Power: National Security, the Truman Administration, and the Cold War*. Stanford Nuclear Age Series. Stanford: Stanford University Press, 1992.

_____. *The Specter of Communism: The United States and the Origins of the Cold War, 1917–1953*. Hill and Wang Critical Issues Series. New York: Hill and Wang, 1994.

Lilienthal, David E. *The Journals of David E. Lilienthal:* Volume II, *The Atomic Energy Years*. New York: Harper & Row, 1964.

Lippmann, Walter. *The Cold War: A Study in U.S. Foreign Policy*. New York: Harper & Row, 1972.

Lundestad, Geir. *America, Scandinavia, and the Cold War*. New York: Columbia University Press, 1980.

MacArthur, Douglas. *Reminiscences*. New York: McGraw-Hill, 1964.

Maddox, Robert James. *From War to Cold War: The Education of Harry S. Truman*. Boulder: Westview Press, 1988.

Matray, James I. *The Reluctant Crusade: American Foreign Policy in Korea, 1941–1950*. Honolulu: University of Hawaii Press, 1985.

May, Ernest R., ed. *American Cold War Strategy: Interpreting NSC 68*. Boston: Bedford Books, 1993.

_____. *"Lessons" of the Past: The Use and Misuse of History in American Foreign Policy*. New York: Oxford University Press, 1973.

_____. *The Truman Administration and China, 1945–1949*. The America's Alternative Series. Philadelphia: J.B. Lippincott, 1975.

Mayers, David. *George Kennan and the Dilemmas of US Foreign Policy*. New York: Oxford University Press, 1988.

McCormick, Thomas J. *America's Half-Century: United States Foreign Policy in the Cold War*. The American Moment Series. Baltimore: The Johns Hopkins University Press, 1989.

McCoy, Donald R. *The Presidency of Harry S. Truman*. Lawrence: University Press of Kansas, 1984.

McCullough, David. *Truman*. New York: Simon and Schuster, 1992.

McLellan, David S. *Dean Acheson: The State Department Years*. New York: Dodd, Mead, 1976.

Merli, Frank J. and Theodore A. Wilson, eds. *Makers of American Diplomacy: From Benjamin Franklin to Henry Kissinger*. New York: Scribner's, 1974.

Mickelson, Sig. *America's Other Voice: The Story of Radio Free Europe and Radio Liberty*. New York: Praeger, 1983.

Miller, Aaron David. *Search for Security: Saudi Arabian Oil and American Foreign Policy, 1939–1949*. Chapel Hill: The University of North Carolina Press, 1980.

Miller, James E. *The United States and Italy, 1940–1950: The Politics and Diplomacy of Stabilization*. Chapel Hill: The University of North Carolina Press, 1986.

Miller, Merle. *Plain Speaking: An Oral Biography of Harry S. Truman*. New York: Berkeley, 1974.

Millis, Walter, ed. *The Forrestal Diaries*. New York: Viking, 1951.

Milward, Alan S. *The Reconstruction of Western Europe, 1945–1951*. Berkeley: University of California Press, 1984.

Miscamble, Wilson D. *George F. Kennan and the Making of American Foreign Policy, 1947–1950*. Princeton Studies in International History and Politics Series. Princeton: Princeton University Press, 1992.

Montague, Ludwell Lee. *General Walter Bedell Smith as Director of Cenral Intelligence October 1950–February 1953*. University Park: The Pennsylvania State University Press, 1992.

Nagi, Yonosuke and Akira Iriye, eds. *The Origins of the Cold War in Asia*. New York: Columbia University Press, 1977.

Neustadt, Richard E. *Presidential Power*. New York: John Wiley, 1980.

Nitze, Paul H. with Ann M. Smith and Steven L. Rearden. *From Hiroshima to Glasnost: At the Center of Decision—A Memoir*. New York: Grove Weidenfeld, 1989.

O'Ballance, Edgar. *The Greek Civil War, 1944–1949*. New York: Praeger, 1966.

_____. *The Indochina War, 1945–1954: A Study in Guerilla Warfare*. London: Faber, 1964.

Pach, Chester J., Jr. *Arming the Free World: The Origins of the United States Military Assistance Program, 1945–1950*. Chapel Hill: The University of North Carolina Press, 1991.

Paddock, Alfred H., Jr. *U.S. Army Special Warfare—Its Origins: Psychological and Unconventional Warfare, 1941–1952*. Washington, D.C.: National Defense University Press, 1982.

Painter, David S. *Oil and the American Century: The Political Economy of U.S. Foreign Oil Policy, 1941–1954*. Baltimore: Johns Hopkins University Press, 1986.

Paterson, Thomas G. *On Every Front: The Making and Unmaking of the Cold War*. Rev. ed. New York: W.W. Norton, 1992.

_____. *Soviet-American Confrontation: Postwar Reconstruction and the Origins of the Cold War*. Baltimore: Johns Hopkins University Press, 1973.

Pemberton, William E. *Bureaucratic Politics: Executive Reorganization During the Truman Administration*. Columbia, MO: University of Missouri Press, 1979.

_____. *Harry S. Truman: Fair Dealer and Cold Warrior*. Boston: Twayne's Twentieth-Century American Biography Series. G.K. Hall, 1989.

Pessen, Edward. *Losing Our Souls: The American Experience in the Cold War*. Chicago: Ivan R. Dee, 1993.

Pfau, Richard. *No Sacrifice Too Great: The Life of Lewis L. Strauss*. Charlottesville: The University Press of Virginia, 1984.

Phillips, Cabell. *The Truman Presidency: The History of a Triumphant Succession*. New York: Macmillan, 1966.

Pisani, Sallie. *The CIA and the Marshall Plan*. Lawrence: University Press of Kansas, 1991.

Pogue, Forrest C. *George C. Marshall: Statesman 1945–1959*. New York: Viking/Penguin, 1987.

Pollard, Robert A. *Economic Security and the Origins of the Cold War, 1945–1950*. New York: Columbia University Press, 1985.

Powers, Thomas. *The Man Who Kept Secrets: Richard Helms and the CIA*. New York: Knopf, 1979.

Prados, John. *Keepers of the Keys: A History of the National Security Council from Truman to Bush*. New York: William Morrow, 1991.

_____. *Presidents' Secret Wars: CIA and Pentagon Covert Operations Since World War II*. New York: William Morrow, 1986.

_____. *The Soviet Estimate: U.S. Intelligence Analysis and Russian Military Strength*. New York: Dial Press, 1982.

Ranelagh, John. *The Agency: The Rise and Decline of the CIA*. New York: Simon and Schuster, 1987.

Rearden, Steven L. *The Evolution of American Strategic Doctrine: Paul H. Nitze and the Soviet Challenge*. Boulder, CO: Westview Press, 1984.

_____. *History of the Office of the Secretary of Defense*: Volume I, *The Formative Years, 1947–1950*. Washington: U.S. Department of Defense, 1984.

Reeves, Thomas C. *The Life and Times of Joe McCarthy: A Biography*. New York: Stein and Day, 1982.

Rhodes, Richard. *Dark Sun: The Making of the Hydrogen Bomb*. New York: Simon & Schuster, 1995.

Ridgway, Matthew B. *The Korean War*. Garden City, NY: Doubleday, 1967.

Rogow, Arnold A. *James Forrestal: A Study of Personality, Politics, and Policy*. New York: Macmillan, 1963.

Roosevelt, Kermit. *Countercoup: The Struggle for the Control of Iran*. New York: McGraw-Hill, 1979.

Rositzke, Harry. *The CIA's Secret Operations: Espionage, Counterespionage, and Covert Operations*. New York: Readers Digest Press, 1977.

Rotter, Andrew J. *The Path to Vietnam: The Origins of the American Commitment to Southeast Asia*. Ithaca: Cornell University Press, 1987.

Rovere, Richard H. and Arthur Schlesigner, Jr. *General MacArthur and President Truman: The Struggle for Control of American Foreign Policy*. 3rd ed. New Brunswick, NJ: Transaction, 1992.

Rubin, Barry. *The Great Powers in the Middle East, 1941–1947: The Road to the Cold War*. London: Frank Cass, 1980.

_____. *Paved with Good Intentions: The American Experience in Iran*. New York: Oxford University Press, 1980.

_____. *Secrets of State: The State Department and the Struggle Over U.S. Foreign Policy*. New York: Oxford University Press, 1985.

Rusk, Dean and Richard Rusk. *As I Saw It*. New York: Penguin, 1991.

Schaller, Michael. *The American Occupation of Japan: The Origins of the Cold War in Asia*. New York: Oxford University Press, 1985.

_____. *Douglas MacArthur: The Far Eastern General*. New York: Oxford University Press, 1989.

_____. *The U.S. Crusade in China, 1938–1945*. New York: Columbia University Press, 1979.

Schilling, Warner R., Paul Y. Hammond, and Glenn H. Snyder. *Strategy, Politics, and Defense Budgets*. New York: Columbia University Press, 1962.

Schoenbaum, Thomas J. *Waging Peace and War: Dean Rusk in the Truman, Kennedy and Johnson Years*. New York: Simon and Schuster, 1988.

Schonberger, Howard B. *Aftermath of War: Americans and the Remaking of Japan, 1945–1952*. Kent: Kent State University Press, 1989.

Shepley, James R. and Clay Blair. *The Hydrogen Bomb: The Men, The Menace, The Mechanism*. Westport, CT: Greenwood Press, 1954.

Shlaim, Avi. *The United States and the Berlin Blockade, 1948–1949: A Study in Crisis Decision-Making*. Berkeley: University of California Press, 1983.

Silverberg, Robert, ed. *If I Forget Thee O Jerusalem: American Jews and the State of Israel*. New York: William Morrow, 1970.

Simpson, Christopher. *Blowback: The First Full Account of America's Recruitment of Nazis, and Its Effects on the Cold War*. New York: Weidenfeld & Nicolson, 1988.

Smith, Gaddis. *Dean Acheson*. Vol. 16 of *The American Secretaries of State and Their Diplomacy*. New York: Cooper Square Publishers, 1972.

Smith, Jean Edward, ed. *The Papers of General Lucius Clay: Germany, 1945–1949*. 2 volumes. Bloomington, IN: Indiana University Press, 1974.

Spanier, John W. *The Truman-MacArthur Controversy and the Korean War*. New York: W.W. Norton, 1965.

Stein, Harold, ed. *American Civil-Military Decisions*. Birmingham: University of Alabama Press, 1963.

Stephenson, Anders. *Kennan and the Art of Foreign Policy*. Cambridge: Harvard University Press, 1989.

Stoff, Michael B. *Oil, War, and American Security: The Search for a National Policy on Foreign Oil, 1941–1947*. New Haven: Yale University Press, 1980.

Strauss, Lewis L. *Men and Decisions*. New York: Doubleday, 1962.

Stueck, William Whitney, Jr. *The Korean War: An International History*. Princeton Studies in International History and Politics Series. Princeton: Princeton University Press, 1995.

_____. *The Road to Confrontation: American Policy Toward China and Korea, 1947–1950*. Chapel Hill: University of North Carolina Press, 1981.

_____. *The Wedemeyer Mission: American Politics and Foreign Policy During the Cold War*. Athens: University of Georgia Press, 1984.

Theoharis, Athan, ed. *The Truman Presidency: The Origins of the Imperial Presidency and the National Security State*. Stanfordville, NY: Earl M. Coleman, 1979.

Theoharis, Athan and Robert Griffith, eds. *The Specter: Original Essays on the Cold War and the Origins of McCarthyism*. New York: New Directions, 1974.

Thompson, Kenneth W., ed. *Portraits of American Presidents*, Volume II. *The Truman Presidency: Intimate Perspectives*. Lanham, MD: University Press of America, 1984.

Trachtenberg, Marc. *History and Strategy*. Princeton Studies in International History and Politics. Princeton: Princeton University Press, 1991.

Troy, Thomas. *Donovan and the CIA: A History of the Establishment of the Central Intelligence Agency*. Frederick, MD: University Publications of America, 1981.

Truman, Harry S. *Memoirs of Harry S. Truman 1945:* Volume I, *Year of Decisions*. Garden City, NY: Doubleday, 1955; reprint, New York: DaCapo Press, 1986.

_____. *Memoirs of Harry S. Truman 1946–1952:* Volume II, *Years of Trial and Hope*. Garden City, NY: Doubleday, 1956; reprint, New York: DaCapo Press, 1986.

Truman, Margaret. *Harry S. Truman*. New York: William Morrow, 1973.

Tsou, Tang. *America's Failure in China, 1941–50*. Chicago: University of Chicago Press, 1963.

Tucker, Nancy B. *Patterns in the Dust: Chinese-American Relations and the Recognition Controversy, 1949–1950*. New York: Columbia University Press, 1983.

Vandenberg, Arthur H., Jr. and Joe Alex Morris, eds. *The Private Papers of Senator Vandenberg*. Boston: Houghton Mifflin, 1952.

Wall, Irwin M. *The United States and the Making of Postwar France, 1945–1954*. New York: Cambridge University Press, 1991.

Weinstein, Allen. *The Hiss-Chambers Case*. New York: Knopf, 1978.

Westad, Odd Arne. *Cold War and Revolution: Soviet-American Rivalry and the Origins of the Chinese Civil War*. The U.S. and Pacific Basin Series. New York: Columbia University Press, 1993.

Whiting, Allen S. *China Crosses the Yalu: The Decision to Enter the Korean War*. Stanford: Stanford University Press, 1960.

Williams, Robert Chadwell. *Klaus Fuchs, Atom Spy*. Cambridge: Harvard University Press, 1987.

Williams, William Appleman. *The Tragedy of American Diplomacy*. New York: World Press, 1959.

Williamson, Samuel R., Jr. and Steven L. Rearden. *The Origins of U.S. Nuclear Strategy, 1945–1953*. New York: St. Martin's Press, 1993.

Wilson, Robert A., ed. *Character Above All: Ten Presidents from FDR to George Bush*. New York: Simon and Schuster, 1995.

Wittner, Lawrence S. *American Intervention in Greece, 1945–1949*. New York: Columbia University Press, 1982.

Woodhouse, C.M. *The Struggle for Greece: 1941–1949*. London: Hart-Davis, MacGibbon, 1979.

Woods, Randall B. and Howard Jones. *Dawning of the Cold War: The United States' Quest for Order*. Athens: The University of Georgia Press, 1991.

Yergin, Daniel. *Shattered Peace: The Origins of the Cold War and the National Security State*. Boston: Houghton Mifflin, 1977.

York, Herbert F. *The Advisors: Oppenheimer, Teller, and the Superbomb*. Stanford Nuclear Age Series. Stanford: Stanford University Press, 1976.

Zubok, Vladislav and Constantine Pleshakov. *Inside the Kremlin's Cold War: From Stalin to Khrushchev*. Cambridge: Harvard University Press, 1996.

UNPUBLISHED STUDIES

Chen Jian. "The Sino-Soviet Alliance and China's Entry into the Korean War." Working Paper #1, The Cold War International History Project, Woodrow Wilson International Center for Scholars.

Guerrier, Steven Warren. "NSC-68 and the Truman Rearmament: 1950–1953." Ph.D. diss., The University of Michigan, 1988.

Hall, David Kent. "Implementing Multiple Advocacy in the National Security Council, 1947–1980." Ph.D. diss., Stanford University, 1982.

Parrish, Scott D. "The Turn Toward Confrontation: The Soviet Reaction to the Marshall Plan, 1948." Working Paper #9, The Cold War International History Project, Woodrow Wilson International Center for Scholars.

Sale, Sara L. "Behind the Iron Curtain: The National Security Council, the CIA, and U.S. Cold War Policy Toward Eastern Europe, 1949–1952." Paper presented at the Mid-America Conference on History, Springfield, September 1991.

_____. "Harry S. Truman, The Development and Operations of the National Security Council, and the Origins of United States Cold War Policies." Ph.D. diss., Oklahoma State University, September 1991.

_____. "Scripting Cold War Nationalism: The Symbolic Systems and Discursive Strategies of NSC 68." Paper presented at the Organization of American Historians Annual Meeting, Indianapolis, April 1998.

_____. "President Truman, the CIA, and the Cold War: A Reassessment." Paper presented at the Mid-America Conference on History, Stillwater, September 1993.

_____. "Rear Admiral Sidney W. Souers: President Truman's Advisory, Cold War Intelligence Gatherer, and Anonymous Servant, 1946–1953." Paper presented at the Southwestern Social Sciences Association Conference, Little Rock, April 1989.

Weathersby, Kathryn. "Soviet Aims in Korea and the Origins of the Korean War, 1945–50: New Evidence from Russian Archives." Working Paper #8, The Cold War International History Project. Woodrow Wilson International Center for Scholars.

Wood, Nelson Ovia. "Strategic Psychological Warfare of the Truman Administration: A Study of National Psychological Warfare Aims, Objectives, and Effectiveness." Ph.D. diss., The University of Oklahoma, 1982.

Acknowledgments

No book is the product of a single individual. Scores of friends, colleagues, archivists, and institutions helped me write this book in different ways and at various stages. I am pleased to acknowledge my debts for the advice and assistance that each extended.

Acknowledgments must begin with a special thanks to many archivists and librarians. The staff of the Harry S. Truman Library were always generous, resourceful, and efficient in aiding my research. I am appreciative especially of the many requests for help filled by Dennis E. Bilger, Raymond H. Geselbracht, Irwin Mueller, Elizabeth Safly, and Pauline Testerman. This book would have never been completed without the knowledge they shared with me regarding the National Security Council and President Truman. In addition, their friendship over the years has made the Truman Library a special place for this researcher. I am also grateful for the research guidance provided by Kathie Nicastro of the National Archives, and Carl Esche and Dan Linke of the Seeley G. Mudd Library at Princeton University. In addition, I owe debts of gratitude to John Phillips of the Edmon Low Library at Oklahoma State University for his help with my earliest research in government documents; and the staff of the George A. Spiva Library at Missouri Southern, particularly Gaye Pate, for their gracious assistance handling of all my requests.

I also owe a great debt for the generous financial support provided by two institutions. Much appreciation goes to the Harry S. Truman Library Institute, which made the greatest amount of my research and a large portion of my initial writing possible with a grant-in-aid and a dissertation fellowship. The Missouri Southern Foundation also helped defray the expenses of later research and travel. My thanks goes to Richard B. Miller and the Faculty Development Committee, and to Vice President of Academic Affairs Erik J. Bitterbaum.

Among my greatest debts are to those colleagues who advised me on this work. I began my study of Truman, the NSC, and the Cold War while I was a doctoral student of Joseph A. Stout, Jr. of Oklahoma State University. His guidance, judicious direction, and friendship were of immeasurable assistance for which I owe enduring gratitude. Special thanks must be extended as well to W. Roger Biles, George O. Carney, and Neil J. Hackett who as members of my dissertation committee provided a multitude of early valuable insights. I also benefited from the generous advice and vast knowledge of Robert H. Ferrell during an important nascent stage of my research at the Harry S. Truman Library. I am especially indebted to Michael A. Barnhart, H. W. Brands, Gary A. Donaldson, Mary Ann Heiss, Virginia Jeans Laas, Walter LaFeber, and Chester J. Pach, Jr., who read the manuscript in later pre-publication stages. Their critical observations helped correct a number of errors on matters great and small, and their scholarly acumen kept me thinking and rethinking. I am indebted as well to the many Truman scholars from whose work I have benefited in varying degrees. Other historians of United States foreign policy on whom I have depended are cited in the notes and bibliography. I respect their consistently high standards of scholarship and thank each for their keen insights.

Robert D. Marcus, the editor of this series, and Charles Peach and the staff of Brandywine Press made the publication process a pleasure. I doubt that I will be able to offer adequate thanks to David Burner and Thomas R. West, who each gave more to this book with their advice, encouragement, and editorial skills than words can say. I owe so much to Betsy Little, for without her time and professional help processing a great many versions of the manuscript, this book would remain unfinished. Lynda Stannard of Thistle Index also deserves my thanks for all of her work during the final production stages.

I am also indebted to all members of my department at Missouri Southern for their continuous patience and support.

Charliene Aldridge and Cindi Spencer deserve great appreciation for rescuing me often; and my gratitude to Cindi for her drawings of the charts. Many thanks goes to Karl J. Schmidt for his expertise and cartographic production of the maps contained herein. Without question, it was my great fortune to have known and learned from three very special colleagues and friends. The late Judith L. Conboy and the late D. David Tate helped show me what can be accomplished in life. The late Robert E. Smith shared generously during my early years of learning how to become a historian his mentorship, devotion to teaching, and love of history. Their strength and dedication will always be remembered.

For all of my students who endured many semesters when I juggled their classes along with work on this book, I must extend a big thank you for understanding. Their numbers are too great to mention; but they know who they are.

The interest and support of family and friends sustained me throughout and contributed in many ways to the completion of this book. Gary Lentz provided his wise counsel in later pre-publication stages. The late Gladys Miles always shared her grandmotherly kindness during revisions. And to Lori L. Bogle, Lentz Galbraith, Shelly Moore Lemmons, Susann, Steve, Kristen, and Greg Schaum, and Ted and Carolyn Stephens, I extend a very special thank you. Spunky and Sissy, as usual, were always there. Last, but certainly not least, through their many years of love, example, and sacrifice, my parents Onal Carter and Margaret Lee Hyde Sale helped keep me committed. This book is dedicated to them as a token of my love and gratitude.

Index